ARE YOU BEING SERVED?

A CELEBRATION OF TWENTY-FIVE YEARS

YEARS

Ground floor perfumery,
stationery, and leather goods,
wigs and haberdashery,
kitchenware and food.

———

Going up.

———

First floor telephones,
gents ready-made suits,
shirts, socks, ties, hats,
underwear and shoes …

———

Thank you so much madam,
and good afternoon …

ARE YOU BEING SERVED?

A CELEBRATION OF TWENTY-FIVE YEARS

Richard Webber with
David Croft and Jeremy Lloyd

Foreword by Joanna Lumley

WELCOME RAIN
NEW YORK

This book is dedicated to Stephen, Diane, Valerie and John, with all my love. RW

First WELCOME RAIN edition 1998
Published by WELCOME RAIN
New York, New York

First published in 1998 by Orion Media
An imprint of Orion Books Ltd
Orion House, 5 Upper St Martin's Lane,
London WC2H 9EA

ISBN 1-56649-042-1
M 10 9 8 7 6 5 4 3 2 1

Library of Congress information available
from the Publisher

Printed and bound in Great Britain by Butler & Tanner Ltd

ACKNOWLEDGEMENTS

Many people have helped during the writing of this book. I would like to thank the staff at Spotlight and Equity, as well as Simon and Amanda at the BBC, for helping put me in touch with many artists, some of whom have left the profession.

I am indebted to all the actors, production crew, and friends and family of deceased cast members who gave up their time to talk to me. I would also like to thank Doremy Vernon, Charles Garland, Douglas Turnbull and Nick Randall; Lisa Anselmi for her contributions; June Hudson for letting me use her costume designs; David Porter, Don Smith and Kerri at Spotlight for their help with photos; as well as David Hamilton, who kindly helped check all those fine details like transmission dates etc.

Thanks to Joanna Lumley for taking time out of her busy schedule to write the foreword, and everyone at Orion, particularly Trevor Dolby. Special thanks to my agent, Jeffrey Simmons. And for her expert guidance, I am, again, grateful to Hilary Johnson.

This project wouldn't have got off the ground if Jeremy Lloyd and David Croft hadn't given their support. I appreciate the time they have given over the last few months, and being allowed the chance to write about their comedy classic.

Finally, my wife Paula has, as always, been very supportive. I'd also like to thank her for surviving the arduous task of sitting through 69 episodes recording the number of times Mrs Slocombe's hair changed colour!

Contents

Foreword

Jeremy had just had one of his brilliant ideas for a television series rejected. 'What *do* they want?' he said. 'They've had hospitals, buses, factory floors, pubs, police stations ... what's missing?' He sat down, twiddled his hair, smoked four cigarettes and said: 'A shop. A department store.' And Grace Brothers was born.

Jeremy had himself worked for a few weeks in a major department store in London during one hot summer. He was sacked for selling soft drinks from a fitting-room, a rather Mr Lucas-type exercise. He knew the exact importance of one's position in the department, one's territorial rights on the shop floor, punctuality, pecking order and appearance.

He and David Croft have a rare knack of seeing the absurdity of some of our most familiar institutions – *Are You Being Served?* is a direct descendant of the *Carry On* films and Donald McGill postcards, taken from the seam of humour which so endeared Benny Hill to his vast American audience.

They very kindly invited me to be a German customer in one episode and Miss French promoting *His and Hers* toiletries in another. It was a huge pleasure to work with the talented regular cast; I must admit that the shows still make me laugh out loud. Just reading about them in this delightful book is enough to whet the appetite. As Young Mr Grace might have said: 'They've all done very well.'

JOANNA LUMLEY

7

Introduction

Jeremy and I got together when I was asked by Bill Cotton to 'funny up' a sitcom called *It's Awfully Bad For Your Eyes, Darling*. Jeremy was playing his usual silly ass Englishman in the piece, which was being received in silence by the studio audience.

I thought the show was beyond redemption, but Bill pointed out that I had been treated pretty well by the BBC in the past – which was true – and this would be a chance for me to 'put a bit back'. We accordingly managed to give the show a few laughs in the first two minutes so that the viewers realized that it was in fact meant to be a comedy and was being played in front of a live audience.

During this rather agonizing process, Jeremy showed me a pilot he had written for ITA about a gentlemen's outfitters called *Fun in Store*. I fancied the idea, and Jeremy managed to get it back from the company which had optioned it but appeared to be taking no steps to put it on the air. It took us about three days to block out a pilot of it and we gave it the title *Are You Being Served?*

A series called *Comedy Playhouse* was being planned by the BBC consisting of six comedy ideas by various authors. I learned that the BBC was one script short and I managed to persuade Bill Cotton that 'he owed me one' for having battled through *It's Awfully Bad...* and he should, therefore, include our effort for the additional reason that it had a non-star cast and would be dead cheap. I seem to recall that the cost of the set was £600, which was cheap even in 1973. We got the go-ahead, were moderately well received and Bill, a born entrepreneur, commissioned the series. It has since been shown countless times all over the world, so I feel I have fulfilled Bill's request to 'put a bit back'!

DAVID CROFT, OBE

Returning to England after writing and acting on *Rowan and Martin's Laugh-In* in America, I found for the first time in my career that I was stuck for an idea, not just for a week but for months. I remember discussing my predicament with Joanna Lumley, to whom I was at that time briefly married. Suddenly I was recalling my life as a young suit salesman at Simpson's in Piccadilly. When we stopped laughing we thought it might work as a situation comedy, and of course it did, and Joanna – from whom I'm now divorced – sportingly made a couple of guest appearances on the show.

I must say I'm surprised I didn't think of *Are You Being Served?* a few years earlier, but then I probably wouldn't have had such a perfect writing partner as David Croft. Not only is he one of the best writers we have, but he also produced and directed most of the shows – so naturally there were no rewrites.

I wasn't aware at the time that I was writing a large part of my pension, but thanks to the continued success of the show that's how it's turned out.

The cast of *Are You Being Served?* were also chosen by David – except Candy Davis, the undulating blonde bombshell secretary assigned to Mr Rumbold. I happened to be doing the auditioning that day and using my considerable experience gained in nightclubs I was able to predict that she'd be a big hit with male viewers – and I was right!

I have a beautiful cut-glass decanter from the cast with the inscription *Jeremy A.Y.B.S. '72–'84*. It's amazing to think that I spent about five per cent of my life writing one show, but I'll drink to the ones who made it possible: David Croft, the cast – oh, and my bank manager whose demands focused my mind enormously; and not forgetting the lovely Joanna Lumley, who was always encouraging, and still is.

JEREMY LLOYD

The First Ever Episode

PRODUCTION TEAM

SCRIPTS: Jeremy Lloyd and David Croft, except episodes 8, 10, 18 & 19 by Lloyd, Croft and Michael Knowles; episode 20 by Lloyd and John Chapman and series 9 & 10 by Jeremy Lloyd

COSTUMES: June Wilson (pilot and series 1); Valerie Spooner (episode 6); George Ward (series 2); Mary Woods (series 3 & episode 21); Andrew MacKenzie (episode 20); Sally Nieper (series 4, except episode 21); Christine Rawlins (episode 27); L. Rowland-Warne (series 5, 6, 7 & 8); Mary Husband (series 9); Irene Whilton (series 10)

MAKE-UP: Deanne Turner (pilot); Lucy Hutchinson (episode 6); Ann Briggs (series 2); Maggie Webb (series 3); Jacqui Fitzmaurice (episode 20); Pauline Gyertson (series 4, episode 27); Jill Matthews (series 5); Dawn Alcock (episodes 35, 36, 37 & 38); Sylvia Thornton (episodes 39 & 40); Jill Hagger (series 7 & 8); Judy Cain (series 9); Pauline Cox (series 10)

LIGHTING: Eric Monk (pilot, series 1, 2, 3 – except episodes 14, 15 & 16 by Clive Thomas – series 4, episode 27, series 5); Warwick Fielding (series 6); Mike Jefferies (series 7); Duncan Brown (series 8 & 9); John Farr (episode 56); Terry Brett (series 10)

SOUND: Larry Goodson (pilot, episodes 3, 4, 5 & 6); John Lloyd (episode 2, series 2); Richard Partridge (series 3, except episode 18 by Mike McCarthy); Adrian Bishop-Laggett (episode 20); Mike McCarthy (series 4, except episode 23 by Richard Partridge); Tony Philpot (episodes 27, 38 & 39); Laurie Taylor (series 5 & 7, except episode 44); Len Shorey (episodes 35, 36, 37, 40, 44 & 68); John Delany (series 8); Bob Foley (series 9 & 10, except episode 68)

DESIGN: James Bould (pilot, series 1); Nigel Curzon (series 2); Rochelle Selwyn (series 3); Gloria Clayton (episode 20); Paul Munting (series 4); Christine Ruscoe (episode 27); Ray London (series 5); Antony Thorpe (series 6); Garry Freeman (series 7); Andree Welstead-Hornby (series 8); John Stout (series 9); Bernard Lloyd-Jones (series 10)

DANCE STAGED BY: Irving Davies (episodes 17, 19 & 56); Frances Pidgeon (episode 22); Michele Hardy (episode 27); Sheila O'Neill (episodes 37, 40 & 42)

CHOREOGRAPHER: Chris Power (episode 69)

VISUAL EFFECTS: Tony Oxley (series 2, episode 19, 22, 24, 25, 26 & 27, series 10); Mat Irvine and Charles Lumm (episodes 43 & 46); Bert Luxford (episode 49); Colin Mapson (series 9); John Horton (series 5)

SENIOR CAMERAMAN: Ian Ridley (episode 51); Peter Ware (episode 52); Garth Tucker (episodes 53, 54, 55 & 56)

CAMERA SUPERVISOR: Ken Major (series 9); Paul Kay (series 10)

VISION MIXER: Angela Beveridge (series 7, 8 & 9); Hilary West (series 10)

VIDEOTAPE EDITOR: Ken Pimenta (episodes 49, 51, 53 & 55); Phil Southby (episodes 52 & 54); Mike Taylor (episode 56); Dave Hambelton (episode 57); Ian Howlett (episodes 58 & 62);

Chris Booth (episode 60); Mykola Pawluk (series 10)

PROPERTIES BUYER: Gill Meredith (episodes 57, 58 & 59); Chris Ferriday (episodes 60, 61 & 62); Pauline Seager (series 10)

ASSISTANT FLOOR MANAGER: Roy Gould (series 9); Peter Laskie (series 10)

PRODUCTION ASSISTANT: Donald Clive (episode 11); Bob Spiers (series 3); Bill Wilson (episode 20); Jo Austin (series 4, episode 27, series 5); Chris Breeze (series 6); Gordon Elsbury (episodes 40, 41 & 44); Sue Bennett-Urwin (series 7); Bernadette Darnell (series 9); Sue Oakey (series 10)

PRODUCTION TEAM: Vicky Pugh & Iain McLean (series 8)

PRODUCTION MANAGER: Susan Belbin (series 8); Robin Carr (series 9 & 10)

DIRECTOR: Bernard Thompson (episodes 3 & 5); Ray Butt (episodes 18, 19 & 20, series 4, episode 27, series 5, except episode 34); Bob Spiers (episode 34, series 6 & 9); Gordon Elsbury (episodes 42, 43, 45, 46 & 47); John Kilby (series 8); Martin Shardlow (series 10). All other episodes by David Croft

PRODUCER: David Croft (all episodes, except series 2 by Harold Snoad, series 9 by Bob Spiers & series 10 by Martin Shardlow)

EXECUTIVE PRODUCER: David Croft (series 2, 9 & 10)

1. THE PILOT

(Transmitted: 8/9/1972 and repeated Wed. 14/3/1973, BBC1, 7.30pm)

Mr Lucas	Trevor Bannister
Mrs Slocombe	Mollie Sugden
Captain Peacock	Frank Thornton
Mr Grainger	Arthur Brough
Mr Humphries	John Inman
Miss Brahms	Wendy Richard
Mr Rumbold	Nicholas Smith
Mr Mash	Larry Martyn
Customer	Michael Knowles
Young Mr Grace	Harold Bennett
Secretary	Stephanie Gathercole

Tempers are frayed when Ladieswear joins Menswear on the same floor. While new recruit Mr Lucas welcomes the change, the older members aren't so keen, especially grouchy Grainger, who's protective of his own space; he nearly blows a fuse when Miss Brahms asks whether he'll take his shirts and trousers down to make room for Mrs Slocombe's strapless bras.

Memories

'The set contained all the contents of a store: suits, shirts, trousers, etc. For some reason a lot of the clothes never got back to the store, so when we did the series all the trousers in the rack had the ass cut out of them, the suits were half suits with a sleeve off and there was only ever one glove or sock. That way we made sure we kept the clothes for the whole series!'

DAVID CROFT

WHAT A SCENE!

(Mr Mash has just had words with Mrs Slocombe.)

MR HUMPHRIES: Having trouble with Mrs Slocombe?

MR MASH: All that Women's Lib has gone to her head, mate.

MR HUMPHRIES: Oh, I hope not. If she burns her bra, we'll have to call out the London fire brigade!

The History of
ARE YOU BEING SERVED?

When it comes to sifting the wheat from the chaff in the congested world of TV sitcoms, the passage of time is a good measure of what can rightly be termed a classic. So when *Are You Being Served?* was revived in 1997 to an appreciative audience exceeding eight million – which translated into an audience share of a staggering 46 per cent – Jeremy Lloyd and David Croft's adventures at Grace Brothers had surely earned the right to be classed as an example of classic comedy.

But why has the show been so successful? 'I think everyone recognized the characters who appeared in the show,' replies Jeremy Lloyd. 'In every walk of life and every company, a hierarchy existed where those in authority made life just a little more difficult than necessary for the people at the bottom.' The familiarity of the scenarios explored in *Are You Being Served?* struck a chord with viewers, who in time found a special place in their hearts for Lloyd and Croft's unforgettable bunch of shop-floor characters, including the redoubtable Mrs Slocombe, the imperious Captain Peacock and the nattily dressed Mr Humphries.

While the sitcom's current success has left many people dumbfounded, it speaks volumes for the style of comedy one associates with Messrs Croft and Lloyd. Whereas contemporary sitcoms bludgeon viewers with blatant images and messages, *Are You Being Served?* simply hinted at such matters, and in doing so created an air of gentleness sadly lacking in many of today's offerings.

Resolute against the arrival of progressive, alternative comedy, David Croft, together with his writing partners, continued delivering shows which boasted all the ingredients of good, old-fashioned comedy, and *Are You Being Served?* was no exception. Some people viewed it as bawdy and smutty, but the show's seaside postcard-style humour, with regular doses of *double entendres* and pure farce, attracted a loyal following for whom the sitcom became part of the fabric of their lives.

Although *Are You Being Served?* didn't contain the degree of pathos and character study that shows like *Dad's Army* offered, and was never a substantial social document, it won respect for being an honest slice of solid, dependable British comedy.

Watching life unfold at Grace Brothers was fascinating. The store was hopelessly antiquated, and

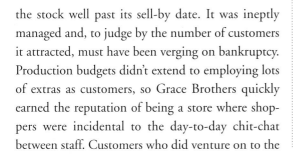

the stock well past its sell-by date. It was ineptly managed and, to judge by the number of customers it attracted, must have been verging on bankruptcy. Production budgets didn't extend to employing lots of extras as customers, so Grace Brothers quickly earned the reputation of being a store where shoppers were incidental to the day-to-day chit-chat between staff. Customers who did venture on to the

shop floor were usually served by the non-speaking sales assistants occupying the background counters, who must have been earning a packet in commission compared with Mrs Slocombe and the others. At times, customers seemed so inconsequential that the staff held informal meetings in the middle of the shop floor – but that was life at Grace Brothers!

The department store was precariously set in its ways: its traditional, hierarchical structure meant it was only a matter of time before the Grace brothers succumbed to the pressures of modern-day retail and closed the business to enjoy their long overdue

LEFT Staff at Grace Brothers were so underworked that they frequently held meetings on the shop floor during the working day. ABOVE Captain Peacock (Frank Thornton) gets a rare chance to sample the culinary delights of the executive dining-room at Grace Brothers.

retirement. Sadly, in Young Mr Grace's case, retirement was short-lived: he died soon after, while on holiday. In an environment where maintenance staff were forbidden from sitting with sales assistants in the canteen, the style of hat one could wear to work was determined by level of seniority, with bowler hats reserved for departmental heads and above, and where female junior assistants were not

13

allowed to wear more frills on their blouses than senior staff, *Are You Being Served?* never failed to tickle the funny bone.

The sitcom may be celebrating its 25th birthday but it's still remarkably fresh. It continues to offer a glimpse into a lost world of innocence, of gentle British humour; and its continued popularity, while new vapid examples of sitcom are languishing, strongly suggests that veterans of British comedy like *Are You Being Served?* will have a place in TV schedules for years to come.

The Idea

Desperation was a key influence behind Jeremy Lloyd's creation. He'd just returned from America, where he'd been writing *Rowan and Martin's Laugh-In*, to find himself out of work. His only job during a barren year was writing a sketch for Jimmy Clitheroe. 'I think people thought I was still in the States,' says Jeremy. 'I was desperate to think of something, so I asked myself: "What do I know best?" The answer was my life at Simpson's department store in Piccadilly. So I wrote an outline about life in a store.'

Jeremy had always admired the work of producer/writer David Croft, so he sent him a copy of his synopsis, as well as posting it to a few TV companies. By the time he received a response from the other companies, Jeremy had already met David to discuss the project. 'David's a man of few words,' smiles Jeremy, 'and when he spoke to me about my idea, he just said: "I think it's very funny, do you want to write it with me?" I agreed, so he told me to meet him the following day. I went over to his house and we started work – it was as simple as that. It was wonderful fun; his wife cooked us delicious meals, and within four days we'd finished the pilot.'

One of the oldest maxims in the world of literature is write from experience, and although *Are You Being Served?* was steeped in comedy and farcical situations, many scenarios explored in the sitcom

were plucked straight from Jeremy's memories of the short time he'd spent working at Simpson's. 'It was very realistic of life in a department store,' he admits. 'All the little nuances like brimming a hat, fluting a handkerchief and the pecking order reminded me of my time at Simpson's. The only things I didn't include were the cardboard collars and cuffs!'

When it came to kneeing the jackets – something that happened regularly at Grace Brothers – Jeremy had first-hand experience. 'It's something I got up to,' he smiles. 'If you only had one jacket and it didn't quite fit because it was too tight under the arms, you'd take it round the back of the counter, stick your knee in the armpit and give it a tug; if you pulled too hard, of course, you'd lost a jacket, so you had to be careful. I was always told: "Wait till you hear the stitches go." So that's what I did!' Jeremy left his job at Simpson's in 1948.

The catchphrases that peppered the scripts are something else he remembers from his days in the retail trade. '"Are you being served?" was a normal shop phrase,' explains Jeremy, 'and "I'm free" was also frequently heard, but as I was a junior and way down the pecking order, I'd only get the chance to say it if the four more senior assistants were busy.'

David Croft liked Jeremy's idea, although he suggested a fundamental change to the format. 'Jeremy's original plan only had a gentlemen's department, so I suggested a joint ladies and menswear department. It needed some girls in it, and Jeremy agreed, so we quickly wrote the pilot. But I really liked the idea, particularly as it was group comedy. Now all we had to do was get the BBC to accept it.'

Getting the Show on Air

The *Are You Being Served?* pilot was transmitted by BBC1 under the *Comedy Playhouse* umbrella, the testing ground for sitcom fledgelings. Although many efforts have sunk without trace after their initial outing, Croft and Lloyd were quietly confident, particularly as their contribution had been shot within the studio and didn't demand expensive location work: its low production costs were a positive factor in the show's ultimate success.

The pilot was given its chance under woeful circumstances: the tragedy of the Munich Olympics, in which eleven Israelis were killed in September 1972, meant that the BBC – whose schedules had been geared around the world event – found themselves with blank screens to fill as coverage of the Games was cancelled. With hours of transmission time to occupy, the *Are You Being Served?* pilot was plucked from the shelf and aired to a captive audience of millions.

Disappointingly, the show met an indifferent response from viewers and BBC executives alike. There was no great rush to commission a series, and it was only because David Croft was in the right place at the right time that the series went ahead at all. 'I was lounging around in the doorway of Bill Cotton's office at the BBC,' he recalls, 'when someone's script for a new series hadn't turned up, so I suggested giving *Are You Being Served?* a chance. I reminded Bill it was cheap and that Jeremy and I could have it ready in six weeks.'

Cotton thought for a while, before agreeing – with one proviso. 'He said: "All right, you can do it, but I don't want the poof in it!" I protested and said: "Without the poof there's no series, Mr Humphries is the funniest character in it." Eventually Bill agreed, but not before warning me against overemphasizing Mrs Slocombe's pussy. He felt two or three jokes of that nature per series would be enough but, of course, we did more.'

'That was how a programme's future was deter-mined in those days. There were no big committees to convince, it was all about one person's hunch; if they felt it seemed right, you got the go-ahead. I miss those days very much.'

And so Jeremy's brainchild hit the screens, with a repeat of the pilot kicking off the first series in 1973. Like most classics, it took a while before the public began viewing it with affection, but Jeremy sensed the feeling of acceptance much earlier.

'When the BBC ordered a second series I suddenly thought the show was a triumph,' he says. 'It was a great time to be writing. The BBC never asked what we were doing; we'd just turn the scripts in, the actors would arrive for rehearsals and before we knew it an episode had been recorded.'

Although the show built up a loyal following of fans, there were factions of the public who disliked aspects of the sitcom. The way Mr Humphries was portrayed angered some in the gay rights movement, but Jeremy Lloyd didn't take much notice of their protests. 'I think 99 per cent of the audience would have loved having Mr Humphries round for dinner, because he was most entertaining, charming and amusing. He was always a friendly, caring sort of character, and I can't see why anyone should have been offended. But you can't please everybody, and I'd rather satisfy most of the audience, as we did, than the minority.'

Concerning Mr Humphries' sexuality, David Croft adds: 'As far as we were concerned, he was just a mother's boy. We never implied he was homosexual, but some people were against him because they thought he was gay yet denying it; we never once suggested anything of the kind.'

The sitcom was also branded politically incorrect by some, but Jeremy feels it pales in comparison with some of today's output. 'We didn't think of it as politically incorrect, that's something that came along after we'd started the show. It may have seemed a little outrageous at times, but it's tame compared with some shows now.'

The Scripts

There was never a dull moment when it came to writing the scripts. Uproarious bursts of laughter were frequently heard as Jeremy and David sat down to pen an episode. In the comfort of either David or Jeremy's home, they took it in turns writing the script in longhand, as Jeremy recalls. 'I'd write five pages, then David five; we'd be talking and writing non-stop. And as soon as the characters fell into place, we'd be imitating them, speaking the lines in their voices – it was hard work but good fun.'

Croft and Lloyd established such a rapport that they found they were able to turn out scripts in days. 'We worked very fast,' explains Jeremy, 'and completed one script in just over two days. I'd got used to working quickly on *Rowan and Martin's Laugh-In*, but as David is also a quick worker we were ideally suited for working together.'

Restricting themselves to around seven scripts a year allowed sufficient time for polishing before rehearsals began. It was an enjoyable period for David and Jeremy. 'We worked well together,' Jeremy says. 'David is the best writing partner I've ever had. As the show progressed we became good friends; initially, we'd go our separate ways when we finished writing a series, but by the third season we'd occasionally have dinner together!'

David found Jeremy an amus-

ing person to work with. 'A stream of comedy pours from him all the time. We'd have hilarious sessions writing the scripts, even though we worked fast. Each episode took just a few days, which is incredible, bearing in mind that included stopping for regular chats and some food.'

Although most scripts were written by the Lloyd-Croft partnership, Michael Knowles – who also appeared in the series – was invited to write a few. 'David was too busy to write them all, so he called me and asked whether I'd like to do some,' says Michael. 'With Harold Snoad, I'd adapted the *Dad's Army* TV episodes for radio, so David knew my writing.' Even though he relished the challenge, Michael was nervous about writing with Jeremy Lloyd. 'Jeremy had just come back from Hollywood, so as a young writer I was worried about working with him. He also writes terribly fast; his brain works like lightning so it's very difficult keeping up with him.'

Michael didn't experience any difficulties writing in the style and manner established in previous episodes. 'It was important I was *au fait* with the show: I watched all the episodes, and read the scripts to understand how the episodes were structured. Although it's strong on character, the object of *Are You Being Served?* is to make people laugh with constant gag lines. And that's something I felt able to contribute to.'

Creating the Characters

Once Grace Brothers – a name influenced by a friend of David's, whose father had inherited a store called Grey Brothers – had been established, staff

Mrs Slocombe (Mollie Sugden) and Miss Brahms
(Wendy Richard) resort to pedal power to get to work.

were required to man the shop-floor. For this, Jeremy relied on his life experiences. After working at Simpson's, he travelled the length of the country as a salesman, selling industrial paint. On his travels he met all sorts of people, many of whom influenced his creations in *Are You Being Served?*

'We created characters who were identifiable,' explains Jeremy, who still spots similar characters in today's department stores. 'Once you've got an ex-army type like Captain Peacock in charge of the floor, you know exactly how he's going to act and talk, and you need to know all your characters that well.'

Peacock, played by Frank Thornton, epitomized

the floorwalkers who patrolled department stores in those days. 'They had usually retired from the army, only to find it difficult getting employment after the war. They always looked smart in a suit, wore their regimental tie with pride and had an air of authority about them.'

As for Mr Humphries, Jeremy believes all stores employ a similar type of character. 'He was bright and enthusiastic, just a mummy's boy, really. I modelled Mr Lucas – who was a thorn in everybody's side – on myself. He'd never be afraid to say how ridiculous things were, challenging traditions like I did until being fired from Simpson's for selling soft drinks in the fitting-room at the height of the summer.

'I've met many Mrs Slocombes in my time, but I don't think she represents anyone in particular, just a northern battle-axe. However, my grandmother was from the north, and a lot of her expressions were fitted in to Mrs Slocombe, so there's an element that was influenced by my grandmother. Miss Brahms, meanwhile, is a typical Essex girl, which will offend some people, no doubt. I borrowed the name from a friend of mine because it was interesting. Miss Brahms was young and more interested in socializing than going to work; she'd never think of her job as a career, it was just a temporary posting she'd held a long time.

'Mr Grainger, the oldest man on the shop floor, was a kind, wonderful old grandfather figure to whom children and adults easily relate. He represents the past, really, and is kind and charming, a loveable character in my view, who was long past retirement even when he joined the department.

'Mr Rumbold wasn't mentioned as often as other characters, but was vital to the show. He was the linchpin because he's the one everyone has to please; Rumbold represents the inefficient management I've encountered several times in my life. He always maintained a tremendous front, but was only in a position of power because of his length of service, not through talent.'

As far as Young Mr Grace is concerned, Jeremy is uncertain what influenced this character. 'He's difficult to place, but I've come across Mr Graces in my time: elderly heads of a company who are very solicitous. By giving him a young secretary we got a lot of fun out of his character. Young Mr Grace was kindly-looking so no one got offended by the remarks he made concerning his secretaries, especially as he was obviously too old to do anything about them!'

In episode 63, a desperate Mrs Slocombe will do anything to keep her job at Grace Brothers – including cleaning the floor!

Mrs Slocombe loved showing off her bras to her colleagues.

The maintenance men, Mr Mash and Mr Harman, adroitly played by Larry Martyn and Arthur English respectively, were treated with disdain by the counter staff and the despotic Captain Peacock. According to their creator, they were the 'below stairs' characters. 'Both Larry and Arthur were in the same happy role, albeit at different times,' explains Jeremy. 'They always got a laugh as they did their best to antagonize authority.' Again, Jeremy Lloyd drew on personal experience when creating these overall-clad maintenance men. 'I knew these characters well,' he says. 'Even before my time behind the suit counter at Simpson's I'd been a "below stairs" person, working in the packing department of an electric light company, starting as a van unloader before working my way up to light bulb inspector. Many of the printable ribald remarks I'd heard in that incarnation appeared in the show. In fact, Mr Mash was based on a Mr Mash I worked with at the electrical company.'

Finally, the shop floor wouldn't have been complete without a few customers wandering around, even if 'few' is the operative word. 'We couldn't afford lots of customers,' explains Jeremy, 'so we got the lift girls and secretaries to walk on the set occasionally, which added extra life to the floor.'

Casting the Roles

Other than playing a fundamental role in securing the services of Candy Davis as Rumbold's final secretary, Jeremy Lloyd was happy to leave the crucial job of casting to David Croft, who already had a great track record in that area. 'Casting is his forté,' says Jeremy, who tried desperately to secure a part for himself. 'I failed to convince David that I should play any sort of role,' he smiles. 'I wouldn't have minded being a customer, but could never get a part. It took about eighty episodes of 'Allo, 'Allo before I made a brief appearance as a German general, and that was because David was away that day!' admits Jeremy, who did manage a cameo appearance as a driver in *Grace and Favour*.

One of the hallmarks of a David Croft production is a fine cast. With a plethora of thespians to choose from, he has a discerning eye when it comes to selecting the right person for the job, and frequently calls upon their services more than once. 'If you know the actor and how they work, it can save a lot of trouble,' he says. 'The wrong person in a company can unsettle a production terribly. I like avoiding hassle and always try to create a family atmosphere.' David's early experience as an actor aids his ability to communicate with the performers he hires. 'Many directors hate actors, but having been one myself I can relate to them and understand the fears they experience. Basically, I listen and treat them as professionals – you have to if you want a happy crew.'

People talk of David Croft's own private repertory company, a cluster of tried and tested actors whom he considers first whenever casting a show. The likes of Jeffrey Holland, Michael Knowles, Wendy Richard and others have popped up in sev-

ABOVE Mr Rumbold's secretaries usually scored top marks in looks, but were bottom of the class in secretarial skills.
LEFT In episode 53, Mr Humphries' mother (played by John Inman) visited the store to quash rumours that her son was heir to the Grace Brothers' throne.

eral shows he's been involved in, and their sterling performances prove that when it comes to picking the personnel, David Croft is a true master.

As far as *Are You Being Served?* was concerned, he knew the people he wanted. 'I first saw John Inman in panto and as soon as I was in a position to use him I did. In *Are You Being Served?* he always gave that extra ten per cent. He knew how to behave in a

store because he'd worked in one, so that was useful. Mr Humphries wasn't a big part to begin with, but John's a wonderful laugh-gatherer and so the role grew and grew as the series progressed.

'Nicholas Smith was a great musician and during rehearsals he'd play anything available – he'd even get a tune out of a teapot if there was one hanging around. Unless it was required for the show I'd have any pianos taken out of the room! But I was very pleased with Nicholas. We wanted a pompous character who was the principal voice of authority. Young Mr Grace was an option, but because of his age I didn't want to lean too heavily on him, and Rumbold worked very nicely.

'I'd worked with Mollie Sugden plenty of times in shows like *Beggar My Neighbour* and *Hugh and I*, so knew her well; she was the only choice as far as Mrs Slocombe was concerned.

'My wife had worked for Arthur Brough in rep at Folkestone, and I'd cast him as a tailor in *Hugh and I* and as a bank employee in *Dad's Army*. A lovely man who was sorely missed, he was very funny during the recordings because occasionally his memory would let him down and he'd get his lines so wrong. He did it once and everyone collapsed in laughter. He turned to me and said: "Is this all the thanks I get for embellishing these otherwise undistinguished scripts!" He was wonderful.

'I'd used Frank Thornton before; he's a fine character actor and absolutely consistent all the way through his performance. Frank's very astute and was heavily employed by the time I came to use him in *Are You Being Served?*

'Trevor Bannister was probably the best known of all the cast. He was a great one for farce and was first choice for Mr Lucas. When he left, Mike Berry was employed and did a good job.

'Harold Bennett was my first choice for Young Mr Grace. I saw him in a panto playing an old bishop. He was marvellous in the part, but I was concerned,

at first, about his age. He looked so old one hesitated before asking whether he still wanted to work. But I needn't have worried because Harold was marvellous: he'd infuriate the rest of the cast because, after they'd played a long scene, he would come on, drop one line and get an almighty laugh from the audience.'

Eventually David noticed Harold beginning to lose his ability to retain the lines. 'His memory was going a little. Harold called me one day and said: "I've had to move house, David, and don't worry about my memory any more: I've been reading lots of books about it and have established a system –

To help push German goods in episode 17, Rumbold's secretary (Moira Foot), Mrs Slocombe and Miss Brahms donned appropriate attire, much to Young Mr Grace's (Harold Bennett) delight.

everything will be all right." I told him that sounded fine, but before finishing the call I said: "If you've got your new address I'd better take it, Harold." He replied: "Oh, yes, it's 40, uh… " There was a long silence before he added: "Hang on a minute, I'll go outside and have a look."'

Jeremy Lloyd watched Harold grow increasingly frail as the series progressed. 'If you made him a cup of tea you couldn't fill it up to the top. He'd say: "Please don't fill my cup up, I'll never get it to my mouth!"'

'Wendy Richard came to the fore after making the record, "Come Outside",' says David. 'I'd used her in *Hugh and I* and she was excellent as Miss Brahms. Larry Martyn, as the stroppy union official Mr Mash, was very good, too, and when he wasn't available, Arthur English, who I'd employed before, was an ideal replacement.'

Jeremy was pleased with the performances delivered by Larry Martyn and Arthur English. 'Of course, Arthur had a very successful stage act as a cockney wide boy and brought the character to life again at Grace Brothers. You can't beat casting an old comedian if the part is right. I was impressed with the entire cast. Trevor was marvellous; I wish he'd stayed longer because he was a competent, well-liked actor. Although it was difficult replacing him, I think Mike Berry worked well. Again, we designed a character who was a thorn in the side of authority. It must have been difficult for him joining a well-established cast, but he coped well.

'Arthur Brough was a fine actor and brilliant in the part,' says Jeremy. 'And John Inman is such an engaging, likeable character, he came across very well. Nicholas Smith is another wonderful actor: he's multi-talented and can play everything from bagpipes to the piano. A very talented person, as were Frank Thornton, Mollie Sugden and Wendy Richard, who were all wonderful.

'One must remember they were all consummate actors who loved the parts they were playing,' Jeremy says. 'They slipped into their characters so

easily, and never really struggled. They always gave it their best shot; one would find it near impossible to form a team like that today.'

Another reason the show ran so smoothly was that no one was the star of the show. 'Someone might have a bigger part to play one week, but that was because it was their turn – it was a gang show and everyone had their chance.'

Changing Faces

One of the risks associated with any long-running production is that unavoidable circumstances can trigger a change in personnel, and *Are You Being Served?* did not survive its twelve-year run unscathed. The first casualty was Mr Grainger, the cantankerous old man who headed the menswear department.

Regardless of how smooth the transition period is, such changes inevitably disrupt the show. Even the die-hard fans would tacitly admit the cast reshuffles were unfortunate. Actor Frank Thornton feels they weakened the programme. 'A few characters were tried out after Arthur Brough died, before it was eventually decided to promote Mr Humphries to head of Menswear. This again weakens the show because a key figure is removed from the situation. The bad-tempered old man was useful for Lucas and Humphries to bounce off, but once he was taken away that avenue had gone. The older character at the head of the department was essential to the success of the show.'

The death of Arthur Brough hit everyone hard. 'He was a funny, warm individual,' says David Croft. 'He always made me laugh because his lips never seemed to synchronize with his words. We missed him terribly when we got together for the sixth series. But his character had to be replaced because Mr Grainger had been important to the show and his absence left a huge gap at the counter.'

Jeremy Lloyd was shocked when he heard the news of Arthur's death. 'It was a very sad day. It was hard to believe that someone you knew so well was no longer around. It was a great sense of loss for everyone.'

Mr Humphries tries his hand at film directing when Grace Brothers decide to splash out on a commercial.

Although it was difficult coming to terms with the loss of Arthur Brough, neither Jeremy nor David considered calling it a day. 'There was never any question of giving up,' explains Jeremy. 'The show was doing terribly well: we were attracting audiences of over twenty million, and enjoying success in countries as far afield as Australia, New Zealand, Zambia and Israel. By this stage the cast was receiving letters from fans around the world. People were telling me how much they loved the show, and I began realizing how lucky I was to have created it. Arthur was unique and no one could have taken over his character, but David and I both felt we had to bring in someone new.'

The first actor to join the cast after Brough's death was James Hayter, a veteran of the profession, playing Mr Tebbs. 'James Hayter was wonderful and we wouldn't have replaced him ever,' says David Croft. 'He was the voice behind the Mr Kipling cake adverts, a valuable contract to him. James lived in Spain and returned to England a couple of times a year to do another advert – he earned a lot of money from it.

'But the advertising agency or the client, I'm not sure which, didn't think his role in *Are You Being Served?* projected the right image for the man who did the voice-overs for Mr Kipling. So James had to elect whether to stay with the adverts, which he'd done for years, or stay with us, and I'm afraid we lost.'

When Old Mr Grace (Kenneth Waller) stepped into his younger brother's shoes at the head of the firm, he shared the same interests!

When Hayter left, Alfie Bass, another actor whose name was already well known among audiences, joined the staff of Grace Brothers, playing Mr Goldberg in the seventh series. 'Alfie was good but decided not to stay around for the following series.'

The eighth season saw two characters join Menswear: Milo Sperber and Benny Lee. 'It didn't quite work out with Milo and he left during the series. I'd seen him give a gorgeous performance in *The History Man* and thought he'd be all right for us, but I don't think he was very happy with the

scripts and so the comedy suffered a little,' admits David. 'But Benny Lee was excellent and he stayed for the rest of series eight.'

A further departure was that of Mr Lucas, another jolt to the backbone of the show. 'Slowly the strong, original team was whittled down,' says Frank Thornton. 'Sometimes changes work, sometimes they don't – it's just that we experienced so many.'

The Signature Tune

Over the years, the *Are You Being Served?* signature tune has become well known. It may not be a catchy number one would constantly hum, but nevertheless it had its own unique style. Over the clanking sound of the cash register, which was rung up more times during the two-minute tune than throughout the entire 69 episodes, a lift girl was heard announcing each floor. The woman's voice belonged not to one of the lift girls, but to Stephanie Reeve (née Gathercole), Mr Rumbold's first secretary.

The tune was written by David Croft. 'One of the problems with signature tunes in those days was that musicians had a tough contract, which meant you didn't get much value for money. I tried eliminating the need to hire musicians, and asked a sound expert to come up with a soundtrack based on the noises heard in a department store: closing lift gates, bells ringing, cash registers opening – anything he could find.

'My idea was that once we'd come up with such a track, we could use it between the scenes, saving a lot of money in the process. Finally, I got Ronnie Hazlehurst and Stephanie to add the finishing touches.'

Jeremy classes it as a 'very catchy tune'. 'We wanted something to represent the store. In the short time you have available, it's difficult writing a song that people will recall and associate with the show, but with sound effects one seems to remember them a lot easier. And I was pleased with the outcome.'

Costumes and Make-Up

In charge of costumes for the pilot episode and the first series was June Hudson (née Wilson). Her designs set the style for future episodes, and she's proud to have been involved with *Are You Being Served?*

When it came to researching life in a traditional, antiquated department store, June turned to her auntie. 'Auntie Mavis had been in charge of a ladies' department in a store in High Wycombe, not unlike Grace Brothers. She dressed and talked just like Mrs Slocombe! Although the costumes were obviously exaggerated, I based them on what my auntie wore.'

Social history is one of June's interests, so she enjoyed the research involved in *Are You Being Served?* She could also relate to the world in which the sitcom was immersed. 'With my auntie having worked in a store, and me living in Chiswick with an excellent example of a hierarchical department store just up the road, I didn't have far to go to observe the environment. The sitcom was my cup of tea, and I loved working on it.'

For a while, June was undecided about what form Mrs Slocombe's and Miss Brahms' uniforms should take. 'I decided against a suit and, as a skirt seemed too much like a waitress, I finally chose a pinafore dress. It's easy to wear because it doesn't ride up, and there wouldn't be any problems with blouses untucking, which would look untidy and possibly lead to continuity problems. A pinafore seemed the ideal solution because it lends itself towards all sorts of possibilities.' As far as the colour was concerned, June chose brown for practical reasons. 'The monitors in the studio were black-and-white, and brown was a good mid-tone.'

There were subtle differences between the women's costumes. 'Mrs Slocombe, who wasn't unlike a pantomime dame, saw everything she had

June Hudson's original designs for Mrs Slocombe's and Miss Brahms'
costumes, which have never before been published, reveal the amount of
detail that went into making the show authentic.

as a badge of office,' says June. 'She was permitted to have a bow, a cravat or frills around the neckline. Being senior, she was also the only one allowed to wear jewellery, that's why early in the series she had a big cameo – it was almost an insignia, a mark of authority. She was a bit of an icon, really, and reminds me of Auntie Mavis every time I watch her. She used to put on a special voice for customers, just like Mrs Slocombe.'

Meanwhile, Miss Brahms had a plain blouse with just a small collar round the neck; she wasn't allowed to wear anything more elaborate – then again, Wendy Richard was so glamorous she didn't need it. 'She was exactly like her character: bright, cheerful, very quick-witted,' says June, who went on to become the first costume designer on *East-Enders*, where she met Wendy again.

As the series progressed, the sexual element, so overtly expressed through the secretaries, became more prominent and important to the flavour of the show, but in the early days when June was involved, it was an area hardly exploited. 'Miss Brahms, for example, was covered right up to the neck – but I did cut her pinafore to miniskirt length.'

When June had completed her designs, she presented her ideas at the regular production meeting that took place with the rest of the team assigned to the show. 'I'd talk to the producer and director, which was David Croft, about what he wanted and I'd tell him my ideas. At that point I'd also be told about the characters and the actors that had been cast. By this time I would have read the scripts, and if necessary completed some sketches – a straightforward procedure that worked effectively.'

The next stage in the process involved the actors coming to the costume department to discuss their outfits. 'I'd call the artist and they'd come in to meet me. We'd discuss the character and I'd show my sketches, then we might have a dummy run: I'd book a fitting-room and I'd give an idea of the sort of clothes the character would wear.'

A lot of fabric was kept in the workroom, but often June would buy material from John Lewis or Shepherd's Bush Market. 'We bought many things at the market,' she recalls, 'because you could find the most wonderful selection of designs and colours.' Once the material was to hand and the actor had been measured, a costume would be made ready for the first fitting. 'That was when I'd make my major decisions regarding the costume's length and final shape.'

June enjoyed working with the cast. 'John Inman was a very quiet, serious actor, whereas Trevor Bannister was just like Mr Lucas: he was a real lad, always laughing and falling about. I had the women's clothes made, but when it came to the men's suits, I bought them from a retailer called Take Six in Bond Street' – an experience she'll always remember.

'We used to travel to the shop on the Tube from Television Centre. Once there, Trevor would get behind the counter and play around; the staff adored him and always looked forward to his arrival. He was always on the go, I don't know where he found the energy.'

With the male characters' suits being bought off-the-peg, June didn't encounter any problems. 'Mr Humphries wore very quiet work clothes; the only thing he did have was a floral tie. Mr Rumbold and Mr Grainger wore the typical bank manager's suit, while Harold Bennett's was hired.'

The walk-ons, normally hired to play customers, a rare breed in the world of Grace Brothers, were required to bring their own costumes. 'Their job was to be in the background and not be eye-catching; normally they'd be given directives like no large patterns, no reds, no logos – just quiet, neutral colours so they remained in the background and didn't distract the eye of the audience, who you wanted watching the principal actors.'

As the costume designer, it was June's job to set the style of the show and establish the characters. The entire mood and feel of the costumes were decided during her time on the show, a responsibility she held for many other popular programmes, including *Till Death Us Do Part*, *The Onedin Line* and *The Fall and Rise of Reginald Perrin*.

During the era of *Are You Being Served?*, the BBC's Costume Department consisted of some sixty designers. 'When a new programme or series was being made, a designer was usually asked whether they wanted to work on it. Being an artistic job, it was important the designer was enthusiastic about their project, or it may have shown in their work.'

When June, who also worked on *Blake's 7* as well as designing more episodes of *Doctor Who* than anyone else, was asked to work on *Are You Being Served?*, she was about to embark on a director's course within the BBC, so she wasn't being allocated any long-running assignments. But she was keen to pick up the show. 'I was pleased to be offered sitcoms,' she says, 'partly because I love expressing humour in clothes, seeking out elements of the costume that are amusing not just in the obvious, but also the subtext, the subtle things which the audience will recognize subconsciously.'

June left the BBC in 1991 and now works freelance as well as lecturing on costume design at Manchester University and acting – she originally trained as an actress – but looks back on her *Are You Being Served?* days with joy. 'It was a delightful time,' she says. 'I adored the actors and it was a very funny programme to work on.'

One of the trademarks of *Are You Being Served?* was the myriad of garish-coloured wigs worn by Mrs Slocombe. The colour combinations became so incredible that one wondered whether the Visual Effects department had got involved with their design! Jill Shardlow, wife of producer and director Martin, worked on make-up during the fifth series and vividly remembers the wigs. 'It became a sort of competition, with people wondering what colour Mollie's hair would be each week,' she says. 'We always tried bettering the previous week's ridiculous colour, which created a rod for our own backs – but it was good fun.'

Before Jill, now Head of Design at the BBC, got involved in the series, Mollie Sugden had dyed her own hair, but by now she was resorting to wigs instead. 'It was much easier for us to stick a wig on a block and colour it, instead of carting Mollie off and torturing her. We used a couple of wigs, which meant one could have a rest each week; recolouring all the time beat hell out of them, so it's hardly surprising Mollie gave up colouring her own hair for the show.'

Jill, too, has nothing but happy memories of the series. 'It was a great team of people. Occasionally when you join an ongoing series you feel like an interloper, which is an uncomfortable feeling. But the team was very welcoming. Such an atmosphere usually stems from the producer, and David was good at creating a family atmosphere; when I was a junior make-up assistant I worked for him on *Dad's Army* and it was just the same on that show.'

Creating the Effects

As the sitcom was shot entirely in the studio, one might think there was little scope for adventurous visual effects, but that was not the case: there was a call for plenty of interesting props, like automatons or illuminating bras! One of the mainstays of the BBC's Visual Effects department at the time was Tony Oxley, whose creative talents were regularly tapped for *Are You Being Served?*

Tony, who left the Beeb to work freelance and is now enjoying his retirement, always enjoyed working on the sitcom. 'All the cast were friendly and there was a good atmosphere, which isn't always the case,' he says. 'I was allowed a lot of freedom in my job. The production team would tell me what it wanted, but I always felt free to develop the idea, taking it a stage further.'

At the start of a new series, Tony would be presented with copies of the scripts and an indication of what was required for any particular episode; he was then responsible for deciding what was possible and subsequently costing the prop. 'There was never much money to play around with. But having been in the job some time, I used to make things in the obvious way, nothing elaborate. While others were using electronics and hydraulics, I was content with elastic bands and springs, which were much cheaper – I think that was another reason the production team liked me,' smiles Tony.

Occasionally he'd be presented with a real challenge, like the time Mrs Slocombe's hair had to stand up on end in the episode 'The Night-Club'. 'I had a great deal of trouble getting it to work, but succeeded in the end,' admits Tony, who resorted to tubes and compressed air. 'Little tubes were embedded in Mollie's wig and I was crouching down

The Visual Effects team could always be relied upon to deliver the goods, as this example from episode 27 shows.

behind her, pumping air up a pipe and into the tubes within the wig. It was often the simple things that caused most headaches.'

In those pre-radio-control days, automatons used in the show were usually controlled by wires, or even strings. 'I remember making an exploding cat for the episode 'The Clock', which was quite difficult. It was meant to be a model cat that went wrong while demonstrating something: it was left to me to decide what should go wrong. They weren't expecting much, so were surprised when I presented a cat whose tail revolved at high speed before exploding and falling flat with its legs stuck out. It was very funny.'

Both David Croft and Jeremy Lloyd hold Tony and the other members of Tony's Visual Effects team in high regard. Aware of their ingenuity and propensity for seeking challenges, David and Jeremy began writing scenes with Tony's team in mind. 'We knew they were clever and very good at their jobs,' says David. 'We'd write a scene that required a model or

something, make suggestions, but they'd always go one step further and improve on our original idea.'

David recalls an example. 'We needed a ventriloquist's dummy that looked like Young Mr Grace. All we wanted was for its arm to lift up and take a hat off. But Tony arranged it so that when the arm tried lifting the hat, the whole head lifted off as well while it remained speaking.'

Jeremy was equally appreciative of the work put in by the Visual Effects team. 'They were excellent. Whatever we wanted, they came up with the goods. In a way, I think they loved being presented with these different challenges, of which many were unusual: after all, what other show would require props that included a revolving bosom and backside?' he smiles.

While writing the scripts, Jeremy and David

Captain Peacock was always leering at Rumbold's secretaries (played here by Isabella Rye) but it never got him anywhere.

roared with laughter as they dreamed up scenes and props to go with them. 'It was a laugh while planning,' says Jeremy, 'but then someone had to actually design and make the prop. However, Visual Effects always did us proud.'

Helping with Production

As with all BBC productions there was always a dedicated team working behind the scenes to ensure the show ran smoothly. Jo Austin worked with David Croft as a production assistant and, later, production manager. 'David kept the same team for years, so I'd be working on *Are You Being Served?* in the early part of the year, *Dad's Army* during the summer, before moving on to *It Ain't Half Hot, Mum*. He liked working with a familiar set of people, and if someone was promoted, he'd always try getting them back in their higher capacity.'

For Jo it was a busy period in her career, but one she enjoyed. 'You'd always be planning ahead. By the time I'd finished *It Ain't Half Hot, Mum* in November or December, I would already have begun planning *Are You Being Served?* But David would always give plenty of notice if something needed investigating, planning or clearing through regulations. He was a perfectionist and easy to work for.'

The fact that it was a studio-based production created a pressure in itself. Although everyone took it in their stride, Jo feels it was a difficult task on the actual day of recording, something that would have been helped if the show had included location shots. 'You had to do thirty minutes' studio filming; there were no five or ten-minute breaks in recording while location filming was shown to the studio audience, which meant there was nothing to lighten the load. The recording day was hectic because we started at 10.30 a.m. and rehearsed a complete thirty-minute episode in order to be ready to go in front of the audience at 8 p.m. But the cast were all pros and just got on with it.'

As to why the sitcom became such a success, Jo, who's retired from the business, says: 'It contained all the right ingredients: it was fun, slightly outrageous without being mucky, and had a brilliant cast. You don't always get a complete cast to gel, but David has a knack of achieving it, and this show was no exception.'

Susan Belbin, who'd worked with David on several of his productions including *Dad's Army* and *'Allo, 'Allo* was assistant floor manager on many *Are You Being Served?* series. She remembers it as one of the happiest periods of her life. 'A little bickering went on at times, but everyone was very loyal to each other.'

One thing she remembers about working for

David was his 'Edward Heath laugh'. 'He'd always be laughing at his own jokes with his shoulders going up and down just like Edward Heath. It was obvious he was enjoying what he was doing, and this would permeate through to everyone else. It was a very happy production and everyone would be in giggles at some point or other; you could see the cast enjoying it just as much as the audience.'

Directing the eighth series in 1981 was John Kilby, who also worked on *Hi-De-Hi!* and *It Ain't Half Hot, Mum* with Croft. He enjoyed being involved in the sitcom. 'I always liked working for David,' he says. 'He's a man of loyalty, and instigates loyalty amongst his team. There was always a great social element in the production and it was marvellous being associated with it – it was also the first show I directed.'

The Set

It took two attempts to get the *Are You Being Served?* set right. Jeremy explains: 'The end result was very convincing, but after the first attempt the set was too up-market for Grace Brothers. So we got another designer who created a set with more of a Harrow Road style to it which was ideal for our show.'

Not everyone felt the same way. Actually working within the set posed its fair share of challenges. For director John Kilby the famous shop floor was 'the set from hell'. 'It was so massive: you had these two main counters, and trying to shoot an intimate conversation across those acres of space was very difficult. But I enjoyed every moment of my time on the show.'

The design of the lifts also fascinated John. 'You had two lifts that presumably came up from somewhere, but as soon as the customers came out of the lift they had to go down some stairs. I couldn't work out the logic behind the design of the building,' laughs John. 'Obviously it was all about entrances for the characters, but it was a fact that always intrigued me.'

Dressing the Set

Authenticity and accuracy were vital elements in *Are You Being Served?* So keen were Jeremy and David to ensure the set looked right that they hired the services of Donald Speake to dress it each week. 'It was important everything was realistic,' explains Jeremy, 'so Donald, who owned his own store, came in each week and made sure that was the case.'

Donald first worked for the BBC in 1965, after opening a general drapery near Television Centre. 'Our place was just down the road from Wood Lane, and one day some BBC buyers came into the shop and my association with the BBC began,' he says. By the 1970s Donald Speake had become well known in the industry and his services were regularly in demand.

'As far as *Are You Being Served?* is concerned, someone contacted me and said they were launching a big new show that required lots of hired clothing – was I interested? I jumped at the chance.' Donald didn't work on the pilot, but when the first series was commissioned he picked up responsibility for supplying all the clothing seen on the shop floor, dressing the set and providing the dummies used in the store.

The day of recording was hard work, as Donald recalls. 'I was at Television Centre at 7.30 in the morning getting everything ready for rehearsals. The dress rehearsal took place in the afternoon, and the actual recording in the evening. Several times during the day sets were changed, which meant moving all the models and clothes, only to put them back again ready for the evening recording. It was extremely tiring. Then, at the end of the day, with only a single light burning, my assistant and I had to pack everything up until the following week.'

After a lot of the clothes borrowed for the pilot episode were never seen again, Donald had to ensure the goods he supplied were totally useless for the purposes for which they were originally made. 'If it was a pair of leather gloves we'd cut bits out of it. They could display the front, but the backs were cut out. Doing that meant no one would want to pinch them. Trousers were cut in half, shirts had the backs removed – it had to be done, or they might have been stolen.'

Donald felt the set was very realistic. 'It had a 1950s feel to it,' he says, 'and we dressed it accordingly; even the dummies were from that era. Although it was exaggerated, the show provided an accurate view of what life was like in a department store of that time.' Even Donald's father, who'd worked in a traditional department store, commented on how much it resembled his days on the floor. 'He told me it was exactly right, particularly the hierarchical attitudes.'

Donald greatly enjoyed the years he spent on *Are You Being Served?*, and he was sad when the series finished. 'Every year someone would call and say: "Hello, Don, they're starting again in April, can you come along to a production meeting?" And off

The snooty Miss Featherstone (Joanna Dunham) rubbed everyone up the wrong way when she replaced Mrs Slocombe in episode 63. Luckily, her stay was short-lived.

we'd go again. I ended up making friends with many people associated with the show. It was a lovely time and when the show finished it felt like part of my life was missing.'

The Final Days

Producing and directing the final series was Martin Shardlow, whose credits include *Terry and June, Only Fools and Horses* and *Black Adder*. He recalls the never-ending farewell parties. 'We had an awful lot of dos, but that was justified when you consider the show ran twelve years.

'It was a brilliant series to work on because everyone got on so well, an essential ingredient for any long-running sitcom. When you're putting a show together you tend to cast not only in terms of who'll play the parts well, but whether they'll get on together – and on *Are You Being Served?* everyone did. In fact, we spent a lot of time falling about with laughter and saying, "We can't possibly put that in!"'

One of the techniques Martin learnt from David

Croft, who was executive producer on the final series, was the 'self-cleaning joke'. 'Basically, you can get away with murder if it cleans itself up in time,' smiles Martin, who left the BBC in 1989 to work freelance. 'David's a great advocate of the self-cleaning joke and, consequently, *Are You Being Served?* is full of them!'

Jo Austin, who worked on earlier episodes, concurs with Martin. 'David's very clever. Whenever he used the "pussy" lines, for example, he always prefaced it with something making the remark perfectly logical, which meant only someone's mind could turn it into anything else.'

By the time Martin Shardlow became involved with the sitcom it was running like a well-oiled machine, but he succeeded in stamping his own style and ideas on the tenth and final series. 'In one episode I was determined to answer the biggest question of all time: "Why do all the people in *Are You Being Served?* sit down one side of the dinner table in the canteen?" I wanted to address that one, so on one occasion I pre-recorded a canteen scene enabling everyone to see all around the table; it confused the cast because they'd never done it before!'

After the show had run for so many years, actor Frank Thornton wasn't surprised when David Croft and Jeremy Lloyd called it a day. 'The show was entirely studio-bound, which had advantages and disadvantages,' he explains. 'The BBC, which was conscious of costs, liked our show because it was cheap – there was no expensive location filming. But as a result of being limited to the studio, it was difficult to think up any new story-lines, so I wasn't shocked when it came to an end.'

Although for many of the actors it was a big disappointment when Grace Brothers finally closed down, even though they were expecting it, David Croft felt the sitcom had overstayed its welcome. 'We'd had an excellent run, but had taken it a bit too far – and I think the cast felt that as well. The scripts were getting tired. In the life of any sitcom you're on borrowed time once you go beyond forty episodes,' he says. 'There's a temptation to go on and on, but Jeremy and I wanted to finish while the programme was on a high, and we achieved that. Any bad press we did receive occurred because the show, having gone on too long, became a little contrived.'

One criticism thrown at the programme during the latter days of its life was to do with the repetition of story-lines, an accusation that Jeremy – who wrote the last two series on his own – disagrees with. 'We never directly duplicated a story-line. There was a familiarity about some episodes, I agree, but that's not a bad thing. When you think about it, coming up with 69 story-lines in a set the size of a large living-room with counters at either side, it's amazing we dreamt up as many plots as we did.'

However, he admits that life became more difficult when David, who was recovering from a heart attack, was unable to co-write the final two series. 'It was less enjoyable working on my own

because we'd become a team as far as *Are You Being Served?* was concerned.'

The last series was transmitted in 1985, but the writers had considered giving up years before, until a BBC executive persuaded them to continue. 'We were in the States discussing the possibility of an American version. One day we bumped into Bill Cotton; he'd heard we had decided not to write any more episodes but was able to convince us it was worth continuing.'

When it did finally finish, Jeremy knew it was the right decision. 'I just couldn't think of any more situations to write about – it had reached a natural end.' To bow out on a high note was important, rather than see audiences gradually dwindle as the format became increasingly tired. 'You never want to write a series until it reaches the point when people don't want to see it any more. Although it's nice to be paid, there's a time when you have to stop.'

The cast was sad at the prospect of no longer working as a team, and so were David and Jeremy. 'The cast presented us with a "thank you" decanter each, which I display proudly in my home,' says Jeremy. 'We had a farewell party and organized a couple of reunions. Working together for more than ten years represented a sizeable chunk of our lives; we were like a close-knit community.'

For David, *Are You Being Served?* was one of the happiest shows he's worked on. 'All the shows were happy,' he says. 'When you're on location there's a holiday atmosphere, which we obviously didn't get with *Are You Being Served?*, but it was still a happy period of my life.'

One wonders whether, with hindsight, they would change anything about *Are You Being Served?* if they were starting over again. 'No,' says Jeremy. 'We were writing for that period, but in saying that, when you watch it today, I don't think it has aged much. The casting was right and the pace of the episodes was as well; David was good at not letting story-lines progress too quickly; he held stories back, which worked well.

In the final episode, Mr Spooner (Mike Berry) becomes a pop star thanks to a winning performance in the London Department Stores' annual concert.

'But if I was forced to think of one thing I'd do differently, it would be to include more departments within the set. Rather than just men's and ladies' wear, different types of goods could have been sold. But the show was a big success anyway, so it doesn't matter.'

Current Success

The recent run of *Are You Being Served?* episodes has entertained millions of viewers on BBC1, many of whom are having their first taste of this classic sitcom. Attracting audiences of over eight million, the repeats have been a great success by anyone's standards, surprising many people as well as the BBC. It's all the more surprising, therefore, to hear that David Croft had been trying to get the Beeb to repeat the show for years. 'I've sent letters as often as I dare without becoming a crashing bore, sug-

gesting the programme be reshown; but it has taken years and years. I reminded the BBC that the show used to attract audiences of twenty million, many of whom would still be alive and, I felt, would probably love the chance to see it again.'

Eventually he convinced the decision-makers at the BBC, who started a run of repeats in the autumn of 1997, with David deciding which episodes to show. 'I've rejected some because they explore subjects that aren't particularly relevant today; those that have been selected are re-edited and the soundtracks polished, so overall the episodes are a little sharper.

'In some cases, it's been over 22 years since the episode was last screened. There was always resistance to it in the BBC,' says David. 'I think it was because many people thought the style of humour was like the *Carry On* films, not the sort of thing the BBC should do. But I was finally able to convince someone to show it, and the results speak for themselves.'

The show's recent success hasn't surprised

Jeremy or David. 'Humour doesn't change. If something is funny, it will always remain funny. The way one presents comedy may change with time, but the basic elements stay the same,' says David, who feels the show has stood the test of time. 'Whenever I see it now I marvel at how professional and competent the team was; they all seemed so confident, mainly because the show was a success and they knew they didn't have to look over their shoulders to see if an axe was going to fall; that made a difference to their morale.'

Director John Kilby believes the sitcom's present success is typical of David Croft's shows. 'It's an institution and doesn't contain any domestic clutter, like all his work; it's almost surreal and, like *Dad's Army*, the show was not contemporary when it was written. There is very little said about what is happening in the world, and these non-contemporary attitudes mean it can be repeated endlessly without appearing too old-fashioned.'

Critics have in the past classed *Are You Being Served?* as smutty humour, but John, who left the

Read all about it!

Over the years, *Are You Being Served?* has often been the butt of jokes for critics and journalists, derogatory in respect of the show's value to the world of television. Occasionally someone would offer a little praise and spot the fact that, as far as the British public was concerned, Croft and Lloyd's creation was half an hour of good, honest fun. The following extracts reveal the thoughts of the media during the life of this classic sitcom:

'It's nice to see that *Are You Being Served?*... has been chosen as a series. There's a gentleness and silly affection about it that is as human as any of those fast-vanishing stores themselves.'

DAILY MAIL, 15.3.73

'There is some fine character acting in *Are You Being Served?*... but what could have been rich play between Mollie Sugden's hoity-toity chief of ladies' wear and the men, led by Frank Thornton as Captain Peacock ... was ruined last night by vulgar knockabout and silly jokes – old silly jokes.'

THE TIMES, 15.3.73

BBC in 1988 and now works freelance, defends the show.

'No one ever does anything, they're all impotent in a sense. You can have a snigger but it's harmless humour, no one ever gets hurt.'

The Future for
Are You Being Served?

The success of repeats across the world proves that Lloyd and Croft's classic sitcom will live on for years to come. Although it has never crossed Jeremy or David's minds to resurrect the sitcom in its original form, offers have been made to reunite the cast once more. 'Recently, we had several offers from America for a show,' says Jeremy. 'The idea was that the cast would take over a floor in an American store in Brooklyn or somewhere. It would probably be a film, showing the cast coming to terms with the American way of life. If someone comes up with a reasonable deal and we're allowed to contribute our thoughts to the project, we may be interested in discussing it further. We'll have to wait and see.'

'If the creation of credible, funny characters is the essence of television situation comedy, *Are You Being Served?* could prove a useful addition to the ranks ... it would be optimistic to suppose that Mr Croft has hit on another *Dad's Army*, but *Are You Being Served?* may be worth watching.'

DAILY TELEGRAPH, 15.3.73

'I missed the comedy series *Are You Being Served?* on its appearance. The fact that it has been brought back must, I thought, have meant that I deprived myself of much-needed laughter in these austere times. Not so, this contrived nonsense ... should have discreetly been left on the shelf ...'

EVENING NEWS 15.3.74

'Candidates for the most inept comedy series of the year so far should definitely include ATV's *It's Tarbuck on Tuesdays* ... marginally worse is BBC1's *Are You Being Served?* on Wednesdays.'

MORNING STAR, 7.4.73

'I would like to be kind. I really would. I would like to say that *Are You Being Served?*, which returned to BBC1 last night, gave us service with a smile. It didn't. I watch grim-faced as the cast plunged despondently deeper and deeper into a predictable situation and struggled with even more predictable lines.'

EVENING NEWS 9.4.76

'*Are You Being Served?* ranks as one of the all-time TV turkeys ... if only the scripts were better ... but the cast do their damnedest to get what they can out of them.'

DAILY EXPRESS 2.4.85

'It served the BBC well for years but as the plots grew thin, it became a parade of pantomime personalities.'

SUNDAY EXPRESS 7.4.85

Episode Guide

SERIES ONE

REGULAR CAST MEMBERS

Mrs Slocombe	Mollie Sugden
Mr Lucas	Trevor Bannister
Captain Peacock	Frank Thornton
Mr Humphries	John Inman
Miss Brahms	Wendy Richard
Mr Grainger	Arthur Brough
Mr Rumbold	Nicholas Smith

2. 'DEAR SEXY KNICKERS'

(Transmitted: Wed. 21/3/73, BBC1, 7.30pm)

ALSO APPEARING:

The 40" Waist	Robert Raglan
The 28" Inside Leg	Derek Smith

Mr Lucas is smitten with Miss Brahms, so composes a love note:

'Dear Sexy Knickers, I don't 'alf fancy you. Meet me outside at 5.30 and we'll get it together!'

But nothing runs smoothly at Grace Brothers and the misdirected note ends up in the hands of Mrs Slocombe, who thinks Captain Peacock is the author. As the mayhem unfolds, Mrs Slocombe and Miss Brahms embarrass themselves, and Mr Grainger is shocked to hear a woman has plans to 'get him on the carpet'!

WHAT A SCENE!

(Mr Humphries tells new recruit Mr Lucas a trick of the trade.)

MR HUMPHRIES: This is a little wrinkle worth knowing; come over here, I don't want Peacock to see. Now you've heard of putting the boot in, this is what's known as putting the knee in.

(Humphries pushes his knee into a jacket sleeve.)

MR HUMPHRIES: See, you put it over like that…

MR LUCAS: Oh, oh, oh, very crafty.

MR HUMPHRIES: And you pull until you break all the stitches. If you listen you can hear them go.

MR LUCAS: *(tapping his nose)* There's a trick in every trade, isn't there?

MR HUMPHRIES: Well the trick in this, Mr Lucas, is making sure the customer gets it home before the sleeves drop off.

3. OUR FIGURES ARE SLIPPING

(Transmitted: Wed. 28/3/73, BBC1, 7.30pm)

ALSO APPEARING:

Young Mr Grace ....Harold Bennett

Secretary...Stephanie Gathercole

The Returned Glen Check.....................Peter Needham

Sales are down and Rumbold suggests a course in salesmanship; initial reluctance to stay behind after the doors close is quashed with the threat of cutbacks unless things improve. Over hot cocoa and rock-hard buns, Rumbold dithers his way through an uninspiring session on sales techniques. The arrival of Young Mr Grace signifies it's time to go home, but not before Mr Lucas impresses the geriatric with his sales techniques by selling him his own vicuna overcoat.

4. CAMPING IN

(Transmitted: Wed. 4/4/73, BBC1, 7.30pm)

ALSO APPEARING:

Mr Mash ....Larry Martyn

The Scot...James Copeland

The 38C Cup......................................Anita Richardson

The Large Brim with Fruit.....................Pamela Manson

Secretary...Stephanie Gathercole

The Man with the Large Bra.................David Rowlands

The Leatherette Gloves ....Colin Bean

A transport strike forces everyone to spend the night in the store. Tents are provided, but Mrs Slocombe worries about sleeping in such close proximity to the men – old Mr Grainger isn't too keen on the idea either, particularly with Humphries around! While Mrs Slocombe wonders who'll zip her up, Grainger leaves his flap open and Peacock wants to share Rumbold's bed.

WHAT A SCENE!

(Mrs Slocombe complains to Mr Rumbold about her cupboard drawers.)

MRS SLOCOMBE: Before we go any further, Mr Rumbold, Miss Brahms and I would like to complain about the state of our drawers. They're a positive disgrace.

MR RUMBOLD: Your what, Mrs Slocombe?

MRS SLOCOMBE: Our drawers, they're sticking and it's always the same in damp weather.

MR RUMBOLD: Really!

MRS SLOCOMBE: Miss Brahms could hardly shift hers at all just now.

MR LUCAS: (*sniggering*) No wonder she was late.

MRS SLOCOMBE: They sent a man who put beeswax on them, but that made them worse.

MR RUMBOLD: I'm not surprised.

MISS BRAHMS: I think they need sandpapering.

WHAT A SCENE!

(Mrs Slocombe tries her best to sell a hat.)

CUSTOMER: Do you think it suits me?

MRS SLOCOMBE: Oh, yes, it does, madam. And those artificial cherries are very youth-making, don't you think, Miss Brahms?

MISS BRAHMS: (*sarcastically*) Oh yes, Mrs Slocombe, takes years off her.

MRS SLOCOMBE: And that green goes so well with madam's eyes.

CUSTOMER: I've got brown eyes!

MRS SLOCOMBE: (*panicking*) That's what I mean… they're the sort of brown that goes so well with green… gives you a sort of film star look.'

CUSTOMER: (*smiling*) Oh.

MRS SLOCOMBE: Marlene Dietrich.

CUSTOMER: But she's in her seventies!

MRS SLOCOMBE: Well she wasn't when she was about forty.

5. HIS AND HERS

(Transmitted: Wed. 11/4/73, BBC1, 7.30pm)

ALSO APPEARING:

Miss French ....Joanna Lumley

Mr Mash ....Larry Martyn

The Customers ....Margaret Flint & Evan Ross

Who's moved the central display stand? Mr Rumbold solves the mystery by announcing that Grace Brothers have signed a deal with His and Hers, a perfumery, allowing an in-store promotional stand. When free ties and stockings are given away with every purchase, Mrs Slocombe and Mr Grainger hit the roof through fear of losing business. When commission is at risk, even Mr Lucas is keen to get rid of the leggy assistant, with the help of a microphone in his hat!

WHAT A SCENE!

(Rumbold tells staff that a new promotional stand for perfume is joining the floor.)

MR GRAINGER: Do you mean we're going to sell scent?

MR RUMBOLD: Yes, you could put it like that.

MR HUMPHRIES: Well, if it's scent why can't you clear some counter space in the ladies' department?

MR GRAINGER: Precisely. Mrs Slocombe's already displaying far too much underwear.

MRS SLOCOMBE: Are you suggesting, Mr Grainger, that I should remove my underwear and put perfume there instead?

MR GRAINGER: Are you suggesting that I should remove my trousers and put perfume there instead?

MR RUMBOLD: Now, now.

6. DIAMONDS ARE A MAN'S BEST FRIEND

(Transmitted: Wed. 18/4/73, BBC1, 7.30pm)

ALSO APPEARING:

Mr Humphries' Customer ....Elizabeth Larner

Mr Mash ....Larry Martyn

Young Mr Grace ....Harold Bennett

Wealthy Customer ....Hilary Pritchard

Secretary...Stephanie Gathercole

The Outsize Dress.......................................Janet Davies

Mr Humphries' Friend ....Vicki Woolf

When a customer loses her diamond ring, she offers a £100 reward for its return. Arguments begin over who will claim the lion's share, but when everyone thinks they've found the diamond, they all keep mum about it and suggest whoever finds it should pocket the biggest share. Eventually it's discovered that lots of artificial stones have fallen off a dress that has been manhandled by Mr Mash. But when one of the stones turns out to be genuine, it's Mr Grainger who gets the last laugh.

SERIES TWO

REGULAR CAST MEMBERS

Mr Lucas ....Trevor Bannister

Mrs Slocombe ....Mollie Sugden

Captain Peacock...................................Frank Thornton

Mr Humphries..John Inman

Miss Brahms..Wendy Richard

Mr Grainger ....Arthur Brough

Mr Rumbold..Nicholas Smith

Mr Mash ....Larry Martyn

7. THE CLOCK

(Transmitted: Thurs. 14/3/74, BBC1, 8.00pm)

ALSO APPEARING:

Young Mr Grace ....Harold Bennett

The Check Jacket ....John Ringham

The Bridal Veil ....Dorothy Wayne

Mrs Grainger ....Pearl Hackney

Elsie ....Hilda Fenemore

The Trio...........Avril Fane, Barbara and Dorothy Loynes

It's Mr Grainger's 65th birthday and the staff discuss his celebratory dinner, the venue being the shop floor. Everyone's hoping it's not a farewell do, with the management forcing his retirement. Mr Grainger is particularly worried and hopes he doesn't receive the dreaded cuckoo clock, always the sign that the company has decided to pension off staff members. When he's summoned to Mr Rumbold's office and hears a clock ticking, he thinks his time is up.

Memories

'I remember clearly the day I sat down with the cast for the first read-through. I'd just taken over the producing from David Croft and wasn't very experienced. The cast sensed this and wondered whether I knew what I was doing. I remember John Inman saying: "Do you think this chap knows what he's doing?" and Frank replying: "We'll have to see." As it happens, I did, and they were very happy. It was said as a joke but they made sure I heard. It was a smashing cast and wonderful fun. This episode was probably my favourite. I thought the storyline was a nice idea.'

HAROLD SNOAD (producer)

WHAT A SCENE!

(Mrs Slocombe and Miss Brahms are trying to convince a customer to buy a wedding veil that is obviously too thick.)

MRS SLOCOMBE: There, how's that?

CUSTOMER: It's a bit thick, isn't it?

MRS SLOCOMBE: Well, it looks lovely from our side.

CUSTOMER: But I can't see.

MRS SLOCOMBE: Well, you'll have someone holding your arm.

CUSTOMER: (*lifting the veil up*) He won't recognize me.

MRS SLOCOMBE: Well, he'll know your voice, won't he?

MISS BRAHMS: Think of the surprise he's going to get when he lifts it up!

8. COLD COMFORT

(Transmitted: Thurs. 21/3/74, BBC1, 8.00pm)

ALSO APPEARING:

Young Mr Grace ....Harold Bennett
Elsie ....Hilda Fenemore
Gladys ....Helen Lambert
Footwarmer ....Robert Mill
The Large Hat......................................Carolyn Hudson
The Fur Gloves ....John Baker

Fuel reserves are in short supply, so Grace Brothers takes action by cutting the central heating, turning staff into iceblocks in the process. Everyone shivers all day, except Rumbold who exploits his managerial perks with an electric fire. Plummeting temperatures call for drastic measures on the shop floor, including hot air up the trouser legs, brandy in the perfume spray and electric blanket footwarmers.

Memories

'I remember David Croft asking whether I'd like to produce and direct the second series. He remained as executive producer, but basically everything was down to me. When he asked, I always wondered if it was because he was unsure whether the series would take off. It just happened the second series was very successful, and the next thing David said to me was, "Thanks for your help, I'll have it back now!" David took back control and I didn't do any more, but I'm grateful I had the opportunity to work on such a fine programme.'

HAROLD SNOAD (producer)

9. THE THINK TANK

(Transmitted: Thurs. 28/3/74, BBC1, 8.00pm)

ALSO APPEARING:

Young Mr Grace. ....Harold Bennett

Sales were £600 down last week, so Rumbold wants ideas to stop the rot. A think tank is formed to generate ideas for increasing trade: after several discarded efforts, Peacock reflects on a study he carried out in sales techniques. He feels the solution to the department's problems is a fashion show, even though Mr Rumbold, as usual, takes the credit. But Young Mr Grace isn't impressed.

Memories

'I loved working with the whole cast, especially Mollie. I'd just bought my first flat in London and was penniless – I even had to borrow a camp bed and cooking stove. I was talking to Mollie one day and she was saying how exciting it was. I agreed but told her it would be if I had some furniture to put in the flat. A week later she arrived at my front door with an armchair, table and other things – I couldn't believe it!'

SUSAN BELBIN (Assistant Floor Manager)

WHAT A SCENE!

(Rumbold asks the staff why sales are down.)

MR GRAINGER: People aren't spending so much money.

CAPT. PEACOCK: Yes, that could have something to do with it.

MR HUMPHRIES: They're not even looking like they used to. There was a time when you'd go up to a customer and say: 'Excuse me, sir, are you being served?' And they'd say: 'No, just looking.' Now they don't even come in, it's most frustrating, isn't it, Mr Grainger?

MR GRAINGER: Most frustrating; trousers are a complete standstill.

MR HUMPHRIES: You're lucky to get your tape up once a day!

MRS SLOCOMBE: Well, my corsets have been down for over a fortnight!

10. BIG BROTHER

(Transmitted: Thurs. 4/4/74, BBC1, 8.00pm)

ALSO APPEARING:

Mr Clegg	Donald Morley
Dr Wainwright	Robert Raglan
Secretary	Stephanie Reeve
The Underwear Customer	Joyce Cummings
The Scarf Customer	Stella Kemball

Shoplifting is on the increase; even Mrs Slocombe's had a skirt lifted and Mr Humphries has had a hand in his Fair Isle drawers! Rumbold recruits Mr Clegg, ex-CID, to tighten security. The installation of security cameras becomes Mr Rumbold's new toy: from his office he can survey every nook and cranny of his domain. But Rumbold sees more than he bargains for – is he really heading for that big department store in the sky?

Memories

'I will always have vivid memories of writing for the second series; while Jeremy and I were in one room bashing out a script, my wife, heavily pregnant, sat in the other. It wasn't long after that she gave birth!'

MICHAEL KNOWLES

WHAT A SCENE!

(*Captain Peacock reminds Mr Lucas that the store shuts at 5.30 p.m.*)

CAPT. PEACOCK: (*looking at his watch*) Mr Lucas.

MR LUCAS: Yes, Captain Peacock.

CAPT. PEACOCK: Am I correct in saying that at Grace Brothers we don't close until 5.30 p.m?

MR LUCAS: Quite correct, sir.

CAPT. PEACOCK: Um. My watch, which is never wrong, says 17.28.

MR LUCAS: Ah, they knew how to make watches in those days, sir.

CAPT. PEACOCK: Don't be facetious, Lucas.

MR LUCAS: Well it's actually 5.30 by the department clock, sir, and that's the one that I set mine by, you see.

CAPT. PEACOCK: Um. Mr Humphries, have you the time?

MR HUMPHRIES: (*turning around*) Depends what you had in mind, Captain Peacock! (*looking at his watch*) Well, I make it 25 past something or other, I must get a new tail for Mickey Mouse.

11. HOORAH FOR THE HOLIDAYS

(Transmitted: Thurs. 11/4/74, BBC1, 8.00pm)

ALSO APPEARING:

Young Mr Grace	Harold Bennett
The Ready-Made Suit	John Clegg
The Dressing Gown	Stuart Sherwin
The Irish Lady	Helen Dorward

The store is being redecorated, and to avoid disrupting the sales figures too much, Grace Brothers is to close for two weeks in August. Management want staff to take their holidays during that period. No one will cooperate until Mr Grace offers to pay for a break in the sun. The staff are placated, but think twice when they discover the destinations aren't up to much.

Memories

'I had a great time working on the show. Whenever you worked for David you'd invariably meet up with someone you knew. He often used actors time and again, it was like one big happy family. It was a very professional atmosphere.'

JOHN CLEGG

Nicholas Smith
(MR RUMBOLD)

CUTHBERT 'JUG EARS' RUMBOLD is the bespectacled store manager at Grace Brothers. During the war he served in the Army Catering Corps, but now dedicates his efforts to mismanaging the archaic department store. Although believing he has the respect and support of all the staff, Rumbold, who spent most of his career in Hardware, is blind to his numerous inadequacies, including always being late for staff meetings.

His outdated, ineffective management style and narcissistic attitudes do nothing for morale, and in his desire to remain in Mr Grace's good books, he's always laying claim to any decent idea submitted by his subordinates. Rumbold's self-centred streak results in him keeping biscuits locked away securely in his office safe; and when the store cut the central heating to conserve fuel, Rumbold, who's married and sleeps with a red koala bear, sneaked an electric fire into his office.

When he picked up the script for the first time, Nicholas Smith had no doubts about how to play Rumbold. 'It was obvious he was an idiot; the man was a fool who understood nothing. How Mr Grace put him in authority will always be a mystery – but then, Grace Brothers was hopelessly inefficient.'

Nicholas suggested that the character should be played with enormous eagerness and enthusiasm, but still as an idiot. David Croft agreed and, with Nicholas donning his own glasses – the first time he'd worn them on screen – the character was conceived.

Nicholas, who lives in London with his wife Mary, had worked for David Croft in *Up Pompeii!* and was pleased to be offered the part of Rumbold.

'The scripts were excellent. Previous experience had taught me that the first couple of days of any TV production are usually spent rewriting scripts, but with Jeremy and David's we hardly ever altered a word. The shows were very coherent, never any loose ends.'

When the series reached the end of its life, Nicholas remembers David and Jeremy breaking the news to everyone. 'They called us around and said the BBC wanted another series, but they felt unable to come up with any more stories within the limitations of the shop set. They wanted to finish while the show was still popular with the viewers, and now was the right time – no one could argue with that.'

Nicholas was born in Banstead, Surrey, in 1934,

and announced to his parents at the age of eight that he wanted to be an actor. 'My mother was a keen amateur actress and singer,' he says. 'She organized a war charity show and got me to sing a song. Walking out on to the stage in front of four hundred people was so exciting. I couldn't have expressed it in words, but even at that young age I knew acting was for me.'

The charity event is a performance Nicholas will remember for the rest of his life. 'I sang "Little Sir Echo" and remember thinking: "Who is this Sur-recko, and why is he so little?" I got rather irritated with this girl standing behind a screen interfering with my song by singing "hello". Of course, she was the echo, but it was all of four years before anyone told me what an echo was.'

During national service with the army, Nicholas gained experience in entertainment via a club in Aldershot which put on variety shows for masonic lodges and other local organizations. 'I once got

Mr Rumbold's ineffective management style did nothing for morale with the shop floor staff, who were forced to tolerate his old-fashioned ways.

paid ten shillings, which was a lot of money then – my weekly army wages were one pound!'

After completing his stint with the army he went to RADA, graduating in 1957, and within a month was touring the country's schools with The English Children's Theatre. But if he hadn't forgotten a pair of shoes, he'd never have known about the job, as Nicholas explains. 'I'd left some shoes in the theatre at RADA and returned to pick them up. Whilst there, I popped in to see the secretary. She'd just spoken to Caryl Jenner, who ran the Children's Theatre and knew auditions were taking place. I went and got my first job.'

The tour lasted nearly nine months, but was followed by six months' unemployment. During this period, taking his mother's advice, he took singing

An early publicity shot of Nicholas Smith, circa 1957 and below, as P.C. Jeff Yates in *Z Cars* (1972–74).

Who as a West Country farmer who leads a revolt against the Daleks; three episodes of BBC's *A Tale of Two Cities* as Roger Cly; *The Frost Report*; *The Champions,* as a Scottish postmaster; and *Z Cars*, as P.C. Jeff Yates. 'Yates was a semi-regular character,' explains Nicholas, 'and a lot of fun to play. I decided to play him as uncouth. He wore a dilapidated uniform, always ate with his mouth open and was a bit rough with the suspects. It was great fun.'

Although he's also appeared in films, his debut being as a non-speaking fireman in *Those Magnificent Men in their Flying Machines*, he'll forever be remembered as Mr Rumbold. 'Without a doubt, appearing in *Are You Being Served?* has restricted my TV career. When we started the show, David Croft warned us that if it took off it would almost certainly kill our chances of other TV roles. That's exactly what happened.'

But his first love is the theatre, for which the link with Rumbold has been a blessing. 'It's given my stage career a tremendous boost: usually anything

lessons, a decision that had a major impact on his professional life. After four decades in the profession, he's appeared in a myriad of musical productions, beginning with *The Beggar's Opera* at Windsor in 1958, and including *Me and My Girl*, *The Mikado* and *My Fair Lady*. 'Singing has been a big part of my career,' says Nicholas, who has written eight string quartets himself. 'When I started in the business you had to be good-looking to get all the young, attractive roles, and I never was. I may have had hair in those days, but not looks,' smiles Nicholas. 'But because of my singing, I was doing chorus work in musicals while other actors my age were assistant stage managers or playing small parts in rep.'

Nicholas made his television debut as a man at an airport in ABC's *Pathfinders to Mars* in 1960, the first credit in a busy small-screen career. Over the years he's appeared in a host of shows, including three episodes of *The Avengers;* three episodes of *Dr*

ABOVE Smith, playing Sir John, and Gary Wilmot, during the 1992/3 national tour of *Me and My Girl*. RIGHT Playing Major Oldfox in the R.S.C. production of *The Plain Dealer* (1988/9)

CROFT
on
SMITH

'THE TOLERANCE AND GOODWILL SHOWN BY NICHOLAS TOWARDS JEREMY AND MYSELF ARE REALLY BEYOND PRAISE. EVERY ONE OF HIS PHYSICAL CHARACTER-ISTICS WAS MOCKED AND LAMPOONED BY US IN EVERY PROGRAMME AND HE NEVER ONCE MADE A MURMUR OF COMPLAINT. ON SCREEN HE CONTINUED TO DISPLAY THAT FAMOUS AIR OF WOUNDED DIGNITY WHICH IS SUCH A HILARIOUS FEATURE OF *ARE YOU BEING SERVED?* PERHAPS THIS BOOK PRESENTS A GOOD OPPORTUNITY FOR JEREMY AND ME TO SAY "THANK YOU, NICHOLAS".'

I've done since the success of the show has been a leading part, and that was purely on the strength of *Are You Being Served?*'

Nicholas, last seen on television in BBC's *Martin Chuzzlewit* four years ago, doesn't regret playing Mr Rumbold. 'There's no doubting the positive impact *Are You Being Served?* has had on my career. It's shown all around the world; I was even stopped in the street while holidaying in Malta one year – I couldn't believe it.'

Frank Thornton

(CAPTAIN PEACOCK)

STEPHEN PEACOCK, who's clocked up more than twenty years with Grace Brothers, is employed as floorwalker, ensuring that customers find what they're looking for. Donning his customary executive carnation, he struts around the floor with an air of pomposity, while derided by other members of staff, particularly Mrs Slocombe.

A reformed gambler, he claims he sold his war medals to finance his habit, but as there's doubt regarding his war service, his claims have to be taken with a pinch of salt.

After beginning his Grace Brothers career sweeping the stockroom, Peacock, who plays table tennis for the firm, worked in Toys and Games, Soft Furnishings and Fabrics, all the time nurturing his snooty, arrogant manner.

Although he's been married fourteen years, Captain Peacock doesn't class it as wedded bliss. Not only did he have a fling with Miss Bagnold from Accounts and got stuck in the lift with Miss Johnson of Novelty Candles, but he's been known to flirt with Mrs Slocombe, leer at Miss Brahms and the voluptuous secretaries, and frequent the seedy Blue Cinema Club.

When asked to play Captain Peacock, Frank Thornton knew immediately the part would suit him down to the ground. 'David Croft's a very perceptive caster,' explains Frank, 'so when he offers a job you know it will be right for you – you don't even need to read the script. Like most of the cast, I'd worked for David before – on *Hugh and I* – so he knew my work and the sort of things I could do.'

Frank believes his height and face were ideal for the type of character he's grown used to playing. 'I call them the "smell under the nose" parts,' he smiles. 'I've played that sort of character often. As Miss Brahms says, he was a "pompous twit" but fun to play.'

Even today, thirteen years and many roles later, Frank is still recognized as Captain Peacock. 'I took my wife, Beryl, to the theatre the other night,' he says. 'We got there early and were standing around in the foyer when this American, in his forties, came up to me and started talking about *Are You Being Served?*, and asked most politely if he could have his photo taken with me.

'The success of the show, particularly in the States, is unbelievable. I still get regular fan mail, with many people referring to Peacock as the "great

English gentleman" – which is absurd because he was anything but.'

Frank is fully aware there's a down-side to being associated with such a popular show. 'Typecasting is an inevitable consequence of being identified with one character for so long,' he admits. 'I played a whole range of characters before *Are You Being Served?*, starting with Michael Bentine's *It's a Square World*, as well as shows like *The World of Beachcomber* and *Scott on* …

'Although I was definitely a light entertainment actor for the BBC, Granada, for whom I worked a few times, saw me as a straight actor, which meant plenty of variety in my work. But when *Are You Being Served?* became a success I realized immediately that I'd always be identified with the character, and consequently most other TV work faded away.'

With only one series of the show being recorded a year, Frank had to find other work to supplement his income and returned to the theatre; but he has no regrets about accepting the part of Peacock. 'There have been

A two-year-old Frank experiments with his father's pipe.

advantages and disadvantages: all the other TV work may have disappeared, but there have been spin-offs, like being invited to Australia to head the cast of a theatre tour purely because of my link with the show.'

But recent events have shown that Frank, now 77, has finally moved away from the shadow of Captain Peacock. After accepting a lunch invitation from TV producer Alan J. W. Bell, he was offered a lead role in the perennial favourite *Last of the Summer Wine*. 'Brian Wilde couldn't make the last series, but I never dreamt for one moment that I'd be asked to replace him; I thought I was going to be offered a one-episode guest role. It was scary at first because it was offered late in the day, but I thoroughly enjoyed it.'

London-born Frank attended drama classes during the evenings, whilst working in the insur-

ABOVE Thornton as a teenager entertaining his dog, Mick, with a tune on his flageolet. RIGHT In 1945 Frank Thornton married his wife, actress Beryl Evans, in West Wickham.

ance business during the day. Although he'd always wanted to act, his father – who worked in a bank – demanded he secure a 'proper' job. 'He said, "Get a steady job and take it up as an amateur." So I spent two years in an insurance office. But when a colleague left to go on the stage, I decided to follow suit and enrolled at a small acting school, the only one offering evening classes.'

When invited to become a day student for his second year, Frank persuaded his father to finance his studies. Shortly after, the Second World War saw him evacuated with the drama school until he secured his first job, touring four plays in Ireland. Three years later he joined the RAF, by which time he'd met his future wife, actress Beryl Evans.

After demob from his position as navigator in 1947, Frank – like millions of others – faced the daunting task of rebuilding his career. 'I struck lucky and got a job in rep almost immediately. I also had the odd day's work in films like *Radio Cab Murder*,' he says. 'If ever I had a big part it was in some cheap picture for little money, and if it was a big picture I was only ever needed for a day!'

His busy career has included over fifty films, including *A Flea in Her Ear* and cameo roles in *Carry On Screaming*, *Victim*, *The Early Bird*, *Crooks and Coronets* and *The Three Musketeers*. Other television appearances include the Reverend in *The Upper Hand*, *Love Thy Neighbour*, *The Tommy Cooper Show* and *Steptoe and Son*.

Whenever Frank reflects on his busy career, he knows that his time walking the floor of Grace Brothers is undoubtedly the highlight of his career. 'Everything seemed to gel: a wonderful bunch of actors working well together, and there were never any problems – what more could one ask for?'

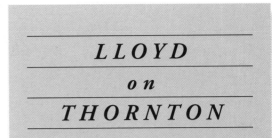

LLOYD
on
THORNTON

'CAPTAIN PEACOCK, AS THE NAME SUGGESTS, WAS SOMEONE WHO LIKED TO STRUT AROUND AND SHOW OFF. I HAD A VERY CLEAR PICTURE OF THE CHARACTER BECAUSE THE DEPARTMENT STORE THAT GAVE ME THE INSPIRATION FOR THE SHOW HAD A NUMBER OF CAPTAIN PEACOCKS TO CHOOSE FROM! THEY WERE ALL EX-ARMY AND PROUDLY WORE THEIR REGIMENTAL TIES AND EXUDED A VERY SUPERIOR AIR OF AUTHORITY.

'ALTHOUGH WE WROTE MANY LAUGHS AT CAPTAIN PEACOCK'S EXPENSE, I MUST CONFESS I HAVE A TRUE FEELING OF SYMPATHY FOR THIS CHARACTER AND HIS COMRADES. AFTER THE WAR JOBS WERE SCARCE, AND FOR SOME LIFE WAS DIFFICULT; TO HAVE A JOB WHERE THEY COULD DRESS SMARTLY AND STILL HAVE SOME AUTHORITY WAS AN UNDERSTANDABLE OPTION.

'FRANK THORNTON PLAYED THE CHARACTER PERFECTLY, AS ONE WOULD EXPECT FROM SUCH AN EXPERIENCED ACTOR, ALTHOUGH I NEVER MET ANOTHER FLOORWALKER WHO COULD DANCE, PLAY THE PIANO AND WAS GAME TO DRESS IN TYROLEAN LEATHER SHORTS TO GET A LAUGH!'

Thornton as P.C. Carp in *The Party Spirit* at The Piccadilly Theatre, 1955.

Wendy Richard

(MISS BRAHMS)

SHIRLEY BRAHMS is the assistant saleswoman whom Mrs Slocombe has taken under her wing. But the leggy Miss Brahms needs little protection: she can easily take care of herself, adroitly rebuking the advances of many would-be suitors, including Mr Lucas.

Shirley, once described by Rumbold as having a sunny, friendly personality who shows plenty of promise, lives in a semi-detached home and has recurrent dreams of flying in the nude while her friends watch.

There was one phone call Wendy Richard longed for each year, and that was to confirm that the BBC had commissioned another series of *Are You Being Served?* She always relished the chance to meet up with old friends on the show. Over the years the cast became so close they celebrated each other's birthdays.

'I'd organize the champagne and Mollie, who's a brilliant cook, would make a birthday cake,' says Wendy. 'The time of year we recorded the series always fell on someone's birthday, although never Mollie's or mine. But one year we didn't start until July, and my birthday is the 20th and Mollie's the 21st. In the rehearsal room Mollie and I were standing behind our mock-up counter, and she said: "Wendy, it's going to be embarrassing this year because it's our birthdays; do I still make the cake and you get the champagne?" I said I'd go and ask. I walked over to John and Trevor, but before I could open my mouth, John said: "It's all under control, bugger off!" Now how did he know what

we were talking about? I sometimes thought we were telepathic.'

Wendy also enjoyed working for David Croft; she had such a strong affinity with the producer that she felt part of 'Croftey's family'. 'I've worked for him so often,' she says, 'beginning way back in the early Sixties with *Hugh and I,* a sitcom starring Hugh Lloyd, Terry Scott and Mollie Sugden.

'He remembers people and is very loyal. When something comes along that is suitable, he instinctively knows you're right for it.'

Wendy had appeared several times in *Dad's Army,* playing Private Walker's girlfriend, for David Croft before joining the staff of Grace Brothers. David knew he could trust Wendy's judgement and skill to develop the character of Miss Brahms, and she was left to decide how to play the role. 'David casts so well, he's always confident the person he has chosen will deliver. I'm not a method actor, I do everything by instinct. Fortunately David was happy with the outcome.'

Wendy was very fond of Shirley Brahms. 'She was brilliant, not as daft as the others. Everyone else came up with crackpot ideas, but Miss Brahms was always level-headed. She was also self-assured: both Mr Lucas and, later, Mr Spooner tried having their wicked way with her but got nowhere.'

One of the show's strengths was the relationship between Miss Brahms and Mrs Slocombe, who used to mother her junior. This bond extended beyond

the camera, as Wendy explains: 'Mollie was such a good sport, she's a wonderful person. But we all got on so well, that's one reason the show clicked.

'I'd worked with Frank in *HMS Paradise* back in 1964, with Trevor in *Don't Turn Out the Lights* for Granada, so it was like meeting up with old friends. And dear old Arthur Brough was lovely. He always called me "that horrid child". I remember standing next to David Croft watching Arthur practising a scene. David turned to me and said: "Wonderful, isn't he? The mouth starts moving four seconds before the voice comes out. It's a nightmare to edit."'

When the doors finally shut at Grace Brothers Wendy was 'devastated'. 'It had been such a joy to work on. In my view, we were one of the best comedy shows on TV. All the jokes were self-cleaning, there was no bad language and we were never offensive or unkind to anyone; I watch some of the so-called "comedy" shows today and wonder what I'm paying my licence for.'

Miss Brahms has always been a popular character, on both sides of the Atlantic, and Wendy holds fond memories of visiting the States to promote the show. 'I went to New York about five years ago to appear on a TV channel's telethon. *Are You Being Served?* was on three times a day, and I was treated extremely well.'

Two years ago she returned, but this time for a holiday with her partner, John. 'We visited LA and San Francisco, and it was amazing. I was wearing my holiday gear with no make-up and was recognized so often,' says Wendy. 'This woman grabbed hold of me, saying, "You're Miss Brahms." She called her husband over, and when he asked how she knew it was me, the woman replied, "By her smile." She was so lovely.'

Such is the popularity of her character, Wendy still receives presents and cards from fans. 'I collect ornamental frogs and the stuff I get from the States is incredible. One fan even sends me a £20 note every so often, telling me to spend it on a nice drink.'

Proposals of marriage are not uncommon either; she received a letter from an admirer just the other day. 'It was written on lined paper by someone with a very shaky hand. He said: "I've seen you on the telly a few times and think you're a bit of all right. At the moment I'm in hospital for my nerves, but I think we should meet." He signed his name and

Wendy Richard as a baby.

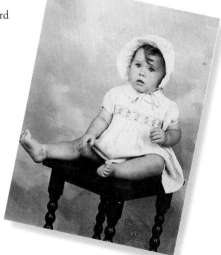

wrote as a PS: "I'm considered to be very good-looking." I'll give that one a miss!'

When Wendy gets time to relax, she enjoys gardening, tapestry work and racing her dogs. 'When we were filming *Grace and Favour* I bought this beautiful blonde bitch from the daughter of someone working at the house. Her dog had just had a litter, and I couldn't resist a puppy. I've called her Shirley Brahms II. I also have two racing dogs: Shirley Brahms and another I bought recently, which I've called Mrs Slocombe. We went to the dogs to see her last night and she ran like a rocket – I wish I'd put more money on.'

Wendy is also an avid fan of the radio soap *The Archers*, and Sunday morning from 10 a.m., when the soap is repeated, is sacrosanct. 'Woe betide anyone who phones while it's on!' laughs Wendy.

Although she's spent most of her life in London, Wendy, 51, was born in Middlesbrough. She moved to the capital as a baby when her parents took over a pub in Mayfair. As a girl she harboured dreams of becoming an archaeologist, but never pursued her ambitions. Upon finishing her education, Wendy completed a course in shorthand and typing, and worked briefly as a sales assistant at Fortnum and Mason's before joining the Italia Conti stage school.

While she was studying she earned some money as a photographic model. 'I did some work for *Woman's Own* and other magazines,' she says. 'I even modelled the bras for Marks and Spencer!'

Wendy made her small-screen debut in the Sixties, playing a runaway teenager in *Dixon of Dock Green,* followed quickly by an appearance with Sammy Davis Jnr in ATV's *Sammy Davis Meets the Girl.* Other credits in a busy TV career include: *On the Buses* (1971) playing Doreen, the clippie; *Please, Sir!*; *The Fenn Street Gang*; a barmaid in ITV's *Not On Your Nellie,* with Hylda Baker; *Up Pompeii!*; *Harpers West One* and *Danger Man.*

In the late Sixties she also spent three years as Joyce Harker in the popular BBC series *The New-*comers, a role Wendy felt was crucial to her career. 'I never did any rep work and, for me, appearing as Joyce knocked me into shape as an actress. The show went out live, so I knew I had to learn my lines and do my job well – it was a good training ground.'

On the big screen, Wendy made her debut with two lines in *Doctor in Clover,* but has appeared in a handful of other movies, including *Bless this House,* Miss Willing in *Carry On Matron,* Ida Downe in *Carry On Girls* and MGM's *No Blade of Grass,* playing Clara, the young wife of a killer.

But her first taste of the entertainment world

Wendy Richard in her days as
a photographic model.

came when she was only fifteen, appearing on Mike Sarne's 1962 chart-topping hit single 'Come Outside', for which she was paid a flat fee of £15. 'I don't get a penny from it, even though it's still being played. And it took me years to shake off the image of the "Come Outside" girl.'

When asked whether she classes *Are You Being Served?* as the highlight of her acting career, Wendy replies emphatically. 'Most definitely. I've been in the business 38 years and it's the icing on the cake. Of course, I am very grateful for *EastEnders* and Pauline, who's a wonderful character, but *Are You Being Served?* was special.

'Everyone was an established performer, so there were no egos fighting to take the lead – it was the same in all of David's shows.'

Wendy will always be grateful to David Croft for helping develop her career. 'When I appeared on David's *This Is Your Life*, I was in tears before even going on – I was so proud of him. I remember looking at all the actors sitting there and thinking: "He's made you all stars, you've got him to thank for your careers."'

CROFT
on
RICHARD

'ON HEARING WENDY'S VOICE ON THAT FAMOUS RECORD "COME OUTSIDE", I COULDN'T WAIT TO TRY HER IN SOME SORT OF ACTING ROLE. I FIRST CAST HER AS MOLLIE SUGDEN'S DAUGHTER WITH TERRY SCOTT AND HUGH LLOYD IN *HUGH AND I*. I FORGOT HOW WE EXCUSED THE FACT THAT MOLLIE SPOKE WITH A NORTH COUNTRY ACCENT AND WENDY WITH A BROAD COCKNEY, BUT THEY MADE A HILARIOUS COMBINATION.

'WHEN IT CAME TO CASTING *ARE YOU BEING SERVED?*, I WAS CONCERNED THAT THE PUBLIC WOULD BE RATHER CONFUSED THAT MOLLIE'S DAUGHTER SHOULD SUDDENLY BECOME MISS BRAHMS. FORTUNATELY, THE PUBLIC WERE VERY QUICK TO MAKE THE ADJUSTMENT AND WENDY CONTINUED THROUGHOUT THE SERIES TO PLAY THE PART WITH HER INCOMPARABLE COMEDY SKILLS.'

Trevor Bannister

(MR LUCAS)

DICK LUCAS is the junior salesman who fancies his chances with the girls, especially Miss Brahms. Unpunctual and not particularly dedicated in his work, Lucas – who'd only been working a month for Grace Brothers when the show started – lives with his mother in Highgate. Always cracking jokes, usually at Mrs Slocombe's expense, his sarcasm and ridiculing of the company's old-fashioned ways are frowned upon by management.

Trevor Bannister's mail bag contains proof that *Are You Being Served?* is already attracting a new generation of fans. Thanks to the recent run of repeats, many youngsters are writing to the actor, none of whom would have been alive when the series was first screened. 'I'm getting masses of mail from people discovering it for the first time,' enthuses Trevor.

'I also receive about thirty letters a week from American fans. It's amazing how popular it is over there. I'm often invited to appear on their public broadcasting stations to help fund-raising by simply talking about the show.'

Shortly after bumping into David Croft in a West London club one evening, Trevor was asked whether he'd be interested in playing Mr Lucas in the pilot. Trevor, who was appearing at the Vaudeville Theatre in the successful play *Move Over, Mrs Markham* at the time, liked the script and agreed to do it. And he had no problems deciding how to play the character. 'To be honest, characters in a show like *Are You Being Served?* are rather one-dimensional,' he says. 'They're surface characters and have little depth, relying a great deal on the actor's personality. So I played him as I saw him: a newcomer to the old establishment, rebelling against authority – the cheerful, cheeky chappie. Mr Lucas was a square peg in a round hole, someone who also took the mickey out of everything, and I enjoyed playing him very much.'

Trevor was hot property in 1972: as well as appearing in the successful West End play, he'd just finished playing Heavy Breathing in the popular sitcom *The Dustbinmen,* and was pleased to be involved in another popular sitcom. 'It was only a pilot, so obviously we didn't know whether it would be a success; but the cast was wonderful – many of them being old friends – and the scripts very funny, so it had lots going for it.'

After playing the unruly Mr Lucas for seven series, another engagement prevented him furthering the role, as Trevor explains. 'A sitcom is about seven weeks' work a year, so you spend the rest of your year earning a living on other projects. The

BBC also never gave us much notice about a new series, and by the time they told me about series eight, I'd already replaced Richard Briers in a tour of *Middle-Age Spread*.

'The play offered months of work and a very good salary, so naturally I accepted it. I tried to arrange it so I could be in the new series as well, but it didn't work out and I stayed with the play.'

Trevor discovered that being involved in *Are You Being Served?* had negative and positive effects on his career. 'I've never had a problem being typecast, but casting directors sometimes have tunnel vision, and playing Mr Lucas seemed to preclude me from doing any more drama. But as far as the stage is concerned, it has helped bring in the audiences. My association with the show has been a blessing in many ways: its appeal is worldwide and consequently I've toured plays all over the world: *Move Over, Mrs Markham* in Canada and Beirut; *Boeing-*

LEFT Mr Lucas (Trevor Bannister) checks that the canteen's custard is up to the usual standard.
TOP Bannister as Morgan Evans with Flora Robson in *The Corn is Green*, 1963.
ABOVE Mr Humphries shows Mr Lucas how to fool a customer into buying a jumper that doesn't fit.

ABOVE Mr Lucas takes a breather while Mr Humphries shows off his ballet skills. RIGHT Bannister in a 1961 production of *Billy Liar* at the Cambridge Theatre.

Boeing in South Africa; *Rattle of a Simple Man* in Australia, and *Bedful of Foreigners* across the Far and Middle East. And, of course, playing Mr Lucas was a happy period of my life.'

Born in Durrington, Wiltshire, Trevor joined LAMDA upon leaving school. After completing national service, during which he was shipped off to Nigeria, he attended a refresher course at the drama school, where he met Arthur Brough. 'He was watching one of our productions and offered me the juvenile lead at his rep in Folkestone. He gave me my big break, and for that, as well as making me laugh during *Are You Being Served?*, I'll always be grateful.'

Eight years of repertory work around the country culminated in a spell at York. 'It was excellent training,' says Trevor, 'but it was the 1960s and time to move to London in an attempt to break into TV.' It wasn't long before he achieved his goal, and besides theatre in the West End, including *World of Suzie Wong* and *Billy Liar,* he's appeared in shows such as *Compact, The Secret Kingdom, Coronation Street, The Saint, The Avengers, Z Cars* and *Softly, Softly.*

'I enjoy TV but prefer the theatre,' admits Trevor. 'In recent years I've done lots of stage work, including *The Odd Couple,* with Jack Klugman, and Ray Cooney's *Funny Money.* And last Christmas I concluded my 27th year as Dame in pantomime.'

Trevor has also recently appeared in three films: *The Hostage,* with Sam Neil, filmed in Argentina, *The Doomsday Gun,* and *An Inch Over the Horizon,* with Bob Hoskins, but still finds time to relax. 'I'm a golf fanatic, and my wife Pamela plays polo, so we keep some ponies and I enjoy riding them. Life has been very kind.'

Bannister as a hopeful
drama student
in 1954.

LLOYD
o n
BANNISTER

'I HAD NO DOUBT IN MY MIND ABOUT THE CHARACTER OF MR LUCAS, PLAYED BY TREVOR BANNISTER. THE ONLY PERSON WHO HAD DIFFICULTY WAS TREVOR HIMSELF AT THE BEGINNING. HE USED TO ASK: "WHO EXACTLY *IS* THIS CHARACTER I'M PLAYING?" AND I'D EXPLAIN THAT HIS MILITANT ATTITUDE TO AUTHORITY WAS SIMILAR TO MY OWN IN MY DAYS AS A SUIT SALESMAN. THEN THE RULES AND REGULATIONS ABOUT CONDUCT WOULD ENCOURAGE JUNIORS TO REVOLT.

'ALTHOUGH TREVOR WAS OLDER THAN A NORMAL JUNIOR, I THOUGHT THIS ADDED TO THE FUN AND, BEING THE WONDERFUL ACTOR HE IS, HE SOON FOUND THE CHARACTER OF MR LUCAS AND GAVE HIM AN AIR OF PERPLEXED FRUSTRATION AS HE BATTLED AGAINST THE PECKING ORDER BEHIND THE MEN'S COUNTER.

'HE WAS ALSO GREAT FUN TO WORK WITH AND OFTEN ADDED MORE TO A SCENE THAN APPEARED ON THE SCRIPT. A MASTER OF THE DOUBLE TAKE AND OUTRAGED INNOCENCE IF CAUGHT MISBEHAVING, HE WAS PERFECT FOR THE PART – I WISH I COULD'VE PLAYED IT MYSELF.'

Mollie Sugden
(MRS SLOCOMBE)

WITH HER MULTICOLOURED coiffure, the man-eating Betty Slocombe lives with her beloved pussy, Tiddles. As departmental head in Ladieswear, no one escapes her bossiness, hectoring and sharp tongue.

Born in 1926, the grumbling queen of hair rinses worked in air-raid precautions during the war. When she met her husband it was love at first sight, but since he deserted her, continuous attempts at trapping any unsuspecting male have failed dismally.

Mollie Sugden accepts that giving autographs is an everyday occurrence for actors involved in popular television programmes, but couldn't believe it when a fan waving an autograph book burst into the changing-room she was using in a Guildford store. 'I was trying on a dress when the curtain was thrust aside; there I was in my bra and pants and this woman asked whether she could have my autograph! I told her to wait until I was fully clothed, but was amazed.'

It wasn't long after *Are You Being Served?* started that people began stopping Mollie in the street asking her about Mrs Slocombe. 'I think everybody knows a Mrs Slocombe, she's quite prevalent. The reaction to the show was tremendous, everyone was always so positive about it.'

Mollie was appearing in a *Comedy Playhouse* with Jimmy Beck and Ronnie Fraser when David Croft, who was producing the half-hour show, intimated that he would be using her in the near future. 'I only had a small part but, as always, he came to my dressing-room to thank me for my performance. He then said: "By the way, I've got a part coming

up which has been written specially for you." He wouldn't tell me what it was, but said I'd know about it shortly.' A couple of weeks later the script for the *Are You Being Served?* pilot landed on Mollie's doormat.

After reading the script, Mollie couldn't see how the show would fail to impress. 'It may have got off to a slow start, but I knew the audience would relate to it because everyone has been in a department store – and the script and characters were so funny.'

She was so impressed with the script that she didn't have to think about how to bring Mrs Slocombe to life. 'The character leapt off the page,' says Mollie. 'As soon as I read the lines I knew exactly what she was like.'

One of Mrs Slocombe's trademarks was her garish, candyfloss-styled hairdos; it was Mollie who suggested the ever-changing hair colours. 'When I watched the pilot, I had to do something about it: I looked such a miserable character with nondescript mousey hair. So when David phoned to tell me a series had been commissioned, I suggested she had different colour hair every week. After all, she was

obviously a bossy soul who would have the hair-dressing department right under her thumb. I never meant for it to become a gimmick, but it's turned out to be a regular talking-point between fans.'

In early episodes, Mollie dyed her own hair, until it began looking the worse for wear. 'The dye washed out, but the problems were caused by having to bleach my hair so the colours showed up,' she explains. 'Eventually the ends became spongy and the colour wouldn't wash out.'

Mollie realized she had to do something about it when one day she met her twins, Robin and Simon, from junior school. 'I was standing there with multi-coloured ends of hair, I looked dreadful. Of course, the boys were very polite and didn't say anything, but I was terribly conscious of it, and when the next series started, I got the BBC to supply wigs.'

Over the years *Are You Being Served?* has built up a big following and Mollie receives lots of fan mail. 'The amount of letters from America is unbelievable,

and now the show is being repeated on BBC1, letters are again flooding in from British fans. It's a bit of a chore replying all the time, but if people enjoy the programme and are nice enough to write – and they say some lovely things – the least I can do is reply.'

Mollie has only ever received one letter that has been assigned quickly to the bin. Writing in response to an episode involving a fur coat, a man said he hoped Mollie 'burned in hell'. 'He lived in the Midwest of America and was angry because Mrs Slocombe wanted a fur coat. Even the most unpractised eye could see it was a terrible fake fur, but the mere fact I was apparently supporting the fur trade had angered this man. But that's the only nasty letter I've ever received.'

Born in Keighley, Yorkshire, in 1922, Mollie always wanted to act. When she was four she heard a woman read a poem at a village concert; it stuck firmly in her mind. 'It was so funny I just remembered it, although I was only young,' she says.

LEFT Mollie Sugden at six months.
CENTRE As an eight-year-old bridesmaid
at her brother's wedding.
RIGHT An early publicity shot.

'The following Christmas, after a relative asked if anyone could "do anything", I stood on a chair and recited this poem. When I finished everyone fell to the floor in laughter. Their response made me realize how wonderful it was to make people laugh.'

Not long after she left school the Second World War broke out, and before she could begin her acting career, Mollie was helping the war effort by working in a Keighley munitions factory making shells for the navy. 'When we'd supplied enough shells about two thousand women were made redundant and I was one of them, which allowed me the chance to attend drama school in London.'

After graduating from the Guildhall School of Drama, Mollie began an eight-year stint in rep, beginning at Accrington with a small company that included Roy Dotrice and Eric Sykes. Three months later she moved to Oldham, earning three pounds a week. Radio work followed, and later her television debut in a live half-hour comedy show with Wilfred Pickles and Paul Whitsun-Jones.

Her first television series was a comedy for Tyne Tees with Glen Melvin and Danny Ross, with whom she'd just worked in summer season. 'It was a big part and marvellous experience,' explains Mollie. 'But because it wasn't networked, any mistakes I made were kept fairly quiet. So it was an ideal situation for someone like me who was beginning their TV career.'

The director was David Croft, who went on to employ Mollie in the early 1960s sitcom *Hugh and I* with Terry Scott and Hugh Lloyd. The show was written by John Chapman, whom Mollie met up with a few years later. 'When John got involved with *The Liver Birds,* he suggested me for the part of Mrs Hutchinson, Sandra's mother.'

Mollie prefers working on TV, and as her career developed she was regularly cast as mothers in shows like *My Wife Next Door, For the Love of Ada* and *Doctor in Charge,* and as Jimmy Clitheroe's mum in *Just Jimmy,* a role she also played on stage. Soon she was being offered lead roles in comedy shows, including BBC's *Come Back, Mrs Noah,* five series as Ida, a doctor's housekeeper in *That's My Boy*, and two series of *My Husband and I* for Yorkshire Television with her real-life husband, William Moore, whom she met at Swansea Rep. 'Starring in a show makes a big difference to your career because people start wanting you in pantomimes and summer seasons.' Mollie also spent 23 weeks working on *That's Life,* and was seen in *Please, Sir!, Oliver's Travels,* as Mrs Robson, in *Coronation Street,* as Nellie Harvey, and many other comedy shows.

In recent years, Mollie – who bought a beige Porsche when she was 62 – has been suffering ill-health which has restricted her work. In 1993 she had a heart bypass, from which she's made a complete recovery. She first knew something was wrong while appearing in an opera in San Francisco. 'I noticed I didn't have to do much before I was out of breath,' explains Mollie, who was informed by a specialist upon her return to England that she'd experience a heart attack. But after surgery she was soon on the road to recovery.

'The horrid thing was that after that I got polymyalgia; that's when steroids entered my life, and it's taking forever to clear up. I did the recent revival of *The Liver Birds* but I'm not sure it was wise because at the time I was on massive doses of steroids and, of course, they don't improve anybody's appearance. But everyone was very sweet to me, and I enjoyed the series.

'I'm not off the steroids yet, but I'm down to a much smaller dose. My appearance isn't quite so bad, but I'm not cured yet. However, life goes on and it's certainly been a wonderful life and career so far.'

To date she has built her career on memorable comedy parts, but she's never hankered after serious roles. 'I love comedy because I still get that great feeling when I hear people laugh.'

LLOYD
on
SUGDEN

'I ALWAYS THINK OF MRS SLOCOMBE AS A CLOSE FRIEND OF MY GRANDMOTHER. WE LIVED IN MANCHESTER AND ALL HER FRIENDS SEEMED TO BE ON THE LARGE SIDE, AND MANY "MRS SLOCOMBE" EXPRESSIONS CAME FROM CONVERSATIONS I HEARD AS A SMALL BOY ON A FAMILY SHOPPING TRIP. AS A MATTER OF ACADEMIC INTEREST, MANCHESTER SEEMS TO BE FULL OF LARGE LADIES AND, I BELIEVE, THE SHOP DUMMIES IN THE NORTH ARE STILL A COUPLE OF SIZES LARGER THAN IN THE SOUTH!

'I'M SURE MANY PEOPLE HAVE MET A MRS SLOCOMBE, AND PART OF THE SUCCESS OF THE CHARACTER IN THE SHOW IS BECAUSE SHE DIDN'T NEED TO BE GIVEN A HISTORY – SHE WAS AN INSTANTLY RECOGNIZABLE CHARACTER, FULL OF SELF-IMPORTANCE DUE TO HER ELEVATED POSITION IN CHARGE OF THE LADIES COUNTER, BUT AT THE SAME TIME VULNERABLE AND QUICK TO TAKE OFFENCE IF A JUNIOR TRIED MAKING FUN OF HER.

'IT TAKES A VERY EXPERIENCED ACTRESS NOT TO OVERPLAY THE ROLE; MOLLIE NEVER DID AND I ALWAYS THOUGHT HER IRREPLACEABLE.'

John Inman

(MR HUMPHRIES)

WILBERFORCE CLAYBOURNE HUMPHRIES, who's always keen to stress he has friends of all shapes, sizes and sexes, is senior assistant on Menswear. With over ten years' service, he could easily have been pursuing a showbiz career: his dancing background includes being a Sunshine Babe at the age of eight, and an instructor at Weston-super-Mare's Twinkle Toes Dance Salon.

With his mincing walk, effeminate demeanour and predilection for making lace mats, Mr Humphries, who's also a palmist, is a colourful character in the department. Single and still living with his elderly mother, who works part-time at a local sex cinema. He was originally refused a job at Grace Brothers until his mother came to the rescue, imploring Young Mr Grace to reconsider.

With a heart of gold, the altruistic Mr Humphries, who warms his slippers in the oven and attends choir practice on Thursdays, is a popular member of staff.

A visit to his local Woolworth's made John Inman realize just how popular *Are You Being Served?* had become. 'The first series had just been shown and I was at home decorating my bathroom. I hadn't shaved for days, was wearing paint-splattered jeans and needed some turps. So I popped down to Woolies to buy some and was attacked by five ladies with prams! They were all shouting: "That's him from the shop!" It was scary, so after that I never went out without shaving and putting on my best suit.'

The offer to play Mr Humphries was perfectly timed because it meant John Inman didn't have to sign on at the labour exchange! 'I was in panto at Coventry, playing an Ugly Sister in *Cinderella,* when a script arrived from David Croft. A little note stated he was doing this one-off *Comedy Playhouse,*

and wanted me to play Mr Humphries, the second assistant in the menswear department. It was wonderful because the panto finished on Saturday, and rehearsals for the pilot started on the Monday. It was an actor's dream because I didn't have to sign on.'

Although John, 62, felt Mr Humphries had little to do in the first episode, it didn't matter. 'The attraction was that it meant a week's wages. There was no artistic attraction to the offer; I'd worked in a shop before and felt qualified to play the character: I knew how to fold a shirt, enjoyed looking smart, so everything seemed right.'

One event that sticks in John's memory is turning up for the rehearsal, and meeting the rest of the cast for the first time. 'I was the only person I'd never heard of!' laughs John. 'Everyone else was known on TV, but I didn't find it daunting because

Mr Rumbold can't believe his eyes when Mr Humphries and Mrs Slocombe are dressed up as punks.

everybody was friendly and we got on like a house on fire – and still do.'

He's particularly close to Wendy Richard, who lives round the corner from him in London. 'She's a lovely person. I think her first words to me were: "'Ere, are you coming to the pub?" Which was music to my ears!'

John, who frequently received letters from women proposing marriage, still gets more letters from women than men. As the series progressed, Mr Humphries' popularity increased as far as the audience was concerned; but not everyone felt the same warmth towards the mummy's boy. John Inman was the target for various gay rights movements, unhappy about how he played the character.

On one occasion he was doing a one-nighter near London when pickets arrived at the theatre. 'There was a handful of people telling everyone to boycott my show, so I chatted with them and asked them to see the show, which they did. I never saw them again. It happened again outside a club in New Zealand, but we talked and smoothed things over.'

As John explains, Mr Humphries never claimed he was gay. 'I used to say to people, the day you see him do it over the counter you can complain, but his sexuality was never mentioned. He was an Auntie really, a little bit precious, lived with his mother and made a very nice Yorkshire Pudding.'

When it came to bringing the character alive, John, who's a bachelor, admits he didn't base Mr Humphries on anyone he'd encountered in his life, but confesses the mincing walk was taken from a colleague he'd met while working at Austin Reed before his acting career took off. 'The character as a whole wasn't influenced by any one person, but I remember a man from the cuff-link counter at Austin Reed who wore steel tips on his shoes. The shop had a marble floor in those days and you could hear him coming a mile off, so I copied his

Tony in a stage version of *Freda,* earning five pounds in the process.'

Upon leaving school he worked in a gents' outfitters in Blackpool, before joining Austin Reed and moving to Manchester. After a spell in London he left to become a scenic artist at a theatre in Crewe. 'I did it so I could earn my Equity card, and then moved on to become a stage manager.'

Whenever John was out of work, he supplemented his income by working for various shops, and it was one Christmas – while he was demonstrating a plastic toy in a store's toy department – that he received a message to call David Croft. 'A friend of mine came to the store and told me I had

TOP Inman with his mother, Mary, who's now 88, and still lives in Blackpool. LEFT On Wimbledon Common in his early 20s, when he was stage manager at the nearby theatre. BELOW Inman in the play *Something About a Sailor*.

walk. But he wasn't really based on anybody because Mr Humphries developed with the series.'

Born in Preston, John moved to Blackpool when he was twelve. His mother ran a boarding house in the town, while his father owned a hairdressing business. John always wanted to work on the stage and his parents paid for him to attend elocution lessons in the local church hall.

His acting debut took place on Blackpool's South Pier, aged thirteen. 'I played a lad called to phone David because he wanted me to appear in one of his shows. I was so excited at the prospect, I didn't bother returning to the shop after lunch.'

David gave John his screen debut in a non-speaking role as a worker in a sherbet factory. Although he appeared in other television productions – including *Grace and Favour, Blankety Blank, Celebrity Squares,* a series of *Odd Man Out,* playing Neville Sutcliffe, a fish and chip shop owner, and ITV's *Take A Letter, Mr Jones* in 1981, playing Graham Jones, a secretary – most of his career has been spent on the stage.

It's in panto that John, whose favourite hobby is work, feels most at home, and every Christmas he is in demand. 'I'm happy on the stage, it's my first love.'

But the time spent in *Are You Being Served?* was the happiest period in his life. 'I desperately tried remembering it, because I knew that such a happy, successful time probably wouldn't happen again,' John admits. 'Such moments can be forgotten quickly, especially when you're leading a busy life, so I purposely made myself slow down a bit to remember those wonderful times.'

Inman appeared in a tribute to his idol, North country comic Frank Randle.

CROFT on INMAN

'I FIRST SAW JOHN WHEN HE WAS PLAYING PC BOOT IN *SALAD DAYS* AT THE GOLDERS GREEN HIPPODROME. THE AUDIENCE WARMED TO HIM STRAIGHT AWAY. AT THE FIRST OPPORTUNITY I GAVE HIM A PART IN ONE OF MY PRODUCTIONS AS THE ASSISTANT TO A FACTORY FOREMAN PLAYED BY A STAR SCOTTISH COMEDIAN. THROUGHOUT THE SCENE JOHN DIDN'T HAVE A WORD OF DIALOGUE. ALL HE HAD TO DO WAS TO REACT IN THE BACK-GROUND. TO THE AMAZEMENT OF THE STAR THERE WERE GREAT LAUGHS IN THE MOST UNEXPECTED PLACES. TO THIS DAY, I DON'T THINK THE STAR COMIC KNOWS WHY THE SCENE WENT SO WELL. JOHN AND I KNOW!'

Arthur Brough

(MR GRAINGER)

THE TRUSS-WEARING Ernest Grainger joined Grace Brothers in 1937. A true veteran in retailing, one wonders why he's not been pensioned off: he's abrupt, irascible, inflexible and always nodding off at meetings – not what you'd expect from a senior salesman.

After growing up at Folkestone, he served with ENSA during the war, entertaining troops with his impersonations of Hitler and Churchill, something he continues to do at a local OAP home's annual do.

With his half-moon specs and tape measure hanging round his neck, Grainger's time at Grace Brothers has seen him spend two years in Haberdashery before getting his own counter in Stationery. Five years in Bathroom Furniture was followed by a transfer to Gentlemen's Shoes and then Gentlemen's Trousers.

Despite his shortcomings, the aged Mr Grainger still occasionally manages to reveal a warm, avuncular manner.

Playing churlish Mr Grainger was undoubtedly the highlight of Arthur Brough's small-screen career, but he spent most of his life running repertory companies around the country.

Although predominantly a stage actor, Arthur did make the occasional excursion into other areas of the business but, as his daughter Joanna Hutton explains, he found it hard adjusting at first. 'One of the first jobs he did away from the stage was the film *The Green Man,* with Alastair Sim, and in that he realized how hammy he was. He used to take the mickey out of himself; he'd always acted in a Shakespearean manner and suddenly realized he had to tone down his performance for film.'

Arthur – real name Frederick Arthur Baker – was born in Petersfield in 1905. He got involved in amateur dramatics, where he first worked with Sim, before studying at RADA in the early 1920s. Soon after graduating he joined a company specializing in Shakespeare and it was there that he met his wife-to-be, actress Elizabeth Addyman. After marrying in 1929, Arthur and his wife, using

their wedding money as collateral, rented the Leas Pavilion, a rep in Folkestone.

Once the rep was up and running, Arthur – who ran the company as well as acting in the shows – turned his attention to other reps. By the eve of the Second World War he'd opened numerous companies, including reps at Oxford, Leeds, Bradford, Keighley, Lincoln, Southampton, Bristol and Blackpool. 'His whole life was dedicated to the theatre,' says Joanna Hutton, 'and in the end he's known for playing one part on television!'

After working at York with Phyllis Calvert, Arthur was enlisted into the navy for the duration of the war. Upon demob, he resumed his career where he'd left off and reopened Folkestone rep. In the 1950s, he went on to establish reps at Southend and Eastbourne.

Arthur retained his involvement with rep for

several years, until he began foreseeing the fall of repertory theatre. 'He was very astute and unsentimental about it,' says Joanna. 'He realized the era was over and that he must diversify, and his film debut in *The Green Man* came soon after.' The rep continued until 1969 before closing.

Excepting his role as Mr Grainger, his screen appearances were restricted to cameo roles in shows like *Upstairs, Downstairs* and *London Conspiracy*, a 1976 TV film of *The Persuaders* in which he played the aged butler Moorehead. He appeared in several theatre productions, including *Half a Sixpence*, playing a shopkeeper.

But everyone identified him as Ernest Grainger, the crusty salesman from Grace Brothers. Throughout his time in the hit show, Arthur lived a life of heartbreak, with his wife seriously ill, as Joanna explains. 'It wasn't a happy time for any of us. Mummy was very ill from 1969 onwards, and they both died within six weeks of each other in 1978.

'After Mummy died he stayed with me a few weeks, during which time David Croft and Jeremy

Lloyd made contact to say they were writing him into the next series,' says Joanna. 'But he died, of course, before he could do it. I had high hopes that if he returned to work it would help, but that never happened.'

Everyone associated with the sitcom has nothing but fond memories of working with Arthur. David Croft recalls the time Arthur would disappear off the set. 'Whenever we were rehearsing he'd vanish at about three minutes to eleven,' he says. 'For a while we wondered where he went, but eventually discovered that he'd nip next door to the pub for a quick pink gin. We'd watch from the window as this little figure hurtled towards the pub – we never spoke to him about it. One day when he returned, John Inman asked where he'd been. He made some excuse, but what he'd forgotten was that it was pouring with rain and his bald head was soaking wet!'

Daughter Joanna is convinced that being involved in such a long-running sitcom helped her

ABOVE Arthur Brough holding his daughter, Joanna, in 1932. LEFT Serving in the navy during World War Two.

father in many ways. 'It was good for his career, which made him happy. But the camaraderie between the cast was wonderful, helping him enjoy the time he wasn't nursing Mummy.'

Arthur was a highly respected actor who'd spent forty years in the profession. It wasn't until he stepped into the shoes of bumbling Mr Grainger that he discovered the success that had eluded him all his career; but he'd achieved a great deal in the world of rep, and there are numerous thespians grateful to the opportunities his life in theatre had brought.

At the time of Arthur's death, David Croft said: 'Arthur created a living character who was the inspiration for much of the humour. His personality made him a pivot round which a whole lot of laughter and affection revolved.'

BALLADE OF A SEPTUAGENARIAN

O glorious day! O shout and sing!
O hang the flags out everywhere!
Let bells in every steeple ring,
And hallelujahs fill the air!
I can't believe it, yet I swear
The Times, the Mirror, and the Sun
With banner headlines all declare
I am a STAR! - at seventy-one!

It makes me want to have a fling,
Throw up my hat, let down my hair,
And dance a frenzied buck-and-wing
From Charing Cross to Leicester Square.
Now my career - it would be fair
To say - has scarcely yet begun,
Since (though not yet a millionaire)
I am a Star - at seventy-one.

Where'er I go, producers bring
Offers of contracts rich and rare
(Commissions, too, from everything
I smoke, or drink, or use, or wear),
And men and women stop and stare,
For after what the telly's done
All Folkestone seems to be aware
I am a Star - at seventy-one.

Envoi:

Age, friends, is neither here nor there;
I've challenged it myself, and won,
And after years of wear and tear
I am a Star - at seventy-one!

-oOo-

Brough enjoyed writing poetry, and this example was about becoming a star at 71!

CROFT on BROUGH

'MY WIFE, ANN, WAS ENGAGED BY ARTHUR TO BE JUVENILE LEAD WHEN HE WAS RUNNING HIS REP COMPANY AT FOLKESTONE. EVEN THEN HE WAS RENOWNED FOR BEING LESS THAN WELL ACQUAINTED WITH THE TEXT OF THE PLAYS HE PERFORMED – A CHARACTERISTIC WHICH REMAINED WITH HIM DURING HIS TIME IN *ARE YOU BEING SERVED?*

'IT WAS ALWAYS FASCINATING TO WATCH THE CAST, PARTICULARLY IN THE CANTEEN SCENES, EAGERLY LISTENING TO HIM IN ORDER TO RESPOND TO THE PARTICULAR VERSION OF THE SCRIPT WHICH HE WOULD PRODUCE ON THE ACTUAL RECORDING. NEVERTHELESS, IT IS STILL A JOY TO WATCH HIM USE HIS WONDERFUL TIMING AND EXPERTISE IN THE SERIES AND THE GREAT TRUTH HE BROUGHT TO THE CHARACTER OF MR GRAINGER. A GREAT, LOVEABLE MAN.'

Harold Bennett

(YOUNG MR GRACE)

A WIDOWER FOR over forty years, Young Mr 'You've all done very well!' Grace reigns autocratically over his department store. Never one to shy away from a tough decision and always prepared to put Rumbold in his place, the lecherous Mr Grace does untold damage to his weakening heart by employing a string of busty beauties to take care of his every need.

Born into a family of cobblers, he grew up in the East End of London. Upon leaving school he became an apprentice haddock filleter, earning the nickname 'Fish Fingers'. After the First World War, he was heading nowhere until, in 1926, an uncle bequeathed him Grace Brothers.

His advancing years have seen a reduction in the time spent at the store, as he prefers idling away his hours on his yacht, visiting strip clubs or doing charity work, like arranging tea parties for distressed night-club hostesses. But while at work he's never without his stress indicator, which he tests by getting his nurse to flash her suspenders.

Young Mr Grace leaves the running of the store to his older brother, Henry, in episode 49. He doesn't officially retire, but leaves to complete the book on ornithology he's been researching for some time.

Harold was already an old man when he joined the cast of *Are You Being Served?*, but he didn't let age hinder his performance as Young Mr Grace. He was a popular member of the cast, as Susan Belbin, who worked as an assistant floor manager on the show, explains. 'He was a lovely man, always cheerful. His timing was superb: he didn't have a lot to say, but whenever he opened his mouth he'd get a laugh.'

Jo Austin, a production assistant on series four and five, also has fond memories of working with Harold. 'He was absolutely wonderful,' she enthuses. 'For someone who wasn't a career actor, he was brilliant – and great fun. His timing was perfect and he never trod on a laugh in his life. He had the enthusiasm of a youngster just starting out in the business. His popularity blossomed as the series progressed; this was reflected in his character, who became more flamboyant.'

At one point, Jo discovered Harold was in hospital, the same one in which she was visiting a friend. So she popped up to see him, but when she entered his room she couldn't believe her eyes. 'There he was in bed surrounded by pretty girls, just like Mr

ABOVE Young Mr Grace (Harold Bennett) celebrates with the rest of the staff. RIGHT Bennett in 1900, aged two.

Grace – I half expected him to say: "You're all doing very well!'"

Born in Hastings in 1899, Harold's packed life resembled a colourful montage. Upon leaving school at twelve he became a jeweller's apprentice, but during his lifetime taught English in the evenings at the Working Men's College, London, studied at art school, painted in Paris and worked as a circus clown.

Harold – who enjoyed painting and motorbikes – was very enterprising and upon demob from the army after the First World War he and a friend hired a coach and took people on tours of the battlefields.

After acting as an amateur he turned professional and embarked on a career involving plenty of

ABOVE LEFT Young Mr Grace can't decide who should play Santa. ABOVE RIGHT One of Bennett's hobbies was fishing. LEFT A ten-year-old Bennett with a friend at a Hastings' carnival celebrating bonfire night.

theatre work, including a tour with Donald Wolfit and numerous West End performances.

When his wife died in the 1930s, Harold took a break from the fickle world of acting while his three children grew up, working as a draughtsman for an electric light company instead. He retained his interest in acting by performing with various amateur companies and, after retiring in 1964, returned to the business professionally. Initially, he did some photographic modelling but was soon offered work as a film extra, before eventually earning the success he deserved appearing in various TV productions, among them as Mr Halliforth in BBC's sitcom *Whack-O!,* Mr Blewitt in *Dad's Army,* a production of Chekhov's *The Three Sisters, Clayhanger,* Dennis Potter's play *Vote, Vote, Vote for Nigel Barton* in 1965, and the 1977 ITC production of *Jesus of Nazareth.* But his most notable appearance was as the doddery Young Mr Grace with his retinue of sexy secretaries and nurses.

His son, John Bennett, describes Harold as a 'strong-willed and independent' man. 'He was very critical about the way the modern world was going, but he loved his life in acting. Although physically he became a little unstable, his mind remained sharp and he was as bright as a button.'

And just like Young Mr Grace, although not to the same degree, Harold enjoyed female company and had an eye for the girls. 'Having any of the ladies around used to buck him up no end,' laughs John.

Harold, who'd clocked up over two hundred stage and screen appearances, looked increasingly frail as the series progressed and, other than a couple of brief appearances in series eight, including the Christmas Special, 'Roots?', the seventh season was his last. Harold, who always looked older than his age, had reached the grand age of 82 when he died of a heart attack in 1981. Paying tribute to the actor, David Croft said: 'Harold was an incomparable actor and comedian with impeccable timing. He presented old age in a way that people accepted. He is a sad loss to us.'

CROFT
o n
BENNETT

'HAROLD WAS ANOTHER RECRUIT FROM THE WORLD OF PANTOMIME. I SAW HIM PLAYING AN INCREDIBLY OLD ARCHBISHOP AT STRATFORD EAST IN *THE ROSE AND THE RING*. WHEN HE CAME TO SEE ME ABOUT *ARE YOU BEING SERVED?* HE ASKED IF HE SHOULD PLAY YOUNG MR GRACE AS OLD OR NORMAL. SINCE HE LOOKED ABOUT 85 AT THE TIME, I PLUMPED FOR "NORMAL"! HAROLD HAD A UNIQUE DELIVERY OF LINES THAT NEVER FAILED TO BRING HIM EVERY POSSIBLE LAUGH. HE WAS IRREPLACEABLE.'

Bennett turned to acting professionally in 1964, initially concentrating on photographic work.

Episode Guide

SERIES THREE

REGULAR CAST MEMBERS

Mr Lucas ....Trevor Bannister

Mrs Slocombe...Mollie Sugden

Captain Peacock....................................Frank Thornton

Mr Humphries ....John Inman

Miss Brahms ....Wendy Richard

Mr Grainger...Arthur Brough

Mr Rumbold ....Nicholas Smith

Mr Mash ....Larry Martyn

Young Mr Grace ....Harold Bennett

---

12. THE HAND OF FATE

(Transmitted: Thurs. 27/2/75, BBC1, 8.00pm)

ALSO APPEARING:

Mr Kato ....Eric Young

Miss Ainsworth ....Nina Francis

Lady Customer................................Therese McMurray

A director is retiring from the board due to ill health and Rumbold is being considered for the vacancy. If he is successful, Captain Peacock will be promoted and the rest of the staff upgraded accordingly, with Mrs Slocombe and Mr Grainger battling for the post of floorwalker. But there's bad news: when Young Mr Grace's tea bag breaks, Lily, the tea girl, reads the leaves and warns him to beware of a bald-headed man with big ears, so that rules out Rumbold for the job!

Memories

'The cast was made up of consummate performers; everyone was very friendly and made it easy for anyone who was inexperienced by feeding you lines in such a way that you just couldn't fail. I picked up the expertise of their timings, and loved it – even though it was extremely nerve-racking.'

NINA FRANCIS

13. COFFEE MORNING

(Transmitted: Thurs. 6/3/75, BBC1, 8.00pm)

ALSO APPEARING:

Miss Ainsworth ....Nina Francis

After Mr Grainger is late returning from his tea break, Captain Peacock takes action: in future everyone must clock in and out whenever they leave the shop floor – and that includes visits to the loo! When the staff refuse to sign the log book and Mr Grainger is made an example of by having 50p deducted from his wages, Mr Mash, as shop steward, stands up for the workers' rights – but they soon regret their stance.

WHAT A SCENE!

(When Mr Grainger is late back from his tea break,
Captain Peacock decides to report him,
much to Grainger's annoyance.)

MR GRAINGER: You don't mean that you're going to report me, Stephen?

CAPT. PEACOCK : Yes, I am, Mr Grainger.

MR GRAINGER: (*angrily*) Very well, Captain Peacock!

CAPT. PEACOCK: I'm sorry but it's my job.

MR GRAINGER: You mean to be a sneak?

CAPT. PEACOCK: It's not easy for me, you know. On the one hand we have our friendship, and on the other I have my job to do. I have to wear two hats.

MR GRAINGER: (*acidly*) Well, you'll find no difficulty in that, you're two-faced!

14. UP CAPTAIN PEACOCK

(Transmitted: Thurs. 13/3/75, BBC1, 8.00pm)

ALSO APPEARING:

The Forty Maternity ....Donald Hewlett

The Bold Check ....Michael Knowles

The Clip-On Bow ....Jeffrey Segal

The Captain's Fancy.................................Maureen Lane

Captain Peacock celebrates twenty years with Grace Brothers and is awarded a coveted key, allowing him access to the executive washroom, much to Mr Grainger and Mrs Slocombe's disgust. But when Peacock is also promoted to the executive dining-room, and the staff's lunch hour is delayed until 2 p.m. each day, Grainger blows a fuse and phones the Factories Inspector, who puts paid to Peacock's days of grandeur.

Memories

'David Croft knew he was about three minutes short on the episode, so he had to write a scene or two to fill up the filming time. He asked me and Donald Hewlett whether we could come in and do something. We agreed, so he wrote us into the episode.'

MICHAEL KNOWLES

15. COLD STORE

(Transmitted: Thurs. 20/3/75, BBC1, 8.00pm)

ALSO APPEARING:

Daphne ....Hilda Fenemore

Forgetful One ....Bill Martin

The Blue Alteration......................................Ann Sidney

Sister ....Joy Allen

Drooping Derrière ....Pamela Cundell

The Fawn Trousers ....Gordon Peters

Mr Lucas has a girl visiting from the country, so he claims he's suffering from a cold and should be in bed, but when Mr Grainger and Mr Humphries arrive for work feeling ill, he knows he's got a battle on if he wants to be sent home sick.

Memories

'I've known David Croft and his wife, Ann, since the age of sixteen – I was a bridesmaid at their wedding; I also went to RADA with Ann. So it was lovely to work for him in *Are You Being Served?* None of the shows David gets involved in ever seem to date; and there's never anything nasty in them, it's wonderful family entertainment.'

JOY ALLEN

16. WEDDING BELLS

(Transmitted: Thurs. 27/3/75, BBC1, 8.30pm)

ALSO APPEARING:

The Small Handicap ....John Clegg

Miss Robinson ....Sandra Clark

The Trousers ....Jay Denyer

Young Mr Grace has been a widower too long. He's got his eye on a member of staff and announces plans to wed, with the identity of his bride to be revealed soon. When Mr Grace invites Mrs Slocombe to his office for a private chat, to discuss a ring, rumours quickly spread that Betty is the chosen one. As she begins throwing her weight about, the rest of the staff are eager to stay in her good books. But there's a shock in store.

WHAT A SCENE!

(Mr Humphries and Mr Lucas try convincing a customer to buy a woollen jumper that's obviously too tight.)

MR HUMPHRIES: What you must remember, sir, is that it will stretch after the first wash.

CUSTOMER: I thought wool always shrank?

MR LUCAS: No, no, that's a popular misconception, that, sir. You only have to think about it to see it couldn't possibly be true, otherwise every time it rained those sheep would get smaller, wouldn't they?

17. GERMAN WEEK

(Transmitted: Thurs. 3/4/75, BBC1, 8.30pm)

ALSO APPEARING:

Miss Thorpe ....Moira Foot

German Customers...........Ernst Ulman, Joanna Lumley

The Lady for 'the Ladies' ....Anita Richardson

Young Mr Grace launches a campaign to push German goods, much to Mr Grainger's distaste and Mrs Slocombe's negativity, especially as the Russian cosmetic week flopped. When the first day's takings are only 32p, the disastrous results are blamed on anti-German feeling. To help get everyone in the spirit, German wine and serving wenches are called for!

Memories

'This is one of my favourite episodes, what with all the slap dancing, and me wearing shorts. Then there's Captain Peacock and Mrs Slocombe having a row and slapping each other across the kisser – great fun.'

FRANK THORNTON

18. SHOULDER TO SHOULDER

(Transmitted: Thurs. 10/4/75, BBC1, 8.30pm)

ALSO APPEARING:

Miss Thorpe ....Moira Foot

The Returned Wig..Kate Brown

Honeymoon Couple.....Jonathan Cecil, Hilary Pritchard

The decorators are in, and as Grace Brothers' finances can only stretch to one section at a time, the ladies have to share the men's department. Trouble ensues when Mr Grainger finds Mrs Slocombe taking down his Y-fronts, so he demands she takes down her underwear in return!

Memories

'I played one of the customers on honeymoon, and when I first got the script I was dismayed because there was nothing particularly interesting about the part. But when I arrived at the BBC, David Croft and Jeremy Lloyd had rewritten the scene, and it turned out to be a nice little job. I'd worked for David before, and Jeremy when he was an actor, so they knew my style. I thoroughly enjoyed my time on *Are You Being Served?*'

JONATHAN CECIL

WHAT A SCENE!

(Rumbold's latest secretary shows her ineptness.)

MR RUMBOLD: (*talking to Peacock*) I want you to advise the staff of the decoration programme. Now, I have the details here. Oh Miss Thorpe, where's the maintenance file?

MISS THORPE: You mean the one marked 'Decoration'?

MR RUMBOLD: Yes.

MISS THORPE: I filed it yesterday under 'A'.

MR RUMBOLD: (*confused*) Under 'A'?

MISS THORPE: Yes, I file most things under 'A'.

MR RUMBOLD: I don't quite follow.

MISS THORPE: Well, *A* letter, *A* sales report, *A* customer's complaint.

CAPT. PEACOCK: A difficult way of finding anything.

MR RUMBOLD: Miss Thorpe is only temporary!

19. NEW LOOK

(Transmitted: Thurs. 17/4/75, BBC1, 8.30pm)

ALSO APPEARING:

Miss Thorpe ....Moira Foot

The Gent for 'the Gents' ....Felix Bowness

After doors close, the staff review ideas from the suggestion box. As the contents consist of a piece of pork pie, a bus ticket, the usual obscenities, and a drawing of a Toby jug with Rumbold's name on it, suggestions to improve the image of Grace Brothers are sought. When it's decided to introduce background music and a recorded voice to help push sales, the question is: whose voice?

WHAT A SCENE!

(Mrs Slocombe recounts her night out – she was chatted up and driven home – to Miss Brahms.)

MRS SLOCOMBE: When we stopped we weren't outside my house at all.

MISS BRAHMS: Where were you?

MRS SLOCOMBE: Outside his place, miles away *(she continues to put on her lipstick).*

MISS BRAHMS: No?

MRS SLOCOMBE: Yes. Anyway, he said: 'Would I like to go in for a nightcap?' Well it seemed harmless enough; it wasn't until he actually produced one with a nightie to match that I realized what was going on.

MISS BRAHMS: Hope you asked him to take you straight home?

MRS SLOCOMBE: Yes … eventually!

Christmas Special

20. CHRISTMAS CRACKERS

(Transmitted: 22/12/75, BBC1, 8.45pm)

ALSO APPEARING:

Waitress...Doremy Vernon

Lady Templewood ....Betty Impey

The staff are summoned to an early morning meeting – so early Miss Brahms is still wearing her curlers. Ideas are sought for increasing the Christmas sales figures. Mrs Slocombe suggests lots of trimmings and something prickly in the underwear, Mr Humphries comes up with kisses for all the gentlemen, and Mr Lucas proposes reindeer and sleigh to transport customers to the counter. But Young Mr Grace decides that the staff must wear novelty costumes – much to their repugnance.

SERIES FOUR

REGULAR CAST MEMBERS

Mrs Slocombe..Mollie Sugden

Mr Lucas ....Trevor Bannister

Captain Peacock....................................Frank Thornton

Mr Humphries ....John Inman

Miss Brahms ....Wendy Richard

Mr Grainger...Arthur Brough

Mr Rumbold..Nicholas Smith

Young Mr Grace ....Harold Bennett

21. NO SALE

(Transmitted: Thurs. 8/4/76, BBC1, 8.00pm)

ALSO APPEARING:

Ivy..Hilda Fenemore

The Wedding Hat ....Hilary Pritchard

The Large Gloves ....Stuart Sherwin

The Check Suit ....John Bardon

Husband ....Gordon Peters

Wife..Anne Cunningham

The Raincoat in the Window.........................Reg Dixon

Grace Brothers are keen to catch any work-bound customers, so doors open at 8.30. Although the initiative is a success, the staff can't hack the early mornings and set about stopping the early shift.

Memories

'Arthur Brough was a wonderful guy, but he splashed a lot when he ate. He wore false teeth, which came from an undertakers, I think, because they didn't look as if they were made for him. When we indulged in our Sunday lunch banquets after rehearsing, we had to cover him in a sheet. It looked like he was having his hair cut, but the sheet was to stop the food going all over him!'

JOHN INMAN

WHAT A SCENE!

(The bell goes to notify staff it's time to open.)

CAPT. PEACOCK: To your places, everybody. Mrs Slocombe, uncover your bust, please.

MRS SLOCOMBE: *(turns round in disgust)* I beg your pardon, Captain Peacock!

CAPT. PEACOCK: Your counter bust, Mrs Slocombe, we're open for business.

22. TOP HAT AND TAILS
(Transmitted: Thurs. 15/4/76, BBC1, 8.00pm)

ALSO APPEARING:

Mr Harman ....Arthur English

Mr Ludlow..Peter Greene

It's time for the Golden Shoes Competition, a national contest between department stores to find the champion ballroom team. Young Mr Grace wants the ladies' and men's departments to form a team. With Mr Humphries utilizing his dancing background as the trainer, the use of the new Dress Hire department for costumes and a £25 bonus, everyone's keen to get involved. But are they up to it?

Memories

'I only appeared in one episode, but it was great fun. There was an element of theatre and old-time music hall about the series, which worked well because most of the cast had experience in those areas. The atmosphere was wonderful and the casting spot-on; everyone complemented each other.'

PETER GREENE

WHAT A SCENE!
(It's dancing rehearsals and Mr Lucas is partnering Mrs Slocombe.)

MR HUMPHRIES: Mrs Slocombe, are you ready?

MRS SLOCOMBE: Quite ready.

MR HUMPHRIES: Hand in the small of the back, Mr Lucas.

MR LUCAS: I can't find the small of her back. (*Shouting*) I can find the big of her back but I can't find the small of her back. (*Mrs Slocombe stamps on his foot.*) Ah!

23. FORWARD MR GRAINGER
(Transmitted: Thurs. 22/4/76, BBC1, 8.00pm)

ALSO APPEARING:

Secretary ....Isabella Rye

Rumbold is in Swansea for a month attending a seminar and, much to Captain Peacock's disgust, Mr Grainger is placed in charge. He soon settles in, puffing cigars, ordering the executive drinks trolley, asking for a rise. But when his colleagues try exploiting his good nature, they discover ol' Grainger has turned into a tyrannical monster.

Memories

'David and his wife had seen Isabella Rye playing a nurse on stage in London; she was in *The Sunshine Boys* with Jimmy Jewel and Alfred Marks. David thought she'd be ideal for playing the secretary in 'Forward, Mr Grainger', and she was great.

'For the episode David really wanted to glamorize her, showing off her cleavage and legs, and I remember sorting out the costume with her. After trying on various tops, she turned to me and said: "I think the first one's best; they're paying for the goodies so they might as well see them." Isabella was great fun.'

JO AUSTIN (former Production Assistant)

24. FIRE PRACTICE

(Transmitted: Thurs. 29/4/76, BBC1, 8.00pm)

ALSO APPEARING:

Mr Harman ....Arthur English

Interpreter ....Ahmed Khalil

The Emir..Ahmed Osman

Head Wife ....Melody Urquhart

Fireman..Hamish Roughead

Chief Fireman..Ken Barker

When an Arab arrives and orders a pair of trousers for one of his wives, Mr Humphries dreams up ingenious ways of obtaining the woman's inside leg measurements without touching her; to do so would result in death! Before business is completed the fire bell rings. It's only a practice, but the poor response means further practices are :quired. But next time they realize it's more than just a drill.

Memories

'One word you couldn't mutter in the studio under any circumstances was "fire" because it always set everything into action. As this episode involved a fire practice we had to invent a word to replace "fire" which could be used during rehearsals. After many suggestions – many not printable – we decided on 'shire'. When it came to the recording we had to tell the audience not to rush out in panic upon hearing the word "fire".'

JO AUSTIN (former Production Assistant)

25. FIFTY YEARS ON

(Transmitted: Thurs. 6/5/76, BBC1, 8.00pm)

ALSO APPEARING:

Mr Harman ....Arthur English

Claude ....Tony Sympson

Mrs Claude..Mavis Pugh

Mr Grace's Secretary...................................Penny Irving

The Six-Pound Fox ....Diana Lambert

To ensure that everyone remembers her birthday, Mrs Slocombe grasps every opportunity to drop unsubtle hints. Believing it's her fiftieth, the gang instigates a collection for a present. After eliminating several ideas, including two cyanide tablets, twelve cut-price vouchers for a canteen lunch and a pet department voucher to help towards replacing her pussy, a mystery gift is presented after a rendition of *Happy Birthday*. But Mrs Slocombe's mood rapidly changes when the specially designed cake is unveiled.

Memories

'On recording day, which was usually a Friday, we'd have lunch in the waitress-service restaurant at the BBC. But sometimes we'd record on Sundays, when the cast treated the production staff to a picnic in one of the dressing-rooms – I remember Mollie was the queen of puddings. Everyone would cook something; it was lovely food and although we only had one hour, it was most enjoyable. The cast were great because they'd always make a fuss of the production team.'

JO AUSTIN (former Production Assistant)

WHAT A SCENE!

(Over a bowl of soup Mr Grainger discusses his wife.)

MR GRAINGER: No, one has to take one's wife out occasionally for an airing.

MR HUMPHRIES: You make her sound like a spaniel.

MR GRAINGER: She doesn't look the least like a spaniel.

MR LUCAS: Mind you, he has to tie her ears back when she's having the soup.

CAPT. PEACOCK: Don't forget you're a junior, Mr Lucas.

MR GRAINGER: She has a very pretty profile – mind you, head on it's a bit of a shock!

26. OH WHAT A TANGLED WEB
(Transmitted: Thurs. 13/5/76, BBC1, 8.00pm)
ALSO APPEARING:

Mr Harman ....Arthur English

Mrs Peacock..Diana King

Monica Hazlewood ....Melita Manger

Mr Grace's Secretary..................................Penny Irving

Mr Hazlewood....................................Michael Stainton

Mr Harman is spreading rumours about Captain Peacock and Young Mr Grace's secretary. Not only were they getting cosy at the Christmas party but they both arrive late for work, and it seems likely they spent the night together. The rumours are fuelled by an irate Mrs Peacock confronting her hubby on the shop floor. There's only one way to sort out the mess: a board of inquiry.

WHAT A SCENE!
(Mrs Peacock, suspecting her hubby of having an affair, confronts him on the shop floor.

MRS PEACOCK: Stephen!

CAPT. PEACOCK: Hello, my dear, I didn't expect to see you.

MRS PEACOCK: Where were you?

CAPT. PEACOCK: When, dear?

MRS PEACOCK: If you're going to prevaricate with me, I shall kick you right in the middle of the gentlemen's department!

CAPT. PEACOCK: Can't we discuss this when I get home, my sweet?

MRS PEACOCK: You won't be going home, they're changing the locks now, my precious.

CAPT. PEACOCK: I thought we were going to the Old Comrades Dance, tonight? You promised to press my dinner jacket.

MRS PEACOCK: I kept my promise. I have pressed it – right down the lavatory!

Christmas Special

27. THE FATHER CHRISTMAS AFFAIR

(Transmitted: Fri. 24/12/76, BBC1, 7.30pm)

ALSO APPEARING:

Mr Harman ....Arthur English

The Plastic Umbrella ....Jeanne Mockford

The Cook...Doremy Vernon

Miss Bakewell..Penny Irving

The Boy ....Donald Waugh

When the electric Father Christmas models are abandoned, the hunt is on for a volunteer to star as the store Santa. Even though there's ten pounds a week on offer, no one's interested. But when the stake is raised to fifty pounds cash, applications flood in. Everyone's up for the part, including Mrs Slocombe, thanks to the recently passed Sex Discrimination Act. While the staff don their suits, Young Mr Grace makes his decision.

Memories

'During this episode there's an automaton dressed as Father Christmas which opens its cloak up, giving everyone a shock. At the end of the recording we needed some shots showing the expressions on the faces of the cast. By this time the model had been taken away and it was too much trouble to set it up again. So I had the bright idea of everyone looking at me, but then realized I had to do something to create a reaction. The only thing I could think of was to lift up my T-shirt! The audience shrieked with laughter and David, not seeing any of this, wondered what was going on.'

JO AUSTIN (former Production Assistant)

WHAT A SCENE!

(At lunch, Mr Grainger joins the rest of the staff at a table.)

MISS BRAHMS: Did you get your 'minute steak'?

MR GRAINGER: No, they said it would take ten minutes, so I settled for spaghetti bolognese, then I'm having some junket.

MR HUMPHRIES: (*knowing Mr Grainger isn't the best of eaters*) Mr Lucas, get in touch with the dry-cleaning department, tell them to stay open late.

MR GRAINGER: (*struggling with the spaghetti*) I'm very fond of this, you know. Yes, Mrs Grainger and I first had it in Sorrento.

MR LUCAS: Did you ever finish it!

Other Memorable Characters

MIKE BERRY, who played Mr Spooner for the last three series, was brought in to fill the gap left by Trevor Bannister. He had little television experience, and the opportunity to join a top-rated sitcom was exciting. 'I was a big fan of the show and loved watching it, so joining the cast was a dream come true,' says Mike, who didn't need to be told how to play the character. 'Like most of David and Jeremy's shows, the character's personality is inherent in the dialogue – you know what they're after. I could see he was a young, cheeky upstart.

'It was a great joy doing those shows and I wish they'd continued,' says Mike, who receives a lot of fan mail, particularly from the States.

For many people, Mike is best known as a singer: his biggest hit, 'The Sunshine of Your Smile', sold more than 300,000 copies in 1980. It was back in the rock 'n' roll era, however, that a fifteen-year-old Mike Berry – real name Michael Bourne – decided he wanted to be a singer. His big break arrived while he was serving a printing apprenticeship. 'I made a demo tape with a group I had, and it wasn't long before we were offered a recording contract.'

His first taste of success was the 1961 hit 'Trib-ute to Buddy Holly', but he'll always remember the one that got away. When a couple of mates offered to write him a song, he was unimpressed and turned them down. Those mates were none other than John Lennon and Paul McCartney! 'They'd only just arrived on the scene and weren't known for their writing skills, so I didn't think anything more of it – I've been kicking myself ever since.'

When the success of his band began to wane, Mike left singing behind in 1969 and invested in a business building racing cars. This venture lasted two years before he returned to the entertainment world, this time doing photographic work and commercials. 'For nine years I earned a decent living, and it was after doing a commercial that I was offered the chance to play Mr Peters, the father of John and Sue, in *Worzel Gummidge*.

After his time in *Are You Being Served?* Mike starred as Captain Beaky in Jeremy Lloyd's West End musical *Heaven's Up,* with Patrick Cargill and Jack Wild. On television he has also appeared in several children's shows, including *Motormouth*.

Now he dedicates most of his time to writing: he has just completed a musical and has developed an idea for a sitcom about an estate agent. 'There's lots going on in my life at the moment,' says Mike, who is married to Sue, and has two children. 'I've also reformed The Outlaws and occasionally play at venues around the country.'

Mike's character, Mr Spooner, had worked in the Paint, Bedding and Sports departments before joining Menswear.

London-born DOREMY VERNON was first seen in the 1976 Christmas Special and appeared a further twelve times, by which time she'd been promoted to canteen manageress. Doremy has a vivid memory of her intro-  duction to the hit sitcom, when she was asked by director Roy Butt, for whom she had worked in *Dixon of Dock Green,* to say just two words. 'I'd just returned from Manchester Rep and Ray called. All he wanted me to say was "plates" and "elbows" – that was it. It was only two words in the Christmas episode 'Christmas Crackers', but I always feel that the smaller the part the more frightening it is, because there's no leeway; you've got to get it right.'

It was a nervous actress that stood in the wings waiting to make her fleeting debut. 'There I was waiting for the scene to begin; I had to carry this stack of plates, but was getting so nervous I was shaking. I always seemed to follow an Arthur Brough line, which was murder because he was a little erratic: it was great for the production team because they could build it into his character, but not so easy if you were following him in the script!'

Doremy became so annoyed with herself for getting nervous that she asserted her anger on the plates she had to place on the canteen table. 'I stormed on to the set, shouted my words and slammed the plates down so hard they spun around,' she laughs. 'The cast loved it and it helped establish her aggressive attitude. Later, I banged the

casserole dish down so forcibly that it cracked and the contents began seeping out!'

The character was a semi-regular and became so popular that fans in America have even dressed up as the boorish canteen manageress at conventions organized to celebrate the classic sitcom. 'Although I usually didn't know until the last minute whether I was needed, I loved being in the show,' says Doremy, who feels her dancing background helped when she had to don a bunny girl's outfit for the episode 'The Night Club'. 'Being a dancer I'd kept myself fit, so I felt fine about it,' she says, 'but I wanted to ensure I was as trim as possible for the role, so I started running around the block at lunchtime. I got on so well I did it more and more, which started an obsession with road running that lasted over two years and included half-marathon races in competitions around the area.'

Doremy's dancing background stems from her teenage years. 'I taught dancing when I was four-

teen, and by the time I was eighteen was running three schools.'

A former Tiller Girl, she danced for three years before turning to acting when she realized she'd never reach the top of the dancing profession. During the 1960s she was an ASM at Bromley, earning £1.50 a week as well as a few pounds from film-extra work. 'Although everything was ticking along nicely, I realized I needed to train professionally, so I joined a drama school.'

Her first job after drama school was with Dick Emery and David Jason at Bournemouth Pier. 'It was a perfect job, a great learning process for me alternating between two plays and appearing with some good actors,' she says.

Doremy's television debut was in the late 1960s, working with Charlie Drake in ATV's *The Worker,* before going on to appear in other shows, including *Softly, Softly.* In recent years, she has found it difficult maintaining her TV career, so she dedicates her time to running a drama workshop for children. She also wrote the definitive history of the dancing troupe the *Tiller Girls,* published in 1988.

The nurse (Vivienne Johnson) was constantly at Young Mr Grace's beck and call, and a flash of her suspenders was enough to make his heart rate spiral.

VIVIENNE JOHNSON played the sexy nurse in three series (1978–81). Her pampering of the frail Young Mr Grace was admirable: she'd escort him wherever he went, but in her sexy uniform, complete with stockings, she usually made his heart rate spiral dangerously out of control.

Sheffield-born Vivienne had been playing a Russian spy in a Jeremy Lloyd play when she was asked to join *Are You Being Served?* So keen were David Croft and Jeremy to recruit her for the show that they presented two options: she could either have a big part in one episode, or appear in the entire series. For Vivienne, who'd always wanted to be an actress, there was no question which one to choose. 'Everyone was lovely, particularly Harold Bennett, who had a real nurse off-screen. He was so frail that when I walked holding him up by the arm, I felt that a breath of wind would blow him away.'

There was no doubt in Vivienne's mind about how the part should be played. 'It was all about short skirts and suspenders! That was part of the fun. But I wish I could have done more. David and Jeremy would have written more for me,' she explains, 'but there was a limit to how much

Harold could do, and as my part was linked with Young Mr Grace, it wasn't possible.'

Vivienne, who normally played mistresses and femmes fatales, trained as a secondary school teacher before working as an acting ASM. Work in numerous reps, including Sheffield, Leicester and Manchester, followed before she made her West End debut. It wasn't long before she was offered film work, and her credits include *Carry On England* and *Yesterday's Hero*, and television appearances in *Odd Man Out, The Sweeney, Potter, Open All Hours,* etc.

After taking a break from the business to bring up her son, Vivienne is now keen to resume her acting career.

Glasgow-born BENNY LEE appeared as Mr Klein, a salesman, in three episodes in 1981, including the Christmas Special 'Roots?'. Always wanting to work in entertainment, he got his first taste of cabaret as a boy. Later, while he worked as a tailor, like his father, he acted in local amateur dramatics.

Also a keen singer, Benny celebrated his stag night in 1941 by accepting a challenge to sing with the resident band at Glasgow's Piccadilly Club. Two weeks later, a telegram arrived inviting him to join the band. His singing career took off and during the war – health reasons prevented him enlisting – he made broadcasts and records with many top bands.

After the war he was busy on radio, working with the likes of Michael Bentine and Bernard Braden, including *Breakfast with Braden.* His television credits include Bentine's *It's A Square World, After Many a Summer* as Mr Clancy, *Friends and Neighbours,* and *That's My Boy* for Yorkshire TV as Mr Thoroughgood.

Benny died in 1995 when complications set in after an operation. He was 79.

KENNETH WALLER, best known for playing Grandad in *Bread,* was called up for series eight when Harold Bennett was unable to continue. Although he was cast as Old Mr Grace (Henry), who grew up in a little gas-lit mining town, Kenneth was only 53 when he appeared. 'I've played old men since the age of eighteen,' he says. 'I'd done odd episodes in various shows, but this was the first time I was in a long-running series.'

Born in Huddersfield in 1927, Kenneth made his stage debut at six, performing in a concert party organized by his mother. Later, when he was carrying out national service on the Isle of Man, he formed a dramatic society with a friend, presenting shows around the island.

Back in civvy street he worked for an auctioneer/estate agent while appearing in amateur dramatics, but when invited to join the local theatre, Kenneth turned professional. After eighteen

months of rep, he moved into the West End in 1960.

On the big screen Kenneth has appeared in a handful of films, beginning with *Room at the Top* in 1958. He later appeared as a dotty professor in *Chitty Chitty Bang Bang*, in *Fiddler on the Roof* and as a party guest in *Scrooge* with Albert Finney.

Other TV appearances include *All Creatures Great and Small*, *Coronation Street*, *Doctor Who*, *Juliet Bravo* and *Big Deal*, playing Ferret.

In 1998 Kenneth toured in *Beauty and the Beast* and recorded *Peter and the Wolf* for Radio 2.

Veteran actor JAMES HAYTER played Mr Tebbs, who joined Menswear after Mr Grainger left. Tebbs served over forty years with Grace Brothers, includ-

In episode 49, Young Mr Grace decided to leave the running of the store to his older brother, Henry (Kenneth Waller).

ing twelve years with Bathroom Fittings. In 1968 he received a pencil and pen set to mark his commitment to the firm. As captain of the company's bowls team, secretary of the darts team and tireless worker for the firm's Benevolent Fund for Distressed Salespersons, Tebbs, who appeared in the sixth series, was a valuable addition to the team.

Hayter was a dependable character actor whose career spanned five decades, incorporating all strands of the business. Often cast in jovial parts, the portly actor was probably best known for his stage appearances as Alfred Doolittle in *My Fair Lady*, succeeding Stanley Holloway in 1959 and

playing the part for five years in the West End and on tour. Meanwhile, he made over a hundred films, most notably playing Mr Pickwick in *Pickwick Papers* and Friar Tuck in *The Story of Robin Hood,* and appearing in *Morning Departure, Oliver!, Tom Brown's Schooldays, A Day to Remember* and *Trio.*

Hayter was born in India in 1907 but brought up in Scotland. After leaving school he studied at RADA before clocking up years of experience in rep. In 1932 and 1934 he combined acting with management, running his own companies in Dundee and Perth; two years later his career took a major step forward when he made his West End debut and appeared in his first film.

After demob from the Royal Armoured Corps at the end of the war, he returned to the theatre, appearing a few years later on the New York stage in a 1951 production of *Romeo and Juliet.*

He made numerous TV appearances, but will forever be remembered as the voice in the Mr Kipling cake adverts. James died in 1983 in Spain, where he'd been living for some years, aged 75.

ALFIE BASS played Mr Goldberg, recruited to replace Mr Tebbs after his retirement, even though Goldberg was in his sixties himself – another exam-

ple of Grace Brothers' policy of employing those long in the tooth rather than young blood. With extensive retail experience, Harry Goldberg, who spent four years with Captain Peacock in the army, stayed with Grace Brothers for the seventh series. A qualified cutting-room fitter, he had his own business above a fish and chip shop for years, but

when it went up in smoke he sought employment at Grace Brothers.

London-born actor Alfie Bass became a household name with television viewers playing Private Bisley in *The Army Game* and the sequel *Bootsie and Snudge,* in which Alfie's and Bill Fraser's characters were back in civvies. But his career also included over sixty films, including, after his 1943 debut in *The Bells Go Down, The Lavender Hill Mob, Brief Encounter, The Night My Number Came Up, A Child in the House, Hell Drivers, I Was Monty's Double* and *Moonraker.*

The youngest of ten children, Alfie left school at fourteen and worked through several jobs as a tailor's apprentice, a messenger boy and a window display fitter before turning his attention to the stage. He acted at the Unity Theatre for several years before turning professional in 1941.

During the Second World War, Alfie served as a despatch rider in the army, but continued his acting by getting involved with concert parties as well as training films and documentaries being made by the Army Film Unit.

When the war ended, he resumed his acting career with many stage and film appearances. He was also seen regularly on the small screen, usually in comedy roles, in shows like *Till Death Us Do Part, Our Mutual Friend, The Dick Emery Show, The Howerd Confessions, Celebrity Squares* and *Minder.* Alfie died in 1987, aged 66.

Playing Mr Grossman for four episodes in series eight, actor MILO SPERBER looked destined for a bright career in Germany during the 1930s before fleeing the Nazis in 1939. He settled with his family in England.

Early in the Second World War he joined the Oxford Pilgrim Players and performed in various venues in the area. But that wasn't his first taste of acting: his career had begun in Vienna several years earlier. While training as a lawyer, he joined a drama school in the city.

Sperber also gained experience in directing the company in *Case 27 VC* on tour and for a season in London. Before the war ended, he got involved in anti-Nazi programmes at the BBC.

His varied postwar career included spells in cabaret, theatre and television, including roles in *Don't Wait Up* and *Maigret.* On the big screen he made sporadic appearances in films such as *Mr Emmanuel, The End of the Road, In Search of the*

Castaways, Operation Crossbow, Billion Dollar Brain, The Spy Who Loved Me and *The Woman in White.* He taught at RADA for a few years and was a published scriptwriter, working for the BBC's German language service.

Milo made his last West End appearance in the 1984 production *The Clandestine Marriage,* at the Albany Theatre. In his final years he travelled the country giving readings from the work of his brother, the writer Manes Sperber. He died in London in 1992.

His character in *Are You Being Served?* arrived on the scene when Young Mr Grace decrees that part of the shoe department is allowed to move to Mr Rumbold's floor. Mr Grossman, who has sold shoes all his life, comes up with the department, and also assists on Mr Humphries' counter whenever possible.

LARRY MARTYN was a regular in the first three series as maintenance man Mr Mash, the militant trade union fanatic who had worked at Grace Brothers for 35 years. The overall-clad men from the basement are not the store's favourite characters, especially when it comes to the likes of Captain Peacock, who is always warning them about not appearing on the shop floor during opening hours, and Mrs Slocombe, who abhors the bawdiness of Mr Mash and his successor, Mr Harman.

Born in London in 1934, Larry entered the industry in the 1950s, working in variety as a singer and comedian until the age of 22. His early small-screen career was dominated by drama until the 1970s, when he was employed more and more in light entertainment. His TV appearances included *Dad's Army, The Dick Emery Show, Up Pompeii!* and *Mike Yarwood in Persons*. He also made several films, such as *Up the Junction, The Great St Trinian's Train Robbery, Carry On at Your Convenience* and *Carry On Behind,* playing an electrician.

Larry, who served with the parachute regiment during the war and continued the activity as a hobby, could not continue his role as Mr Mash because he was already booked for a new series of *Spring and Autumn*, in which he played Joe Dickinson. Later TV appearances included *Never the Twain* and *The Bill.*

He died in 1994.

ARTHUR ENGLISH joined the cast in 1976 after the departure of Larry Martyn. Playing bolshy Mr Harman from maintenance, an avid gambler who also runs a pawnbrokers on the side, he aggravates Peacock and Slocombe just as much as his predecessor.

Born in Aldershot in 1919, Arthur began entertaining fellow soldiers during the Second World War and turned professional shortly after demob, having worked as a waiter and shop assistant before the war, and as a navvy and painter and decorator afterwards.

Beginning his career as a light comedian, he toured music halls for years, after initial success at the Windmill Theatre. He became well known for his spiv character Tosh, and Prince of the Wideboys, wearing a white trilby, outrageously shoulder-padded suit, pencil moustache and kipper tie.

A radio favourite in the early 1950s – he became resident comedian on *Variety Bandbox* in 1951 – Arthur realized his variety days were numbered and

moved towards television and straight theatre roles during the 1960s. After several lean years, he began a busy small-screen career which included *How's Your Father?* playing Ted Cropper, the stablehand in the 1970s children series *Follyfoot,* Doolittle in a production of *Pygmalion, Never Say Die,* a traffic warden in *Bless this House, Dixon of Dock Green* and Alf Garnett's mate in *In Sickness and in Health.*

He appeared in a handful of mainly low-budget films, including *The Hi-Jackers* as a lorry-driver, *Echo of Diana* as a bookmaker, *Percy, Love Thy Neighbour* and *For the Love of Ada.*

Arthur died in 1995, aged 75.

Episode Guide

SERIES FIVE

REGULAR CAST MEMBERS

Mr Lucas ....Trevor Bannister

Mrs Slocombe...Mollie Sugden

Captain Peacock....................................Frank Thornton

Mr Humphries ....John Inman

Miss Brahms ....Wendy Richard

Mr Grainger...Arthur Brough

Mr Rumbold ....Nicholas Smith

Mr Harman ....Arthur English

Young Mr Grace ....Harold Bennett

28. MRS SLOCOMBE EXPECTS

(Transmitted: Fri. 25/2/77, BBC1, 8.00pm)

ALSO APPEARING:

Cleaner ....Hilda Fenemore

Customers ....Geoffrey Adams, Jennifer Lonsdale,

...............Elizabeth Morgan, Jeffrey Gardiner,

....Raymond Bowers

The men get the wrong end of the stick when they hear Mrs Slocombe discussing a happy event with Miss Brahms. After first thinking that the pink-haired tyrant is expecting, they're relieved to discover her cat is having kittens. Against management's wishes, Mrs Slocombe smuggles the expectant moggie into the store, but it gives birth at the most inopportune moment!

Memories

'Mollie Sugden used to get lots of fan mail from cat lovers asking about her pussy. One old lady wrote a twelve-page letter explaining she'd lost her cat. It rambled but was quite touching; I told Mollie we had the letter, held up the twelve pages and she went white! The old lady was lonely and a cat lover, so I wrote back on Mollie's behalf. To my horror, I got twenty pages back, complete with photos. Mollie couldn't believe it.'

JO AUSTIN (former Production Assistant)

29. A CHANGE IS AS GOOD AS A REST

(Transmitted: Fri. 4/3/77, BBC1, 8.00pm)

ALSO APPEARING:

The Red Indian Father.............................Terry Duggan

The Bridal Doll ....Jacquie Cook

Miss Bakewell...Penny Irving

When the staff are summoned to see Young Mr Grace in the boardroom, everyone's imaginations run wild over the reasons for the meeting. Mr Grace puts them out of their misery by announcing another brainwave: everyone should learn each other's jobs, so they're swapping roles with the toy department. Initial objections soon disappear as the staff enjoy their experience – Mr Humphries is even talking to the toys!

Memories

'I enjoyed making this episode because it meant David and I spent a wonderful afternoon in Hamley's toy shop buying the toys ourselves. It was great fun; I wonder how many writers get that sort of opportunity? We enjoyed ourselves so much I don't think we bothered even charging the BBC for them.'

JEREMY LLOYD

WHAT A SCENE!

(The staff wonder why they've been called to the boardroom.)

MRS SLOCOMBE: I wonder if we're all going to get a rise?

MISS BRAHMS: Or a cut.

CAPT. PEACOCK: Perhaps it's a take-over by the Army and Navy.

MR HUMPHRIES: (*grinning*) That would be nice!

MISS BRAHMS: Perhaps some Arab sheik has bought us all.

MR LUCAS: Oh, Mrs Slocombe will come into her own then, won't she? (*laughing*) They like 'em big in the east – come to think of it she's very big in the south as well!

MRS SLOCOMBE: Mr Lucas, just because we're in the boardroom and on our best behaviour doesn't mean that I won't give you one up the bracket!

30. FOUNDER'S DAY

(Transmitted: Fri. 11/3/77, BBC, 8pm)

ALSO APPEARING:

The Two Fur Coats ....Tim Barrett

The Top-Pocket Handkerchief ....Bill Martin

The French Underwear ....Carolle Rousseau

Miss Bakewell..Penny Irving

Miss 38-22-36...Jenny Kenna

It's Young Mr Grace's eightieth birthday and the staff organize *This Is Your Department,* a spoof *This Is Your Life*. With the help of Mr Grace's half-completed memoirs, and Mr Lucas adopting a thick Irish brogue, the tribute looks back over the life of this octogenarian.

Memories

'During rehearsals I discovered Mollie Sugden shared my passion for flowers. That evening she must have gone into her garden and dug up a massive day lily, because the following morning she presented it to me. Even now, twenty years later, that plant has quadrupled in size and flowers every summer, and whenever it does I think of Mollie!'   JENNY KENNA

WHAT A SCENE!

(Over lunch, the staff discuss plans for Young Mr Grace's birthday.)

MISS BRAHMS: Well, why do we have to think about it?

CAPT. PEACOCK: It's our turn.

MRS SLOCOMBE: Catering did him last year.

CAPT. PEACOCK: Well, of course, they went too far. It should've been obvious that a topless go-go dancer leaping out of a cake would have been a terrible shock for a man of his age.

MR LUCAS: That was his second heart attack, wasn't it?

MR HUMPHRIES: His first one was when Mr Lucas phoned up, said he was Hugh Fraser, and how much did he want for the shop.

MRS SLOCOMBE: They should've known that a scantily clad young girl would've had that effect.

MR LUCAS: (*laughing*) It's a pity. If you'd volunteered, Mrs Slocombe, you could've saved him six months in hospital.

MRS SLOCOMBE: You wouldn't catch me doing that.

MR LUCAS: No, you wouldn't get in the cake!

31. THE OLD ORDER CHANGES

(Transmitted: Fri. 18/3/77, BBC1, 8.00pm)

ALSO APPEARING:

The Afro Pants..Jeffrey Holland

Cynthia..Bernice Adams

Back from the States, a stetson-wearing Young Mr Grace introduces a host of new sales techniques, including everyone being on first-name terms and dressing to express their personalities, and using background music. But no sooner has the firm adopted the new image than Mr Grace returns from Peking and scraps the American look.

Memories

'During the recording of this scene, Mollie came up to me wearing her stern look and said: "Captain Freecock, are you pea?" It got a big laugh from the audience and Mollie's face dissolved into howls of laughter. We tried several times but she couldn't complete the scene without cracking up. Finally, she got it right, but the audience gave her a round of applause which messed it up again! So the audience were told not to laugh or applaud and eventually we finished the scene.'

FRANK THORNTON

WHAT A SCENE!

(Peacock reminds Mrs Slocombe of Grace Brothers' procedure.)

MRS SLOCOMBE: Captain Peacock!

CAPT. PEACOCK: Mrs Slocombe, go back to your counter and stand behind it. When I happen to look in your direction, raise your hand a little. If I nod, say: 'Captain Peacock, are you free?' If I am I will beckon and you may then approach me – that is correct procedure, do I make myself clear?

MRS SLOCOMBE: *(angrily)* Yes, Captain Peacock.

32. TAKE-OVER

(Transmitted: Fri. 25/3/77, BBC1, 8.00pm)

ALSO APPEARING:

Lady Weeble Ablesmith...............................Mavis Pugh

Henry Grant Hopkins ....Donald Bisset

Miss Bakewell...Penny Irving

Rumbold – with the unwanted help of Mr Harman – tells everyone there's a take-over bid in the air. While the staff scan the 'situations vacant', Mr Rumbold and Young Mr Grace cook up a plan to help swing the vote, thus killing off the bid. Dressed up as shareholders, Mr Grainger, Mrs Slocombe, Miss Brahms and Mr Harman put the plan into action.

Memories

Arthur Brough, who was wonderful, was wearing a toupée for this episode. Every time we did the scene it was positioned at a different angle. When it came to the actual recording it was at an even more ridiculous angle – I just managed to get my words out before cracking up.'

TREVOR BANNISTER

WHAT A SCENE!

(After hearing news about the possible take-over, the staff scan the 'situations vacant'.)

MRS SLOCOMBE: Glamorous personal assistant required by director of film company; much travel, must be under thirty – oh dear, just too late.

MR HUMPHRIES: Listen to this: organ demonstrator wanted!

MR GRAINGER: The only job for which I seem qualified is that of a chair man.

CAPT. PEACOCK: Company chairman?

MR GRAINGER: No, deck chair man!

33. GOODBYE MR GRAINGER

(Transmitted: Fri. 1/4/77, BBC1, 8.00pm)

ALSO APPEARING:

The Corset Customer ....Peggy Ashby

Mr Grainger is annoying everyone with his grouchy manner, which isn't helped by the fact that he's losing the use of the central stand display for 'bra week'. Everyone agrees his time is up at Grace Brothers, but before he can be told, he resigns. But it's not long until everyone feels sorry for the old-timer and sets about retaining his services.

34. IT PAYS TO ADVERTISE

(Transmitted: Good Friday 8/4/77, BBC1, 8.15pm)

ALSO APPEARING:

The Ten-Pound Perfume ....Ferdy Mayne
The Porter..Freddie Wiles
Miss Bakewell...Penny Irving
Mr Crawford ....Raymond Bowers

Not only have Mrs Slocombe and Mr Humphries been chosen as models for the store's latest display dummies but, along with the rest of the staff, they're appearing in a Grace Brothers advert, for screening at local cinemas. The commercial is set in a cocktail bar, but to save money the shop floor is used. With Mr Humphries directing, the usual mayhem ensues, particularly when Mrs Slocombe loses a mike down her cleavage.

Memories

'In this episode two display models resembling Mrs Slocombe and Mr Humphries are seen. I remember having to chaperone Mollie and John when they had their face masks done. They had

WHAT A SCENE!

(Mrs Slocombe is using her normal sales patter.)

MRS SLOCOMBE: There you are, madam, I hope the garment gives every satisfaction.

CUSTOMER: And you really think that this type of corset will keep my figure under control?

MRS SLOCOMBE: Well, the stiffeners are the best quality whale-bone.

CUSTOMER: Yes, but will they be strong enough?

MRS SLOCOMBE: Well, they're strong enough for the whale!

the full plaster works, bandages around their faces, and between Make-up and Visual Effects we came up with very accurate face masks. I think they found it a horrid experience, so I stayed chatting with them – not that there were any answers!'

JO AUSTIN (former Production Assistant)

WHAT A SCENE!

(The lifelike Mrs Slocombe display model is unveiled by Mr Harman.)

MRS SLOCOMBE: Oh! They've got me to a tee. You know, looking at that face is a very eerie experience.

MR LUCAS: That's what I said to Mr Humphries the first day I met you.

CAPT. PEACOCK: Mr Lucas, if you're going to be rude you can return to your counter. I think Display have done a wonderful job, it's absolutely lifelike.

MISS BRAHMS: There's not so many wrinkles.

MR HARMAN: Well, they would have got them all in only Mr Grace wouldn't pay the overtime!

SERIES SIX

REGULAR CAST MEMBERS

Mrs Slocombe	Mollie Sugden
Mr Humphries	John Inman
Mr Lucas	Trevor Bannister
Captain Peacock	Frank Thornton
Miss Brahms	Wendy Richard
Mr Tebbs	James Hayter
Mr Rumbold	Nicholas Smith
Mr Harman	Arthur English
Young Mr Grace	Harold Bennett
Miss Bakewell	Penny Irving
Nurse	Vivienne Johnson

35. BY APPOINTMENT

(Transmitted: Wed. 15/11/78, BBC1, 6.45pm)

ALSO APPEARING:

Ivy	Hilda Fenemore
Lady Customer	Joy Harington
Radio Voice	Colin Ward-Lewis

The staff are back from their holidays, and with Rumbold bearing scars from a falling coconut, Peacock sounding like Donald Duck and Mr Lucas with burnt feet, it seems their vacations were eventful. As Mr Tebbs joins the department as head of Menswear, news breaks that Royalty are visiting the area and may pay a visit to Grace Brothers. In preparation, everyone stays late and rehearses, with Captain Peacock – wearing his blue Y-fronts – and Mrs Slocombe doubling for the Royal couple.

WHAT A SCENE!

(Mr Lucas arrives with burnt feet.)

MR RUMBOLD: What on earth is the matter with you, Mr Lucas?

MR LUCAS: I burnt my feet in Skegness.

MR RUMBOLD: In Skegness?

MR LUCAS: Well, there was this female acrobat, you see, and she took me back to her flat. She was just showing me how to juggle with a couple of grapefruit and a cucumber standing on my head, when her father came in.

MR RUMBOLD: Well, what's this got to do with burnt feet?

MR LUCAS: Well, he's a fire-eater on the pier and he took a swig of paraffin from his hip flask, flicked his Ronson, breathed out and it was *Towering Inferno* with me going head first down the fire escape.

36. THE CLUB

(Transmitted: Wed. 22/11/78, BBC1, 6.45pm)

ALSO APPEARING:

Roger's Master.....................................Raymond Bowers

Roger's Mistress..Mavis Pugh

Flexibra Customers.......Dominique Don, Tony Brothers

The staff are offered a room in the basement as a social club, but before the doors can open, the place needs a face-lift. With the decorators quoting five hundred pounds for the work, the plan looks doomed until the staff muck in and do it themselves, earning fifty pounds each in the process. But it soon becomes clear that decorating is not their forte.

Memories

'I had a habit of appearing with animals. It was a cat in *Close to Home,* a dog in *Fawlty Towers* and, of course, a poodle in *Are You Being Served?* The owner was terribly anxious and thought there might be some problems, but to everyone's relief the dog took to me straight away.'

MAVIS PUGH

WHAT A SCENE!

(A customer unintentionally insults Captain Peacock.)

CAPT. PEACOCK: Are you being served, sir?

CUSTOMER: No. Are you an assistant?

CAPT. PEACOCK: (*annoyed*) No! Actually I'm in charge of the floor.

CUSTOMER: (*looking down at the floor*) Oh. Well, I must say it looks very nice.

CAPT. PEACOCK: Perhaps I should rephrase that: I'm the floorwalker, it's my job to help you find what you're looking for.

37. DO YOU TAKE THIS MAN?

(Transmitted: Wed. 29/11/78, BBC1, 6.45pm)

ALSO APPEARING:

Wendel P. Clark ....Norman Mitchell

Mr Tomiades ....Gorden Kaye

The Matching Pantaloons........................Felix Bowness

Greek Band Leader....................................Stelios Chiotis

Mrs Slocombe has met a new man, who is well known for his bazouki. When the secret of her impending marriage to the Greek is out, the rest of the staff decide to help Mrs Slocombe with all the arrangements, including a reception on the shop floor to help keep costs down. As the bride gets ready, Mr Tomiades arrives with bad news.

WHAT A SCENE!

(Over lunch, the staff talk about Mrs Slocombe's news.)

MR HUMPHRIES: D'you know, when Mrs Slocombe told us the news yesterday, you could've knocked me down with a feather.

CAPT. PEACOCK: She didn't look too happy this morning.

MISS BRAHMS: She's worried about the cost of the wedding; it's the bride's family what pays and she's the only one what's left.

MR HUMPHRIES: Catering can cost a fortune these days.

MISS BRAHMS: Well, I know. She started out getting a quote for champagne and smoked salmon, and now she's working on meat paste and brown ale!

38. SHEDDING THE LOAD

(Transmitted: Wed. 6/12/78, BBC1, 6.45pm)

MAIN CAST MEMBERS ONLY

Sales are so low, again, that someone will be made redundant and it's down to the staff to decide who'll be collecting their cards. The claws are out as everyone fights for survival. No one can decide who must go, so Mr Harman suggests a secret ballot. But the final decision is down to Young Mr Grace, who observes the staff at their jobs. Just when things are getting out of hand, Mr Grace announces the cutbacks are cancelled: he's saving money by taking a three-day week instead.

39. A BLISS GIRL

(Transmitted: Wed. 13/12/78, BBC1, 6.45pm)

ALSO APPEARING:

Lady Customer...Jan Holden

Typist..Bernice Adams

The Bliss perfume has arrived but not the assistant to sell it. When someone is required, Mr Humphries is chosen, even though no commission is involved. And with Captain Peacock replacing Mr Humphries on Menswear, it's all change.

40. HAPPY RETURNS

(Transmitted: Tues. 26/12/78, BBC1, 7.00pm)

ALSO APPEARING:

Fairy Prince ....Michael Halsey

Waitress..Doremy Vernon

To celebrate Young Mr Grace's birthday each department gives the annual rendition of 'Happy Birthday' and enjoys the nosh – although the spread is rather spartan – at the free luncheon. After work they party at the celebration do, but when it comes to providing the cabaret, there's a surprise in store.

Familiar Faces

During the life of Grace Brothers a myriad of characters ventured on to the shop-floor or risked their health at the staff canteen. Some of the actors who brought them to life were employed more than once, while others made a fleeting appearance and were never spotted again. In this section I have included mini profiles, which I hope are informative, of the actors who, whether they were regular or only made one appearance, all played their part in the success of *Are You Being Served?* Although it has not been possible to include every character, I hope your favourites are here.

JOY ALLEN (b. Werrington)
Roles: Sister (episode 15); Staff Nurse (episode 42)
Joy always wanted to become an actress and after leaving school took elocution lessons before joining RADA.

After drama school she was offered the chance to join a production of *King's Rhapsody* in two capacities: as an understudy and as a member of the chorus. Then, when the principal girl in a Peterborough panto was taken ill, Joy took over within three days. Shortly afterwards, Joy got married, raised a family and gave up acting until the early 1970s when the manager of a theatrical company in Corby, Northants, spotted her in an amateur production and invited her to join his company. She stayed three years, by which time she'd made her first television appearance, playing a clippie in *Dad's Army.*

Joy has been in other TV shows, including several non-speaking roles, and appeared in a recent series of David Croft's *Oh, Doctor Beeching!* Nowadays she mostly works as an extra.

AVRIL ANGERS (b. Liverpool)
Role: Miss Comlozi (episode 44)
Avril, born of theatrical parents, pursued a career in entertainment because it seemed the logical thing to do. She made her debut as a dancer at the age of fourteen.

She went on to write her own material for a stand-up comedy routine before moving into television. She had her own series, *Dear Dotty,* but has also been seen in *All Creatures Great and Small, Coronation Street* (in two different roles), *The Dustbinmen* and *Just Liz.* Avril appeared with Arthur Lowe in the 1970 series *The More We Are Together.*

While still busy on TV, Avril has performed extensively on the stage, and has made many West End appearances in *Oklahoma!*

LISA ANSELMI
(b. Clacton-on-Sea)
Role: His Secretary (episode 61)
After leaving drama school, Lisa earned her Equity card by modelling and dancing in Paris. Her first TV appearance was as an extra in *Hi-De-Hi!,* before playing the secretary, her first speaking role, in *Are You*

Being Served? She worked for David again in *'Allo, 'Allo* and has also worked in the theatre.

For the past eleven years Lisa has been living in the USA; based in New York, she's now a scriptwriter.

PATRICIA ASTLEY
(b. Blackpool)

Role: Nurse, a non-speaking role (series 5)

Patricia, who is now in her fifties, worked in insurance for five years before moving to London. When her daughter started school she replied to an advert for models and her career began.

Most of her career was spent as a model, and her role as the nurse was only her second TV appearance – her debut was in *The Dave Allen Show*. She appeared in the occasional bit-part while continuing her modelling career before giving up the business and moving back to Blackpool. Nowadays she works two days a week for a friend's furniture store.

JOHN BAKER (b. Newport)

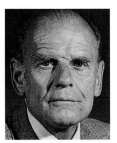

Role: The Fur Gloves (episode 8)
After drama school John – often cast as butlers and footmen – worked for years in rep before making his TV debut in the 1950s. He appeared in several episodes of *Z Cars* and *Blake's 7*. On film he made a cameo appearance in Laurence Olivier's 1948 production of *Hamlet*. John, who is now 81, has retired.

KEN BARKER (b. London)

Role: Chief Fireman (episode 24)
Actor/stuntman Ken Barker began acting in 1949 and for fifteen years appeared in such shows as *Z Cars*, *Dixon of Dock Green* and *New Scotland Yard*, before concentrating on stunt work. He has been a stuntman in many films, including *Superman*, *Indiana Jones* and *Octopussy*, as well as TV shows such as *Last of the Summer Wine* and *The Fall and Rise of Reginald Perrin* (he's the swimmer who appeared in each episode's opening credits).

Until recently Ken was also a busy after-dinner speaker, but is now suffering ill-health.

TIM BARRETT (b. London)

Role: Two Fur Coats (episode 30)
Originally known as Arthur Barrett, Tim worked extensively in rep before entering TV, the medium for which he's best known. He quickly established himself as a popular, reliable character actor who was always in work, appearing in *The Dick Emery Show*, *Terry and June*, *The Janet Brown Show*, *The Fall and Rise of Reginald Perrin*, etc. He never reached leading status, but his familiar face led to a fruitful small-screen career.

Tim hadn't been well for some time when, after returning from a Greek holiday, he died at the home he shared with his mother.

MORRIS BARRY
(b. Northampton)

Role: Customer (episode 41)
After attending drama school, Morris worked for several years on the stage before the outbreak of the Second Word War, during which he served as a major in the army. After demob he returned to the stage, but gave up acting in 1956 to join the BBC. He began as a floor manager before becoming a director on shows including *Z Cars*, *Compact*, *The Newcomers*, *Doctor Who* and *Softly, Softly*. He later became a producer on shows such as *Angels* and *Poldark*.

On retiring from the Beeb in the 1970s, Morris returned to acting in small parts, including *Blake's 7* and *Doctor Who*. He also worked as a freelance trainer for television, and lectured at Loughborough University for two years. Now 80, Morris has retired.

COLIN BEAN (b. Wigan)
Role: The Leatherette Gloves
(episode 4)
Colin wanted to act from child-hood. After leaving school in 1944 he joined the army for four years and began acting whilst in Japan. He graduated from drama school in 1952, but stayed on to teach for a year before joining Sheffield rep as ASM. He also worked with the Court Players for four years.

His early career was dominated by theatre. He had his first TV speaking role in 1961, in *Richard the Lionheart* with Richard Greene. Working for Jimmy Perry at Watford's Palace Theatre in 1962 led to a non-speaking part in *Dad's Army*. He eventually appeared on the credits as Private Sponge in 28 episodes. He played policemen in *Z Cars* and *No Hiding Place*, and was also seen in *The Liver Birds*, *The Goodies*, *The Harry Worth Show* and fourteen episodes of *Michael Bentine Time* in 1973. He appeared in the penultimate episode of *Hi-De-Hi!* in 1988 as the Verger alongside Frank Williams (as the Vicar) at Gladys's wedding. He also made three films.

Colin, who gained a master's degree in Speech and Projection during the 1980s, now suffers from arthritis, and is restricted to radio work.

HAROLD BERENS
(b. Glasgow).
Role: Customer (episode 41)
Harold worked in the shirt industry in London for several years before turning to entertain-ment, concentrating on rep and vaudeville. He also did plenty of radio work, including his own show, *Beat the Band*. He made cameo appearances in over twenty films,

notably in *Carry On Columbus* as Cecil the Torturer, *Third Time Lucky*, *The Big Money*, *The Pure Hell of St. Trinians* and *Trail of the Pink Panther*.

On TV, he played an aristocrat in *Crossroads*, and was seen in *The Prisoner*. Harold, who took up jazz singing in his eighties, died in 1986, aged 92.

RAYMOND BOWERS
(b. Swansea)
Roles: Customer (episode 28);
Mr Crawford (episode 34);
Roger's Master (episode 36);
The Shrunken Sock (episode 45)
Raymond's first taste of acting was in amateur dramatics while

studying philosophy at Swansea University. After failing to get a two-year scholarship for drama school, he was offered a year's free tuition instead. After graduation he worked in rep, initially at Salisbury, but his West End debut quickly followed. He began working on television in *The Newcomers* in 1967. Other credits include *The Dick Emery Show*, *Odd Man Out*, *Come Back Mrs Noah*, a porter in *Crossroads*, *How Green Was My Valley* and *To Serve Them All My Days*.

Raymond, also seen as the camp hairdresser in the *Are You Being Served?* movie, last appeared on TV in 1994. The last fifteen years of his career have been dominated by his work with the RSC.

FELIX BOWNESS (b. Harwell)
Roles: The Gent for 'the Gents'
(episode 19); The Matching
Pantaloons (episode 37)
Felix has been in the entertain-ment business for over four decades, performing in variety shows around the country. Win-

ning a talent contest in Reading encouraged him to turn semi-pro. Whilst working in cabaret, he was spotted by a BBC producer and given a small part in radio. With great tenacity, Felix – an amateur boxing champion in his late teens – kept plugging away, eventually making his TV debut as a stand-up comic before moving into comedy roles in shows such as *Porridge*, playing Gay Gordon.

A veteran warm-up man – he did the *Are You Being Served?* warm-ups – Felix is best known as jockey Fred Quilley in *Hi-De-Hi!* He has frequently worked for David Croft, appearing in *Hugh and I*, *Dad's Army*, as a grocer in *You Rang, M'Lord?* and as a relief guard in the last series of *Oh, Doctor Beeching!*

MARY BRADLEY (b. Windsor)
Role: Cleaner (episode 69)
Mary began acting in her thirties after working in a legal office. She attended drama school in 1979 and was soon working in theatre. After background work in several series of *Hi-De-Hi!*, the cleaner in *Are You Being Served?* was her first speaking role on television. Other small-screen credits include *The Bill*, *Indelible Evidence*, *The Legacy of Reginald Perrin* and *As Time Goes By*.

For the last ten years Mary has been raising her son, but is keen to resume her career.

RONNIE BRODY (b. Bristol)
Roles: Signor Balli (episode 46);
Man in Cinema (episode 67)
Son of music-hall artistes Bourne and Lester, Ronnie joined the merchant navy at fifteen, before serving with the RAF in North Africa during the Second World War.

After demob he spent several years in variety and rep, but by the 1950s his career was dominated by film and television. Over the years he became one of the nation's most recognizable comedy character actors.

During his career Ronnie worked with many top comedians in shows like *Dave Allen at Large*, *The Dick Emery Show*, *Rising Damp*, *Bless This House*,

Home James, *The Lenny Henry Show* and *The 19th Hole*. He has also been seen in films such as *Help!*, *A Funny Thing Happened on the Way to the Forum*, *Superman III*, as the Little Man in *Carry On Don't Lose Your Head* and as Henry in *Carry On Loving*. Although he concentrated on comedy, he appeared occasionally in TV drama. He died of a heart attack in 1991, aged 72.

KATE BROWN (b. Manchester)
Role: The Returned Wig
(episode 18)

Kate, who got the part of the wig customer when Julia McKenzie was unavailable, wanted to act since childhood, and after leaving school went to drama school. When she graduated she spent three years as a singer in musicals and pantomimes around the country, before moving into rep.

Her first taste of television arrived with *Z Cars* in 1963, in which she played an information officer for seventeen episodes. Other small-screen credits include *Dixon of Dock Green*, *Last of the Summer Wine*, *Chinese Puzzle*, two series of *Now Take My Wife*, *Softly, Softly*, *Owen MD*, and *Some Mothers Do 'Ave 'Em*, as a hospital patient.

In 1976 Kate left the profession and fulfilled a childhood dream by going to live in America. For twelve years she worked on a jewellery counter in a Californian department store. She has now returned to the acting business and concentrates on commercials.

JONATHAN CECIL
(b. London)
Role: A Man on his Honeymoon
(episode 18)

Jonathan got involved in acting at Oxford. On the strength of a university performance at Stratford, he was told he had a future in the profession, so on graduating he joined LAMDA.

Rep work followed before he moved into television. Early screen credits include *Ben Travers Farces, The Goodies, Dad's Army, The Dick Emery Show,* and playing snooty Jeremy Crichton-Jones in two series of *Romany Jones.* As well as an extensive TV career, Jonathan has made over twenty film appearances, including *Rising Damp, The Yellow Rolls Royce, Up the Front* and *Alice Through the Looking Glass.*

Jonathan's career has graced all areas of the profession, and he remains busy today.

JEAN CHALLIS (b. Cheadle Hulme)
Role: Mrs Rumbold (episode 68)

Jean, who describes Mrs Rumbold as 'fat and nasty', trained as an infant teacher, but after a successful appearance in a college production joined drama school. Seven years of rep followed before the occasional television job arrived. She worked as a radio announcer for BFBS in Cyprus, and upon returning in 1966 began working on television in earnest, her last appearance being as a bossy matron in *Goodnight Sweetheart.*

Other TV credits include several episodes of *Hi-De-Hi!, Terry and June, No Place Like Home, Alas Smith and Jones* and *Bread,* but Jean is best remembered for playing Mrs Arnott in two series of *Dear John,* with Ralph Bates.

Jean, who has spent more than forty years in the profession, mainly works in theatre now, and was recently seen in the stage version of *Animal Crackers.*

STELIOS CHIOTIS (b. Famagusta, Cyprus)
Role: Greek Band Leader (episode 37)

Stelios grew up in Cyprus, but on leaving school moved to London to study music. After playing the guitar and singing in coffee bars, he went on to make a career as a musician and singer.

When he was 35, he began to get offers of walk-on parts and roles in TV shows. He was seen in the BBC play *One Last Chance,* an episode of *Inspector Morse, The Bill, Surprise, Surprise* and *The Big E.* As well as appearing in Channel 4's documentary *Landscapes of Childhood,* about Cypriots living in London, he had his own radio programme on LGR, discussing social and topical events.

After 36 years in London as a musician, band leader and singer, Stelios returned to Cyprus with his wife and youngest son and has opened a restaurant/night club near Nicosia.

SANDRA CLARK (b. Glasgow)
Role: Miss Robinson (episode 16)

Sandra intended to be a PE teacher but joined drama school instead. Since graduating she has worked in every medium.

Television credits include *Dr Finlay's Casebook, Sutherland's Law, Barlow, EastEnders* and *Taggart.* Her biggest small screen roles are thirteen episodes of BBC's *The MacKinnons* and 31 instalments of *Me and My Girl,* playing the housekeeper. Her movies include *The Gift of the Nile* and *Five Castles,* and she has made over five hundred radio appearances. She is currently on an extensive RSC tour.

PETER CLEALL (b. London)
Role: Mr Winston (episode 62)

Peter, best known for playing Eric Duffy in *Please Sir!,* wanted to be a writer but changed his mind when a friend asked him to join a local amateur play. After drama school he worked in theatre and soon made his television debut in *Dixon of Dock Green.* He also appeared as Stephen Crane in *Dempsey and Makepeace,* as Percy Foreman in *London's Burning,* and in *Minder* and *Silent Witness.* Today, as well as acting, Peter helps run a co-operative theatre agency in Brighton with other actors.

JOHN CLEGG (b. Murree, Pakistan)

Roles: The Made-to-Measure Customer (episode 11); The Small Handicap (episode 16)

John was eighteen months old when he moved to England (his father was in the army). He always wanted to be an actor, so after national service he joined RADA. On graduating he worked in rep, including Coventry and Liverpool.

He is best known as Gunner Graham in *It Ain't Half Hot, Mum,* a role he played for seven years. Other TV roles include a calligraphist in *Mr Bean,* Mr Franklyn in *You Rang, M'Lord?,* Clifford Howes in *Crossroads* and vicars in *Keep it in the Family* and *Spooner's Patch.* He has also appeared in several films.

His one-man show, based on Kipling's Indian writings, won much acclaim, winning an award at the Edinburgh Festival.

CAROL CLEVELAND (b. London)

Role: Lady Customer (episode 68)

Carol, who was offered her part after writing to Martin Shardlow, appeared in *Only Fools and Horses* straight after episode 68.

Her parents met on a film set, so it was no surprise that Carol wanted to act. She grew up in California, returning to England to attend RADA. After graduating she worked in theatre and television, including *Randall and Hopkirk (Deceased), The Saint, The Lotus Eaters* and *About Face* with Maureen Lipman. She also worked as a 'glamour stooge' for Ronnie Corbett, Roy Hudd and Spike Milligan, but she's best known for appearances in every series of *Monty Python,* as well as the films and stage spin-offs. Recent work has mainly been in the theatre.

PEGGY ANN CLIFFORD (b. Bournemouth)

Role: Mrs Maxwell (episode 47)

Peggy worked in rep before establishing herself as a supporting actress, normally cast as a jolly character, on film and television. She was particularly busy during

the 1950s, and appeared in many films, including *Kind Hearts and Coronets, Man of the Moment, Brothers in Law* with Ian Carmichael, *Doctor at Large* and *Under Milk Wood.* She appeared on television with Tony Hancock on several occasions.

Peggy sold a block of flats in Fulham in order to buy a grocery shop in Chelsea, which she ran for three years while not acting. Peggy died in 1984, aged 65.

JOHN D. COLLINS (b. London)

Roles: Doctor (episode 49); Second Waiter (episode 54); Secretary at Number Ten (episode 61)

After leaving school John worked as a shop assistant for a year before joining RADA. A busy

career has included a ten-year association with Spike Milligan as assistant director and actor. Television appearances include *Get Some In!, A Family at War, Peak Practice* and several shows produced by David Croft, including the Q series, *Hi-De-Hi!, 'Allo, 'Allo, You Rang, M'Lord?* and *Oh, Doctor Beeching!* He also ran his own theatre in Essex for a year.

JESS CONRAD (b. London)

Role: Mr Walpole (episode 59)

Jess started out as a rep actor before succeeding as a pop star in the 1960s, when he appeared frequently on the *Oh Boy!* shows, and was voted England's 'Most Popular Singer' in 1961. On

television he's appeared on *The Des O'Connor Show,*

Jim Davidson Special, and *Big Break,* as well as playing cameo roles in *Crossroads,* as Phillip Bailey, and a *Miss Marple* series. Film credits include *The Great Rock 'N' Roll Swindle, Rag Doll* and *Follow a Star.* He has also made many stage appearances.

BRENDA COWLING
(b. London)
Role: Lady Customer (episode 55)

As a child, Brenda Cowling wanted to be a film star, but after leaving school she trained as a shorthand typist. Eventually she changed direction and joined RADA (she was in the same class as Warren Mitchell and Jimmy Perry). While still at RADA she appeared as a drama student in Hitchcock's *Stage Fright.*

Plenty of rep work followed before her television break. Early appearances include several series of an afternoon keep-fit show and *The Forsyte Saga.* Her career has focused mainly on TV but she is seen occasionally on the stage. She has also appeared in films, notably *The Railway Children, International Velvet, Carry On Girls* and *Carry On Behind,* and made brief appearances in two Bond movies.

Brenda has worked for David in *It Ain't Half Hot, Mum* as a WVS lady, *Dad's Army* and the final instalment of *Hi-De-Hi!* She has played many nurses, including a sister in *Fawlty Towers* and a matron in *Only When I Laugh.* She was cast as Jane in three series of *Potter,* two of which starred Arthur Lowe.

Recent years have been dominated by four series of *You Rang, M'Lord?* playing Mrs Lipton. Brenda was also seen in *Follyfoot, The Detectives, Casualty* and *The Legacy of Reginald Perrin,* as C.J.'s housekeeper, Mrs Wren.

JOYCE CUMMINGS (b. Bristol)
Role: Underwear Customer (episode 10)

Educated in Belgium and trained at RADA in 1939, Joyce worked in rep at Bristol for four years, before touring. She has worked in theatre, recently playing Margaret Thatcher in *Her Royal Highness,* and in television, where her debut was in *Cinderella.* She was also seen in *Z Cars, Angels* and *The Dick Emery Show.* Her film appearances include *Second City* and *The End of the Bridge.* Joyce, who has taken several breaks during her career, is still active in the profession.

PAMELA CUNDELL
(b. Croydon)
Role: Drooping Derrière (episode 15)

Both Pamela's parents were in the entertainment business and she never wanted to do anything else.

Training at the Guildhall School of Music and Drama was followed by plenty of work in rep and summer tours, mainly as a stand-up comic. She made her television debut in *Yes, It's the Cathode-Ray Tube Show!* in 1957 with Peter Sellers and Michael Bentine, and worked on *Jim's Inn* during the same period.

Pamela has been fortunate enough to work with all the great comics, including Benny Hill and Frankie Howerd. In recent years, she's played Vi Box in three series of BBC's *Big Deal,* and Mrs Monk, the housekeeper, in *The Choir.* She is also well known for playing Mrs Fox in *Dad's Army.* Pamela is still busy, particularly on stage, and appeared recently in the Far East with Derek Nimmo.

JANET DAVIES (b. Wakefield)
Role: The Outsize Dress (episode 6)

Janet's father, a solicitor, died in his early thirties, and as a result she was sent to boarding school. Deciding not to train as a solicitor, she qualified as a shorthand typist and worked for the BBC before eventually moving into rep in 1948.

She worked at various reps at Leatherhead, Watford

and Northampton and early television work included several episodes of *Dixon of Dock Green* and *Z Cars*. She also made a few films: *Under Milk Wood* with Richard Burton, *The Hiding Place, In This House of Brede* and *Something in Disguise.*

Her TV work includes *The Last of the Summer Wine, The Professionals, General Hospital, The Fall and Rise of Reginald Perrin* and *All Creatures Great and Small*. But she is best remembered as Mrs Pike in *Dad's Army.*

When she wasn't acting, Janet utilized her typing and shorthand training in work for various theatrical agencies. A true jobbing actress, she kept busy throughout her career. She died of cancer in 1986, aged 56.

REG DIXON (b. Coventry)
Role: The Raincoat in the Window (episode 21)
Reg left school at fourteen to work in a factory, singing with a local dance band at weekends. During his varied life he worked in a circus, was a call-boy for a touring revue and half of a double-act, before turning to acting professionally.

After serving with the RAF in the Second World War he worked in theatre, taking over from George Formby in a West End production in 1952. He went on to do lots of radio work and was resident comedian on *Variety Bandbox* in 1949.

Reg made two films, including *No Smoking* with Belinda Lee. Most of his career was spent in variety, but he made occasional TV appearances, for example in *Meet the Wife* and *Citizen Smith*. He died of kidney failure in 1983, aged 69.

JOANNA DUNHAM
(b. Luton)
Role: Miss Featherstone (episode 63)
After training as a painter at art school, Joanna joined RADA.

Graduation was followed by a busy period of work, in which she played a damsel in *The Adventures of William Tell* and made several stage appearances. She played Juliet in a production of *Romeo and Juliet* in the UK, America and Europe, and Mary Magdalene in Hollywood's *The Greatest Story Ever Told*, during which time she was expecting her first child.

She appeared on television in the TV play *In the Night* with Adam Faith; as the high-spirited Sister Benedict in Rediffusion's *Sanctuary,* as Arlette, the detective's wife, in *Van der Valk*, and in *Churchill Said To Me,* a series with Frankie Howerd.

Joanna, who's just finished a film about Princess Diana, appears less frequently on TV these days, earning her living as a painter in Suffolk.

HILDA FENEMORE
(b. London)
Roles: Elsie (episodes 7 & 8); Daphne (episode 15); Ivy (episodes 21, 28, 35, 41 & 48)
Hilda is a veteran character actress of film, TV and stage. For four years she played Jack Warner's

affable neighbour who frequently brought him meals in *Dixon of Dock Green*. Among many other TV credits are appearances in *Dad's Army, Goodnight Sweetheart, Crown Court, The Duchess of Duke Street, Minder, Brookside* and *French and Saunders.*

Hilda always wanted to become an actress, and when she acted as an amateur in a play directed by Bill Owen (Compo in *Last of the Summer Wine*) everybody thought she was a professional, so she decided to make it her career.

In over four decades in the profession, Hilda – who's still acting – has appeared in ninety films, including *Esther Waters* (her debut), *Room in the House, The Tommy Steele Story, Clash by Night* and two *Carry Ons,* as Rhoda Bray in *Nurse* and an agitated woman in *Constable.*

Playing the cleaner in *Are You Being Served?* led to the successful adverts for Mr Sheen polish.

MARGARET FLINT
(b. London)

Role: Customer (episode 5)

Margaret, who served with the WRAF during the war, began her career in rep in 1949. Her extensive small-screen career included appearances in *Hadleigh,* playing a housekeeper, as Mrs Bannister in *Coronation Street,* Sister Frazer in *Angels* and Elsie in *Shoulder to Shoulder,* as well as various comedy parts in shows such as *Little and Large, Morecambe and Wise, The Kenny Everett Show* and *Porridge.*

Usually cast in working-class parts, she also appeared in several films, including *Scandalous, The Charge of the Light Brigade* and *No Diamonds for Breakfast.* Margaret died of a heart attack in 1993, at the age of 68.

JEFFREY GARDINER
(b. Richmond)

Roles: Customer (episode 28);
Mr Bakewell (episode 41)

Jeffrey served with the army during the war. After demob he joined drama school, then spent several years in rep, including Oldham. One of his early appearances on television was in an episode of *The Larkins* in 1959. He has been seen on stage and TV in numerous roles, *The Canterbury Tales* being a favourite. He was also in *Sherlock Holmes, Hugh and I* – his first job for David Croft – *My Wife Next Door, Terry and June, You Rang, M'Lord?,* etc. Jeffrey is still working.

RUSTY GOFFE
(b. Herne Bay)

Roles: Monkey (episode 61); also
appeared in a non-speaking role in
episode 55, as a man who replied
to a 'lonely heart' ad.

Rusty started out as a musician, but turned to acting during the

1960s. Early television appearances include *Play for Today* and *The Dave Allen Show.* Since *Are You Being Served?* he's appeared in *'Allo, 'Allo, The Goodies* and *The Two Ronnies.* He has also appeared in several films, such as *Willy Wonka and the Chocolate Factory, Star Wars* and *Funny Bones.*

Currently, he's working as a hippo for Carlton's *Potamus Park* and reading the weather for *Live TV* while bouncing on a trampoline!

PETER GREENE (b. London)

Role: Mr Ludlow (episode 22)

Peter, whose mother was a professional actress, worked as a student ASM at Watford Rep for writer Jimmy Perry before joining drama school. After graduating, he toured, worked in rep and made commercials before making his TV debut in *Whack-O!* A role as a vicar in *Doctor on the Go* during the 1970s was followed by many one-off comedy appearances, notably in *Some Mothers Do 'Ave 'Em* and *It Ain't Half Hot, Mum.* He also understudied in the *Are You Being Served?* stage show for two weeks, and has made cameo appearances in a handful of comedy films.

Today, Peter works for an independent research company, but still does corporate work and directs local shows.

JENNIFER GUY (b. Carshalton)

Roles: Second Customer (episode
42); Miss Hurst (episode 51)

Jennifer always wanted to act but, after discovering she was too young to attend drama school, opted for an alternative two-year drama course instead. A grounding in rep followed; her first job was on the Isle of Wight during the 1970s. Her appearances in *Are You Being Served?* occurred early in her television career, and were followed by shows like BBC's drama

Horseman Riding By, two episodes of *Bergerac, One by One, Birds of a Feather* and *Room at the Bottom.*

Jennifer, who is still in the business, has also worked a lot in the theatre, including spells with The Young Vic and at the Chichester Festival. She's also appeared in a handful of films such as *Razor Blade Smile, Willow, Without a Clue* and *Phantom of the Opera.*

PEARL HACKNEY (b. Burton)
Role: Mrs Grainger (episode 7)
Pearl, who spent nearly five decades in showbusiness, trained as a ballet dancer from the age of five. After leaving school she moved to London and became principal dancer at The Windmill Theatre for four years. During the late 1930s acting began to dominate her career, and she worked chiefly in rep and radio. Her numerous TV appearances include *Coronation Street, Hi-De-Hi!, Meet the Wife, The Liver Birds, All Creatures Great and Small* and *Terry and June.* She made several films, including *There's a Girl in My Soup, The Hound of the Baskervilles, Yanks* and *Laughterhouse.* Pearl retired from acting in 1994.

JOY HARINGTON
(b. London)
Role: Lady Customer (episode 35)
After drama school Joy went straight into rep. In her early career she spent a season at Stratford – making her professional debut in 1933 – and worked in America. For a while she was employed by Paramount film studios in Hollywood. In addition to script editing, she made thirteen films and directed dialogue for nine others, including *National Velvet,* with a young Elizabeth Taylor.

Between 1951 and 1961 she worked for the BBC, producing children's drama. She was responsible for the original screening of *Heidi, Treasure Island, Billy*

Bunter and *Vice Versa,* among others. But she's best remembered for *Jesus of Nazareth,* for which she won a BAFTA Award, the first to be given for a children's serial.

After retiring from the Beeb in 1970, she returned to acting, one of her roles being a neighbour in *Sykes.* She toured the Far East with Jimmy Edwards, Hattie Jacques and Eric Sykes in *Big Bad Mouse,* and appeared as the housekeeper in *The Moon Stallion.* Joy died in 1991, aged 77.

DONALD HEWLETT
(b. Manchester)
Role: The Forty Maternity (episode 14)

Donald was studying meteorology and geography at Cambridge when the Second World War broke out. Although he was unable to complete his degree, he joined the navy as a meteorologist, based in the Orkneys, where he helped establish an arts club in Kirkwall. He was later drafted to Singapore where he was in charge of Japanese POWs and helped with the entertainments.

After demob he studied at RADA, winning the Athene Seyler prize for comedy, and went on to work in rep at Oxford with Ronnie Barker. Several years of stage work followed before his television debut in *Mick and Montmorency* in the early 1950s, when he was also a co-presenter on BBC's Children's Television. Preferring TV work, Donald has appeared in many shows, notably playing Carstairs in *Come Back, Mrs Noah,* Colonel Reynolds in *It Ain't Half Hot, Mum* and Lord Meldrum in *You Rang, M'Lord?* He's also popped up in *Rings On Their Fingers, The Avengers* and *Whose Life Is It Anyway?*

Donald, who also appeared in several movies, including the 1986 film *Saving Grace* with Tom Conti, *A Touch of Class* with Glenda Jackson, and *Carry On Behind,* remains busy in pantos and the occasional TV show. He's married to Therese McMurray, who also appeared in the show.

JEFFREY HOLLAND
(b. Walsall)

Roles: The Afro Pants (episode 31); The Blazer (episode 43)

Jeffrey didn't contemplate acting as a career until joining an amateur company at fifteen. Unsure about what to do with his life after leaving school, he worked first at a wine merchants, and next in the office of a cardboard box manufacturer. It was then that he decided to become an actor.

After more than four years in theatre at Coventry, small TV parts came his way. His first speaking role was a young husband in *Dixon of Dock Green,* but he also played a market stall trader in ten episodes of *Crossroads* in the mid-1970s.

His career blossomed in the 1980s: he spent seven years playing Spike Dixon in *Hi-De-Hi!* and appeared with Russ Abbot on his *Madhouse* shows. He has appeared in two successful 1990s sitcoms, as James Twelvetrees in *You Rang, M'Lord?* and Cecil Parkin in *Oh, Doctor Beeching!*

STELLA KEMBALL
(b. London)

Role: The Scarf Customer (episode 10)

Stella began her career in rep and has done just about everything in the profession. She started off in television by working in children's productions like *Great Expectations* and *The Treasure Seekers* in the early 1960s. Since then her numerous TV credits have included cameo appearances in many top shows, including *The Two Ronnies, Oh Brother!* with Derek Nimmo, *Steptoe and Son, Hancock, The Dick Emery Show, Harry Worth* and *Keeping Up Appearances,* her last TV role.

She also appeared in films such as *The Knack* and *Here We Go Round the Mulberry Bush,* playing a customer in a fish shop. Stella works less frequently these days.

JENNY KENNA (b. Farnham)

Role: Miss 38-22-36 (episode 30)

After training as a dancer, Jenny spent six months as a typist for an electrical company. Before long she was singing and playing small parts in panto. She eventually moved into acting in the theatre and, in 1969, on television, appearing with Les Dawson in *Living Legends* and *The Generation Game,* utilizing her art skills. She also worked in Germany on the German version of the hit show.

Other than the occasional stage play, in recent years Jenny – who worked with John Inman several times on stage – has been concentrating on writing. During the 1980s she wrote three series of her own, *Windfalls,* two of which she presented. She also helps run her husband's drama school.

MICHAEL KNOWLES
(b. Midlands)

Roles: Customer (episode 1); The Bold Check (episode 14)

Michael had considered studying medicine before turning his attention to acting. Graduating from RADA, he worked at reps in Richmond, Bromley and Watford. Appearances in *Dad's Army* began a twenty-year career in television, with notable appearances as Captain Ashwood in *It Ain't Half Hot, Mum,* Fanshaw in BBC's 1978 sitcom, *Come Back, Mrs Noah,* and in *The Dick Emery Show* and *Brush Strokes.*

With Harold Snoad, he was responsible for adapting 67 episodes of *Dad's Army* for radio. He also helped write a number of the *Are You Being Served?* episodes. Michael is still a regular face on TV, particularly in sitcoms.

DIANA LAMBERT
(b. London)

Roles: The Six-Pound Fox (episode 25); Mrs Peacock (episodes 64 & 68)

Diana wanted to act since childhood, and after leaving school she worked in a nursery until she was old enough to join a repertory company. Quickly realizing the acting world was for her, she spent the majority of her career in theatre, beginning with several years of rep.

From the 1950s onwards, she popped up on TV, including an episode of *William Tell, Fair Passenger, Blue Murder, The Sandcastle, Our Man at St Mark's* and *Cakes and Ale.* She also made a few films. Diana died in 1995, aged 66.

JIMMY MAC (b. Glasgow)

Role: Warwick, Mr Harman's assistant (episodes 41 & 46)

Jimmy started his career in a circus at twelve. He worked as a boy entertainer in Blackpool before later managing his own summer shows and pantomimes. A famous panto performer, he appeared at the Theatre Royal, Bath, for 31 years. He was also seen in numerous TV shows, including *The Two Ronnies* and *Dad's Army,* where he was a regular as a non-speaking member of the platoon. He died in 1984.

PAMELA MANSON
(b. London)

Role: The Large Brim with Fruit (episode 4)

Pamela entered the industry in 1952 and after years of theatre work began what was to become a busy TV career, with appearances in *The Good Life, Dad's Army, Jackanory, The Professionals, Charles and Diana,* etc. Though Pamela was a versatile actress, working with the likes of Tony Hancock and Peter Sellers, she spent most of her career in comedy.

Before turning to acting, Pamela was a secretary on the *News Chronicle.* For a while she worked as a public relations officer in the fashion industry and did a spell managing theatrical artists. Pamela died in 1988 at the age of 59.

NICHOLAS McARDLE
(b. Bournemouth)

Role: Head Waiter (episode 54)

Nicholas, who also worked for David Croft as a British officer in an episode of *It Ain't Half Hot, Mum,* moved to Scotland as a boy, and as a consequence is frequently cast in Scottish parts.

He originally trained as a teacher, specializing in English and drama, before attending drama school in his twenties. After graduating he spent a year at Salisbury Rep, two years at Lincoln and a year at Liverpool, before joining various other reps around the country. With seven years' theatre experience under his belt, he turned his attention to television, making his debut in a play for Granada with John Thaw. He worked on two series of BBC2's *Broaden Your Mind* with Tim Brooke-Taylor, a series of *Colditz* as Captain Walters, *No Place Like Home, Marty, Taggart, Strathblair* and four episodes of *To the Manor Born* as the farm foreman. In 1997 he recorded ten episodes of the radio version of *To the Manor Born* (playing the aged butler Brabinger) for Radio 2.

Nowadays Nicholas usually works on TV or radio.

THERESE McMURRAY
(b. Herne Bay)

Role: Lady Customer (episode 12)

Therese, who made her acting debut in *Snow White* while at St Mary's Convent, Whitstable, believes it was a foregone conclusion that she would become an actress. Previous generations of her family had had successful stage careers, including her aunt, who was the world-famous contortionist, Cochran's Eve.

She grew up in Whitstable and was attending Saturday drama classes at the Italia Conti stage school when Lord Grade, her godfather, offered to pay the fees for five years' full-time tuition. She quickly established herself as a leading child actress and appeared in many stage and television productions. At eighteen she was cast as Nurse Parkin in *Emergency – Ward 10* for two years. In 1968 she was back in the nurse's uniform for an appearance in *Hugh and I Spy*, produced by David Croft, which led to appearances in *Dad's Army*.

Other TV credits include two series of *The Dick Emery Show, Second Time Around* and *The Brighton Belle*.

Married to actor Donald Hewlett, Therese retired from acting in 1981 to bring up her family. She now runs a production company, writing and producing corporate videos.

ROBERT MILL (b. London)
Role: Footwear (episode 8)

After finishing national service, Robert began reading Classics at Oxford but left before gaining a degree. He moved between jobs for two years before joining RADA.

Robert became an ASM at Margate, and had spells at Cambridge, Coventry and Northampton in the early 1960s. Theatre work is his great love (he appeared in Tom Conti's 1991 production *Otherwise Engaged* at Windsor), but he has appeared on television in *Enemy of the State* in the 1960s, a version of Oscar Wilde's *The Canterville Ghost* with Bruce Forsyth, as a vicar in *In Sickness and In Health*, and in *The First Churchills*. He has also made a few films.

Robert hasn't worked on TV or stage for over a year, but is an active member of the Equity Council.

NORMAN MITCHELL
(b. Sheffield)
Role: Wendel P. Clark (episode 37)

Norman, a veteran character actor, studied medicine at Sheffield University for three years before turning to the stage. Since his screen debut in the 1950s, he's notched up over two thousand television and one hundred movie appearances, including *Barry Lyndon, Revenge of the Pink Panther, A Night to Remember, Carry On Spying, Legend of the Werewolf* and *Goodbye Mr Chips*.

Norman has popped up more recently in *All Creatures Great and Small* and *Yes, Minister*.

JEANNE MOCKFORD
(b. London)
Role: The Plastic Umbrella (episode 27)

Jeanne, who first appeared for Croft as the soothsayer in *Up Pompeii!*, worked in a bank for eighteen months before joining RADA. Her first job was in a tour of *St Joan*, followed by stints at reps, including Manchester, Liverpool, Oldham and Bath.

She made her TV debut in the 1950s before appearances in numerous shows such as *Dixon of Dock Green, Angels, The Liver Birds, Only Fools and Horses, Hi-De-Hi!, Dear John* and *Last of the Summer Wine*. Nowadays she mostly works in the theatre, her preferred medium.

DONALD MORLEY
(b. Richmond-upon-Thames).
Role: Mr Clegg (episode 10)

Although Donald hasn't appeared on stage or television recently, he has enjoyed a full career. On TV he's been seen in *Coronation Street* as Walter Fletcher, *Compact, Bless*

This House, Van Der Valk, Dad's Army, Open All Hours and *Bergerac*. More recent appearances include *The Brittas Empire* and *Grace and Favour*, playing Mollie Sugden's husband, Cedric. His film appearances include *Blowing Hot and Cold* and *Out of Sight*.

PETER NEEDHAM
(b. Nottingham)

Role: The returned Glen Check (episode 3)

Peter, who has been an actor for over forty years, began acting at his local boys' club. He enjoyed it so much that after completing national service he joined RADA. Upon graduation in 1953, he worked at the Old Vic for eighteen months.

As well as acting, he used to arrange sword fights, and he first met David Croft on *Up Pompeii!*, one of Peter's early small-screen appearances, while planning a sword fight for Frankie Howerd. When offered the role in *Are You Being Served?* he had just joined the RSC.

Other TV work includes ATV's *Crime of Passion* during the 1970s, as the defence counsel, *A Touch of Frost*, *Inspector Morse*, and providing fencing instruction in *Pride and Prejudice*. But Peter's first love is the theatre, a medium that has dominated his career. He is currently working for the RSC.

JACKIE 'Mr TV' PALLO
(b. London)

Role: Mr Franco (episode 45)

Before entering the world of wrestling, Jackie led a varied life. He was a motor mechanic for ten years before replacing his father as boxing instructor at a public school in London. He worked at the school for 25 years, by which time he'd begun his successful wrestling career in 1950.

Jackie became a household name in the world of wrestling, which led to various media assignments during the 1960s, such as appearances on *The Dickie Henderson Show*, *The Avengers* and *Emergency – Ward 10*, in which he made his debut.

Today Jackie, an active 72-year-old, produces wrestling shows for American TV and travels regularly to Las Vegas.

DAWN PERLLMAN
(b. London)

Role: Miss Hepburn (episode 51)

Dawn left school at fifteen and took up acting immediately, beginning with *TV Club*, a BBC schools programme. Just before *Are You Being Served?* she appeared in *The Sweeney*. Other TV credits include *Slinger's Day*, *Home James!*, *General Hospital*, *Only Fools and Horses*, *Dempsey and Makepeace*, *Shine On Harvey Moon* and *The Gentle Touch*. She has also worked in the theatre.

Nowadays Dawn – whose last TV appearance was in *The Bill* – does a lot of corporate work.

GORDON PETERS
(b. Co. Durham)

Roles: The Fawn Trousers (episode 15); Husband (episode 21)

A chorister at Durham Cathedral for six years, Gordon worked for Standard Bank as a bank clerk, and emigrated to Southern Rhodesia with the job. Whilst there he rekindled his acting interests, winning a talent contest in the process.

At 25 he returned to the UK and kicked off his acting career. He worked mainly as a stand-up comic, until club work became scarce, and then regularly worked as a warm-up artist. He also appeared in *Now Take My Wife* and a series of his own, *The Gordon Peters Show*. Recent work includes cameos in *Keeping Up Appearances* and *One Foot in the Grave*.

Lately Gordon has toured with his old-time music-hall act and done cabaret work on cruises.

NOSHER POWELL
(b. London)

Role: Truck Driver (episode 60)

Nosher, who's now 69, left school at fifteen and worked in Covent Garden market before becoming a professional heavyweight boxer, later winning several championships. After being offered a small part as a boxer in a 1949 TV show, he turned his attention to the entertainment business. He was a stuntman for many years, and appeared in several *Carry On*'s, such as *Cruising* and *Spying*. Other TV credits include *The Saint, The Avengers, The Prisoner* and *Morecambe and Wise*.

Nosher also acts, and has just returned from Morocco where he has appeared in *The Mummy*, the third film he's made in the country.

MAVIS PUGH (b. Kent)

Roles: Mrs Claude (episode 25); Lady Weeble Ablesmith (episode 32); Roger's Mistress (episode 36)

As a child Mavis was a keen dancer and fond of literature, so her decision to study drama at Oxford's International School after leaving boarding school came as no surprise to her family.

Until her television debut in the 1970s as the haughty Lady Maltby in *Dad's Army,* she spent many years on the stage. Beginning her career in rep at West Hartlepool, she had spells at other theatres before making her West End debut in *Little Women* at the Westminster Theatre.

Among her TV credits are appearances in *Fawlty Towers, Spooner's Patch,* as a belligerent army official in *It Ain't Half Hot, Mum* and as Lady Lavender Meldrum in *You Rang, M'Lord?* She is normally seen in comedy roles.

Her film appearances include *A Class of Miss McMichael* with Glenda Jackson in 1978, as an expletive-spouting teacher, and the third *Pink Panther* movie. Mavis is still acting and does a lot of TV commercials.

ROBERT RAGLAN (b. Reigate)

Roles: The 40" Waist (episode 2); Dr Wainwright (episode 10)

After joining a water company straight from school, Robert – whose brother James was also an actor – soon left to attend drama school. He worked in various reps until war broke out, during which he served in the REME before touring overseas with ENSA.

Frequently cast as policemen or military officials, he resumed his acting career after demob and quickly made his film debut. An illustrious big-screen career boasts over seventy films, including *Brothers in Law, Private's Progress, A Night to Remember* and *Jigsaw.*

After suffering two heart attacks while appearing with Robert Morley in the West End, he retired from the stage and concentrated on TV in shows like *George and Mildred, Shelley* and *Bless this House.*

Although never a star name, he was always a solid, dependable supporting actor. He died in 1985.

HARRIET REYNOLDS
(b. Hampton)

Role: Customer (episode 66)

Harriet joined a drama school at Bristol's Old Vic in 1961. Rep work soon followed, her debut being with Paul Eddington at Bristol. After working in the theatre for several years, TV began to dominate her career. She was mostly seen in small comedy parts in shows like *Ever Decreasing Circles, Butterflies* and *Yes, Minister*. She was also seen as Dame Josie in *The New Statesman* and Madge in *Lovejoy*.

Harriet played Susan in the award-winning play *Abigail's Party* in Hampstead and for the BBC.

West End credits include the Headmistress in *Daisy Pulls It Off*, Sergeant Fire in *Dry Rot* and Miss Casewell in *The Mousetrap*. Among her big-screen credits are appearances in *Loser Takes All, The Pumpkin Eater* and *The Secret Life of Ian Fleming*. Whenever she wasn't acting, she worked at a theatrical costumier.

Her last role was in 1991, a production of *A Woman in Mind* at Exeter, where she was playing the lead. She died in 1992 of cancer, aged 47.

JOHN RINGHAM
(b. Cheltenham)
Role: The Check Jacket (episode 7)
Primarily a classical actor, John has spent over fifty years in the profession, subsidizing his theatrical career with television and radio work. During the war he joined a teenagers' amateur dramatic society, performing highbrow material which fuelled his enthusiasm for serious roles. He turned pro in 1948 and after eleven years in rep, made his TV debut. During the 1960s he appeared in *The Forsyte Saga, The Railway Children, War and Peace* and *David Copperfield*.

Most recent television work has seen him in an episode of *The Governor* and an advert for vegetarian sausages. He has made over two hundred appearances on the stage, including the National, three hundred on TV, and one film, *Very Important Person*, in 1961. John, who writes his own plays, works mainly in the theatre now.

EVAN ROSS (b. Cardiganshire)
Role: Customer (episode 5)
Evan, who worked for David Croft as a regular non-speaking member of the platoon in *Dad's Army*, won a scholarship to the Royal Academy of Music. He was an opera singer before moving into acting with work as an extra. He was a regular on *Crackerjack*, as a policeman in comedy sketches. As well as being a freelance singer, Evan continues to work in commecials.

DAVID ROWLANDS
(b. Abergavenny)
Role: The Man with the Large Bra (episode 4)

David won a scholarship to Guildhall School of Music and Drama at the age of fifteen. He made his television debut in Rediffusion's *All About You*. Shortly after appearing in the sitcom *The Fall and Rise of Reginald Perrin*, he left acting to take a degree in International Relations. Other TV appearances include *'Allo, 'Allo*, as a doctor, *Dr Who, The Two Ronnies* and *Rising Damp*, as a curate.

In addition to acting, David worked for Radio Sussex as a reporter for seven months and qualified as a teacher. Today he does supply teaching in secondary schools and lives on a 130-acre farm in west Wales.

JEFFREY SEGAL (b. London)
Roles: The Clip-On Bow (episode 14); The Loud Sweater (episode 47)

Jeffrey, always an active amateur actor, left school with the intention of becoming a Civil Servant. But the war put paid to his plans and he joined the army, serving in Italy and Germany. When a recruitment drive was launched for people who could help entertain the troops, Jeffrey seized the opportunity and joined a theatrical unit.

He continued acting after the war and has remained busy ever since. He first worked at the Mercury Theatre, Notting Hill Gate, and various reps including Watford and Leatherhead.

On moving into television, he worked as a back-up news commentator. He has since worked in all genres of television, including appearances in shows like *It Ain't Half Hot, Mum.* He appeared as Mr Perkins in *Rentaghost* for five years and has been seen in many other shows, including *Love Hurts* (the final series), *Bergerac, Lytton's Diary* and *David Copperfield.*

On radio, Jeffrey was one of the writers behind the much-loved soap *The Dales.* He made his film debut at the age of thirteen as a schoolboy, and went on to make a handful of cameo appearances. Now 76, Jeffrey is not only acting; he also writes.

STUART SHERWIN

(b. Stoke-on-Trent)

Roles: The Dressing Gown (episode 11); The Large Gloves (episode 21)

Stuart's father was a travelling pottery salesman. When he arrived home on Fridays, the family would visit the local theatre, and that's where Stuart's interest in the stage originated.

Before joining the army in the Second World War, he worked on the railways, and after demob he returned to the job for a while before joining an estate agents. He eventually joined a rep in Leeds after seeing an advert in *The Stage.*

Small parts in TV came along, including *Emergency – Ward 10,* work with Les Dawson and Terry Scott, and parts in *Keeping Up Appearances, Rumpole of the Bailey,* as a clerk of the court, and *Fawlty Towers,* as a hotel guest.

Although he recently filmed a part in *The Find,* the last few years have been dominated by long theatre stints. He recently finished a two-year spell in *Oliver!* at the Palladium.

DEREK SMITH (b. Tooting)

Role: The 28" Inside Leg (episode 2)

Derek had a variety of jobs,

including being a surveyor, clerk and labourer, before turning to acting in his late twenties. After leaving RADA he worked in rep before making his television debut in 1960, playing a barrister in *The Baccarat Scandal.*

Since playing a private investigator in *The Forsyte Saga* in 1966, Derek has made over two hundred appearances, notably in *EastEnders, Coronation Street, Hannay, Lovejoy* and *The Duchess of Duke Street.*

In recent years he's acted in Vienna and Frankfurt, as well as over twenty roles with the RSC, and is still busy in the theatre.

ELIZABETH STEWART

(b. Bristol)

Role: Customer (episode 63)

Elizabeth frequently appeared in small parts on television. She turned professional in the 1960s after directing amateur productions. She had previously worked

as a typist for an insurance company. Her first professional job was in rep in Perth. Her first television work came in the 1971 play *The Silver Sword* and an episode of *Z Cars.* Three years later she appeared at Folkestone with Arthur Brough. She was also seen in *Poldark, Pride and Prejudice* in 1980, playing Lady Lucas, and *Spatz* for ITV, her final TV appearance, in 1991.

For the last two years of her life, she worked with the RSC in London. Her final job was at Chichester in a Noel Coward play. Elizabeth, who suffered congenital heart problems, died in 1991, aged 62.

TONY SYMPSON (b. London)

Roles: Claude (episode 25); Mr Webster (episode 41); Mr Wagstaff (episode 49)

Tony Sympson, instantly recognizable with his snow-white hair and beard, was an insurance

inspector turned actor. He spent much of his career in musicals, panto and opera, making his stage debut as a speciality dancer in *Dear Love* while in his early twenties. In 1930, when things went wrong on the first night of *The Intimate Revue* at the Duchess Theatre, he ad-libbed for over an hour.

During the Second World War he toured extensively with ENSA. Tony died in 1983, aged 76.

RON TARR (b. London)
Role: Truck Driver (episode 60)
After *Are You Being Served?*, Ron worked with Wendy Richard in *EastEnders,* playing Big Ron, a market stall holder; it was a job he knew well because after leaving school he had worked as a market trader. In the early 1970s his distinctive features led a friend to suggest he tried his hand at acting.

Ron, who usually played small parts, popped up on television in shows like *Hale and Pace* and *Cannon and Ball* and in several commercials. He also appeared in a few films, including *A View to a Kill*, playing a guard. He died of cancer in 1997, aged 60.

DOROTHY WAYNE
(b. Harrogate)
Role: The Bridal Veil (episode 7)
After leaving school, Dorothy worked in a bank for three years until invited to join a summer season at Filey in 1956. Her television appearances, in which she has often played old ladies, include *David Nixon, Barrymore, That's Life, Kindly Leave the Stage* and, most recently, *The Generation Game*. She has also had her own show on Radio 2, *Saturday Sounds*.

Today Dorothy works mainly in cabaret around the country as well as on cruise ships.

FREDDIE WILES (b. London)
Roles: The Porter (episode 34); many other episodes in non-speaking role as Young Mr Grace's chauffeur.

Freddie worked in a confectionery factory before becoming a sales rep for an asphalt company either side of the war. He'd always fancied acting, so upon retiring from the industry he registered with an agency and started appearing as an extra on television. His biggest TV role was as a non-speaking platoon member in *Dad's Army.*

He appeared in BBC1's comedy series *A. P. Herbert's Misleading Cases*, in 1967, and played a diplomat in *Edward VII*, a monk in the series *Come Here Often?*, and a vicar in the ATV thriller *Only a Scream Away.* He appeared in several commercials, including one advertising Qantas, the Australian airline, and in numerous schools programmes. His last job was in a chocolate cake commercial in Rome. He died in 1983, aged 78.

EILEEN WINTERTON
Role: A regular extra, usually playing a non-speaking shop assistant (various episodes)
After leaving school, Eileen trained as a professional dancer, including three months in Paris. In 1939 she formed a dancing

trio, *The Winterton Trio*, dancing and acting in variety for five years. She worked in pantomimes, operas and concert parties before eventually giving up.

In her late fifties she turned to walk-on work in TV and commercials, including a recent Jacob's Cream Cracker advert. Her TV credits include *Dad's Army, Only Fools and Horses* and *One Foot in the Grave.* Eileen, who's over 90, only officially retired from acting two years ago.

Episode Guide

SERIES SEVEN

REGULAR CAST MEMBERS

Mr Humphries ....John Inman

Mrs Slocombe.......................................Mollie Sugden

Captain Peacock...............................Frank Thornton

Mr Lucas ....Trevor Bannister

Mr Goldberg ....Alfie Bass

Miss Brahms ....Wendy Richard

Mr Rumbold ....Nicholas Smith

Mr Harman..Arthur English

Young Mr Grace................................Harold Bennett

Miss Bakewell ....Penny Irving

Nurse ....Vivienne Johnson

41. THE JUNIOR

(Transmitted: Fri. 19/10/79, BBC1, 7.05pm)

ALSO APPEARING:

Mr Webster ....Tony Sympson

Mr Beauchamp.....................................Jeffrey Gardiner

Ivy..Hilda Fenemore

Customers ..Harold Berens, Morris Barry, Bernard Stone

Warwick..Jimmy Mac

Mr Tebbs retires after sixty years' service at Grace Brothers. With Mr Humphries becoming the new senior salesman and Mr Lucas also promoted, there's a vacancy for a junior. To ensure the right candidate is selected, the entire staff conduct the interviews. After several inappropriate interviewees, Mr Goldberg turns up and, to Captain Peacock's horror, claims to have served with the floorwalker in the army. Peacock, afraid that Goldberg will reveal the truth about his suspect war career, votes against him being hired, but is out-voted. When sales rocket thanks to the new recruit and he demands a pay rise, Peacock threatens to walk out.

Memories

'I worked for David many times. Whenever he offered me a job I wouldn't even want to read the script. It didn't matter that there might not be much to do, one just knew it would be a lovely week working for him.'

JEFFREY GARDINER

42. STRONG STUFF, THIS INSURANCE

(Transmitted: Fri. 26/10/79, BBC1, 7.05pm)

ALSO APPEARING:

Ballet Mistress ....Amanda Barrie

Staff Nurse ....Joy Allen

Doctor.....................................Imogen Bickford-Smith

The Dressing Gown ....Geraldine Gardner

Second Customer ....Jennifer Guy

Grace Brothers launch a pension bonus scheme and will pay for it if everyone passes a medical. To get in shape, Captain Peacock suggests an intensive fitness course, while Mr Goldberg decides to take up jogging. Meanwhile, Mr Humphries, with the help of his ballet dancing friend, gets everyone dancing into shape. But it's a nervy time as they await the results of their medicals, particularly when they overhear Young Mr Grace being warned of false knockers, dry rot and saggy middles!

Memories

'I always enjoyed working for David Croft. He's very friendly, funny and approachable, and a lot of the success of his productions is down to his personality. He'll share a joke, be one of the "lads" and is never remote – it all helps in making a pleasant working atmosphere.'

JENNIFER GUY

WHAT A SCENE!

(An attractive woman wants to buy a dressing gown. Mr Humphries and Mr Lucas try to help.)

MR HUMPHRIES: What length do you have in mind?

MR LUCAS: Yes, we have knee-high, thigh-high and eye-high!

CUSTOMER: No, I like them round my ankles.

MR LUCAS: (*eyeing the woman up and down*) I expect your husband does as well.

CUSTOMER: (*looks at the gowns on the rack*) They all look very nice; I'm never quite sure what men like.

MR HUMPHRIES: No, it is a bit of a puzzle sometimes.

43. THE APARTMENT

(Transmitted: Fri. 2/11/79, BBC1, 7.00pm)

ALSO APPEARING:

The Blazer ....Jeffrey Holland

Life is hectic for Mrs Slocombe when she moves home. Before her furniture can be off-loaded it's discovered that she's got squatters. To help, Young Mr Grace offers the use of a vacant department on the fifth floor until she gets her problems sorted. When none of her colleagues is prepared to take her in, Mr Grace also allows her to sleep alongside her furniture in the store. A transport strike prevents her workmates reaching home, and the first night in her temporary home is far from smooth because the doorbell doesn't stop ringing.

Memories

'Last year I went to Boston for a wedding. I was in the ladies' loo combing my hair when this woman came in. She said, rather excitedly: "Gee! you're on *Are You Being Served?*" I couldn't believe it.'

VIVIENNE JOHNSON

44. MRS SLOCOMBE, SENIOR PERSON

(Transmitted: Fri. 9/11/79, BBC1, 7.00pm)

ALSO APPEARING:

Miss Comlozi ....Avril Angers

The Plastic Mac ....Gorden Kaye

First Customer ....Derrie Powell

When Rumbold is taken ill and rushed to hospital, Mrs Slocombe is placed in charge. Even though she has an ally in Mr Humphries, who sucks up to her at every opportunity, the rest of the staff resent the situation and try everything to make her life hell, including cold-shouldering her in the canteen.

But life in the management chair isn't what Mrs Slocombe expected, and when she admits to wanting her shop-floor position back, Mr Rumbold's meringues come to the rescue.

45. THE HERO

(Transmitted: Fri. 16/11/79, BBC1, 7.00pm)

ALSO APPEARING:

Mr Franco ....Jackie 'Mr TV' Pallo

The Shrunken Sock............................Raymond Bowers

Captain Peacock is in a foul mood and all because Mr Franco, from the Sports department, spotted a huge boil on the floorwalker's backside while he tried on jogging shorts. Peacock is fuming when he discovers the whole store knows about his embarrassing problem and rashly threatens Mr Franco, who calls his bluff and suggests a boxing match to settle their scores. As the big day approaches, Peacock gets cold feet and tries wriggling his way out of the battle in the ring. Eventually it's left to Mr Humphries and Mrs Slocombe to save the day.

Memories

'Playing the cleaner in the series, I was frequently stopped in the street by fans of the programme. One woman thought I seemed so real on screen that I must have been like that in real life. Then there was a man who said: "You don't speak anything like your character, so you must be an actress." It was a lovely compliment.'

HILDA FENEMORE

WHAT A SCENE!

(Mrs Slocombe is excited and can't wait to tell Miss Brahms her news.)

MISS BRAHMS: Now, what's this big news you had to tell me?

MRS SLOCOMBE: Today is a very special day.

MISS BRAHMS: And what's so special about today?

MRS SLOCOMBE: Today's the day my pussy comes of age.

MISS BRAHMS: Oh! You mean it's 21 years since you first had it?

MRS SLOCOMBE: No, it's three years since I first had her.

46. ANYTHING YOU CAN DO

(Transmitted: Fri. 23/11/79, BBC1, 7.05pm)

ALSO APPEARING:

Canteen Manageress..............................Doremy Vernon

Signor Balli..Ronnie Brody

Warwick..Jimmy Mac

Mohammad ....Mohammad Shamsi

Lift Girls ....Sue Bishop, Belinda Lee

Standards in the canteen hit rock bottom, and when Captain Peacock and the others complain, the kitchen staff walk out, forcing the staff of Menswear and Ladieswear to see if they can do better. Compliments flow, even though the food comes courtesy of the local takeaways. But when the books at the end of the first day show a loss, it's time to get the regular staff back.

47. THE AGENT

(Transmitted: Fri. 30/11/79, BBC1, 7.05pm)

ALSO APPEARING:

Mr Patel ....Renu Setna

The Long Sweater..Jeffrey Segal

Mrs Maxwell ....Peggy Ann Clifford

Amanda..Marcella Oppenheim

To help supplement his pittance of a wage, Mr Goldberg runs his own employment agency and touts for business on the shop floor, quickly recruiting Mr Humphries, Mrs Slocombe and Miss Brahms. He impresses everyone with his wheeling and dealing. He secures jobs for Humphries and Slocombe at a rival firm, as manager of the Unisex Clothing Department and Pussy Shampoo Parlour respectively. But when the management of Grace Brothers finds out, it offers its experienced workers pay rises.

Christmas Special

48. THE PUNCH AND JUDY AFFAIR

(Transmitted: Wed. 26/12/79, BBC1, 6.40pm)

ALSO APPEARING:

Canteen Manageress..............................Doremy Vernon

Ivy..Hilda Fenemore

With most of the store on strike, the staff of Ladieswear and Menswear – who broke the picket line – are resigned to doing all the work, including cleaning the floor. But when the strike is

resolved, there is plenty of resentment towards Peacock and the rest of the gang. To aid staff relations, they stage a Punch and Judy show for the children of the store employees.

Memories
'This is one of my favourite episodes because it was so ludicrous. I loved Wendy with her false chin and nose, and me trying to kiss her also wearing a false chin and nose – what fun we had!'

TREVOR BANNISTER

SERIES EIGHT

REGULAR CAST MEMBERS

Mr Humphries ....John Inman

Mrs Slocombe.....................................Mollie Sugden

Captain Peacock...............................Frank Thornton

Miss Brahms ....Wendy Richard

Mr Rumbold ....Nicholas Smith

Mr Harman...Arthur English

Mr Spooner ....Mike Berry

Old Mr Grace...................................Kenneth Waller

Nurse...Vivienne Johnson

49. IS IT CATCHING?

(Transmitted: Thurs. 9/4/81, BBC1, 8.00pm)

ALSO APPEARING:

Mr Grossman..Milo Sperber

Young Mr Grace ....Harold Bennett

Canteen Manageress............................Doremy Vernon

Secretary ....Debbie Linden

Doctor..John D. Collins

When Mr Humphries feels unwell and faints on the shop floor, the doctor is summoned. Blood tests reveal that he's suffering from the rare marines' disease, which has bizarre side-effects. Anyone who has been in contact with him needs to be isolated for seven days, which wipes out the entire staff of Menswear and Ladieswear.

50. A PERSONAL PROBLEM

(Transmitted: Thurs. 16/4/81, BBC1, 8.00pm)

ALSO APPEARING:

Mr Grossman..Milo Sperber

Secretary ....Debbie Linden

Mrs Peacock ....Diana King

Tramp ....Jack Haig

Warwick..Jimmy Mac

The Mohair Jumper...Pat Keen

The Silk Handkerchief ....Andrew Davis

Captain Peacock's marriage has hit the rocks and his wife has threatened to boot him out the house. Believing he's having an affair, she warns him she's found another man – but is it really Mr Rumbold? When Mrs Peacock joins Grace Brothers as Rumbold's new secretary, it seems there could be truth in the rumour – or is she just intent on making her husband jealous?

51. FRONT PAGE STORY

(Transmitted: Thurs. 23/4/81, BBC1, 8.00pm)

ALSO APPEARING:

Mr Grossman ....Milo Sperber

Secretary ....Debbie Linden

Man with Moustache ....Michael Sharvell-Martin

Miss Hurst ....Jennifer Guy

Miss Hepburn ....Dawn Perllman

Miss Coleman ....Denise Distel

Old Mr Grace launches a store magazine, titled *What's Up in the Store*. As editor, Mr Humphries has the photo department at his disposal for those exclusive shots and puts to good use for the first edition, which carries a photo of Mr Grace in a group pose with his leggy nurse and sexy secretary. The responsibilities of running the mag take up much of Humphries' time, not least the arrangements for the Holiday Girl beauty contest – especially as he's also the winning contestant!

Memories

'I was about eighteen when I appeared in the show, and loved every minute. I was so excited when offered a part that I couldn't wait to tell everyone! I'd been watching the show and was a big fan, but to actually appear in it was something else. The cast was lovely, particularly Frank Thornton – a real gentleman.'

DAWN PERLLMAN

52. SIT OUT

(Transmitted: Thurs. 30/4/81, BBC1, 8.00pm)

ALSO APPEARING:

Mr Grossman ....Milo Sperber

Secretary ....Debbie Linden

Virginia Edwards.......................................Louise Burton

Fireman..Martin Cochrane

Customers are so scarce that there's even time for the crosswords. Business is so bad Old Mr Grace cuts everyone's wages by ten per cent – much to the staff's anger. They feel so strongly about this drastic action that they carry out a rooftop protest.

53. HEIR APPARENT

(Transmitted: Thurs. 7/5/81, BBC1, 8.00pm)

ALSO APPEARING:

Mr Klein..Benny Lee

Secretary ....Debbie Linden

It's sale time and Mr Klein joins the team from the cutting department to help. Meanwhile, Mr Humphries is nominated for Grace Brothers' Sales Person of the Year Competition. When he has to supply a photo to support his nomination, Old Mr Grace gets to see one of Humphries' mother, back in 1938, and admits she was an old flame. There's even more shocking news: he claims Mr Humphries is his son – and heir to the Grace Brothers throne. But is it a case of mistaken identity?

Memories

'It's amazing how successful the show has become. I was visiting the Gulf recently and saw several episodes on TV. It was transmitted in English with Arabic subtitles – I can't imagine what the Arabs think of it!'

ROGER REDFARN (Director of the stage show)

WHAT A SCENE!

(Captain Peacock completes a report on Mr Humphries to help his nomination.)

CAPT. PEACOCK: (*reading aloud*) Progress report on Wilberforce Claybourne Humphries, age …

MR HUMPHRIES: (*interrupting*) Sshh! Keep your voice down, please, that's private and confidential. I don't want the whole world to know that I'm accelerating down the road of life towards forty.

CAPT. PEACOCK: According to this form, you can see it clearly in your rear-view mirror!

54. CLOSED CIRCUIT

(Transmitted: Thurs. 21/5/81, BBC1, 8.00pm, postponed from 14/5/81)

ALSO APPEARING:

Mr Klein..Benny Lee

Secretary ....Louise Burton

Mr Fortescue ....Gorden Kaye

Head Waiter......................Nicholas McArdle

Second Waiter........................John D. Collins

Lord Hirly ....John Oxley

Rabbi...Marty Swift

Lady Customer ....Margaret Clifton

It's a late night conference and, as usual, sales figures are down. To help, closed-circuit TV is installed which projects on to a big screen outside the store, showing the public what's going on inside. While Mr Rumbold's head fails the screen test and Mrs Slocombe has to slap on gallons of anti-wrinkle cream, Miss Brahms – miming to the nurse's deep, seductive voice – rescues the poor attempt at making an advert, and receives a surprise dinner invitation in the process.

55. THE EROTIC DREAMS OF MRS SLOCOMBE

(Transmitted: Thurs. 28/5/81, BBC1, 8.00pm)

ALSO APPEARING:

Mr Klein...Benny Lee

Secretary ....Louise Burton

Old Man ....Jack Haig

Lady Customer ....Brenda Cowling

Is Mr Humphries really the man of Mrs Slocombe's dreams? The blue-rinsed battle-axe thinks so; she's been dreaming of him enough. But Humphries isn't too keen, so with the rest of the staff they devise a way of steering her attention elsewhere. After advertising in a 'lonely hearts' column, Mr Humphries arranges for all respondents to come and view Mrs Slocombe – the trouble is, they're quick to turn on their heels. There's only one thing for it: Mr Humphries will have to steel himself and return the one-sided affections – but is he up to it?

WHAT A SCENE!

(In the canteen, the staff discuss Mrs Slocombe's sudden liking for Mr Humphries.)

MR HUMPHRIES: I had no idea any of this was happening.

MISS BRAHMS: She's had a thing about you for weeks, that's why she's been hitting the bottle.

MR HUMPHRIES: Why didn't you tell me?

MISS BRAHMS: I thought it would wear off.

MR KLEIN: She's a fine woman. There's a lot of love going to waste there.

MR HUMPHRIES: First time I've felt sorry for her cat.

MR SPOONER: I expect it's a new experience for you, Mr Humphries?

MR HUMPHRIES: On the contrary, Mr Spooner, quite a lot of ladies have thought twice about me. Trouble is, it's usually the second thought that puts them off!

Christmas Special

56. ROOTS?

(Transmitted: Thurs. 24/12/81, BBC1, 7.15pm)

ALSO APPEARING:

Young Mr Grace ....Harold Bennett

Mr Klein...Benny Lee

Secretary ....Louise Burton

To celebrate Old Mr Grace's ninetieth birthday, the team decides on something that will help him remember his roots. They plan a Welsh song, but when they find the Grace family is traced back to Somerset via Scotland, a Scottish dance and West Country song are prepared. At the last minute, it's discovered that the true family origin goes beyond Somerset; the staff's attempt at a Black and White Minstrel routine fits the bill.

The Secretaries

If you wanted a job as a secretary at Grace Brothers, it helped to be aware that there were certain prerequisites any hopeful applicant would need. No longer was there a place for the proficient, hardworking, archetypal secretary in this antiquated emporium. Instead, an endless stream of curvaceous beauties was employed, which satisfied the lascivious Mr Grace. It didn't matter whether

their typing and shorthand were up to scratch, so long as their figures were right.

The increasing presence and stature of the role developed as Young Mr Grace became a more important member of the cast. Susan Belbin, assistant floor manager on the show, says: 'I feel they provided a good juxtaposition between the ancient old boy and the fact that he still had an eye for the girls; there was an underlying statement saying it doesn't matter what age you are, you can always have an eye for the girls.'

Jeremy Lloyd felt the secretaries were an important part of the show. 'Over the years, we had some very good people playing the part,' he says. 'We got a lot of fun out of sexy secretaries causing a bit of excitement for Young Mr Grace and the male staff.

It's always nice having a pretty face in a show – without being sexist, of course.'

Stephanie Reeve, the sitcom's first secretary, enjoyed her time with the series. 'The atmosphere was great. Mollie, Frank and Nicholas were particularly warm personalities. And David Croft is lovely to work for, he's got such a calm temperament.'

After being given the freedom to play the character as she saw fit, Stephanie, whose dream role would have been Miss Brahms, decided not to play around with the character. 'I would've played it like Wendy did Miss Brahms but, of course, I couldn't duplicate a similar voice for the secretary. So I decided to play it fairly straight because there wasn't much more I could do with it.'

Stephanie gave up the business after failing to secure the classical-style roles she yearned for. 'I also got a little fed up hanging around in studios for parts that had very few lines.' But even though it's 24 years since she appeared in *Are You Being Served?*, friends frequently remind her of the days spent on the show. 'They come up and say: "I saw you, didn't I, in *Are You Being Served?* on Saturday? I still recognize you." And that's a nice compliment.'

Nina Francis, who took over the role of Mr Rumbold's secretary for the first two episodes in series three, was excited about joining *Are You Being Served?* 'It was my first live TV job, and I'd always wanted to do comedy, so I was very pleased when I got the part.

'The series was gorgeous because it was totally apolitical, encapsulating an old-fashioned, wonderful, sweet world with a touch of innocence,' says Nina, who believes audiences are crying out for similar ingredients in today's helping of sitcoms. 'It's years since the show was made, but people are still attracted to these sorts of shows because they're dying to see something that isn't too manufactured, that highlights people's foibles and sweetness. After all the violence on TV people feel refreshed watching the show.'

Two decades have passed since Nina was Rumbold's incumbent secretary, so she's surprised when people remind her about the role, particularly if it's her son after a day at school! 'When I picked him up from school the other day, he said: "Mummy, you've been on television." I replied: "Don't be daft!" But he told me his friends had watched the show and kept asking him about it – I couldn't believe it.'

In 1976 it was decided to employ a secretary for Young Mr Grace. By this stage in the show's life,

OPPOSITE Captain Peacock couldn't keep his mind on his work when Miss Belfridge (Candy Davis), Mr Rumbold's final secretary, was around.

ABOVE RIGHT In episode 51, Old Mr Grace (Kenneth Waller) poses for the store magazine with his dutiful nurse (Vivienne Johnson) and secretary (Debbie Linden).

RIGHT Young Mr Grace (Harold Bennett) was a glutton for punishment when he continued to employ sexy secretaries who carried a health warning!

Louise Burton (Old Mr Grace's last secretary) was 'over the moon' to be working on the show when she took over from Debbie Linden.

Harold Bennett's character had become immensely popular, and David Croft and Jeremy Lloyd wanted to exploit this adoration. They needed to create the opportunities for this to happen, and installing a secretary provided the ideal platform.

Penny Irving was first to take up the post. She remained with the show until the eighth series, when Debbie Linden, another former Page Three girl, became the next beauty to pamper the doddery store owner, although by this time Old Mr Grace, played by Kenneth Waller, had taken charge.

One of the girls who was unsuccessful when Linden was hired was called upon later in the eighth series. Louise Burton was 25 when she appeared in *Sit Out,* playing Virginia Edwards. 'I'd just returned from the rehearsals for that episode and David Croft called and asked whether I'd like to play the secretary for the rest of the series. I was over the moon to be part of this wonderful show.'

Louise, who went on to work with John Inman in *The Pyjama Party,* always found herself being cast in glamorous roles. 'My figure turned out to be a real negative for me,' she explains. 'If I'd had a different shape, a different figure, I would have had a lot more opportunities to do other types of roles. I found it very frustrating.'

Even after seventeen years Louise, who ended up being Old Mr Grace's final secretary, is still receiving the occasional fan letter. 'I couldn't believe it when one letter arrived about a year ago. Someone had seen me in an episode on a flight back from their holidays, and wondered whether I still looked the same. He wanted to know what I was doing now – it was incredible.'

Playing Rumbold's final secretary before Grace Brothers closed its doors for the last time was Candy Davis, whose generous curves were admired by the male staff, particularly the leering Captain Peacock. When Candy went along for the audition, she didn't think for a moment she'd get the part. She explains: 'For booby blondes in those days, this was *the* part everyone wanted to get.'

Candy took topless photos along to the interview. 'I didn't have any others, so I had to take them along – maybe that's what got me the job!' she laughs. At the end of the audition, Jeremy Lloyd and David Croft asked her out to lunch. 'I had a feeling I'd got the job, particularly when they invited me for something to eat.'

The secretarial role was all about having the ability to exude glamour and sex appeal, particularly in the later appointments. But playing the typical Grace Brothers secretary didn't worry her at all. 'I was like that anyway, the role was very much me,' smiles Candy, who received sackloads of fan mail. 'I used to get some bizarre requests, and was also sent lots of scripts for porno movies! But I just ignored them.'

Candy has happy memories of *Are You Being*

Served? 'It was a great time. I was twenty, having fun, living in London and had a job on television. So I enjoyed myself.'

Candy was a popular member of the cast, and well liked by David Croft and Jeremy Lloyd. 'She was bright academically and sensational to look at,' enthuses David, who admits that not everyone

Captain Peacock (Frank Thornton)
and Miss Belfridge (Candy Davis)
get down to business.

shared his and Jeremy's enthusiasm. 'Bob Spiers wasn't so keen, so we told him not to be so daft. He thought we could find someone who would act a little better, but even if we could, we wouldn't have found anyone prettier.'

Jeremy was equally keen to recruit Candy. 'She was terrific, and although she probably wasn't the best at the auditions in terms of reading the script, she looked jolly good and had a great sense of fun – it worked very well.'

When Candy joined the cast to play Mr Rumbold's secretary, Nicholas Smith, who played her incompetent boss, was a little worried. 'When I saw her, I thought: "She's very pretty but, oh God, not another glamour-puss!" I could imagine having the greatest difficulty getting laughs with somebody who looked terrific but didn't know what she was

doing. As it turned out, she was perfectly capable of feeding me lines and everything worked out well.'

While spending a few years in America recently, Candy experienced the popularity of the sitcom at first hand. 'I was living in the middle of the country, miles from anywhere. One day the family at the nearest house, which was about a mile away, invited me to dinner. The last thing on my mind was *Are You Being Served?* I hadn't thought about it for years. So I couldn't believe it when the subject came up and one of them asked whether I'd seen the programme. I never told them about the part I played in the show, but just couldn't believe their enthusiasm for it.'

Candy, who was seen in a handful of shows around the time of Miss Belfridge, only stayed in the acting business a couple of years. 'I don't think I was cut out for it,' she claims. 'I enjoyed the lifestyle associated with acting, but not the actual process.'

Now 36, she recalls seeing a recent repeat of an episode she appeared in. 'I thought I'd cringe and hide under the sofa, but I managed to stick it out,' she laughs. 'But I've changed so much, no one would recognize me now – all that hair and eyelashes have gone.'

LOUISE BURTON (b. Brighton)
Roles: Virginia Edwards (episode 52); Old Mr Grace's Secretary (episodes 55 & 56)
Louise began acting professionally at the age of thirteen, working on commercials and a special *Jackanory* series. After studying at the Italia Conti stage school on leaving school, she appeared in two *Carry On* films, playing Private Evans in *England* and a girl at a zoo in *Emmanuelle*. Plenty of stage and television work followed, including *The Dick Emery Show*.

Louise gave up acting in 1988 when her first child was born. At that point she'd spent seven years on the afternoon show *That's My Dog.*

CANDY DAVIS
(b. Essex)
Role: Miss Belfridge,
Mr Rumbold's Secretary
(series 9 & 10)

Candy, who was twenty when she first appeared, left home as a teenager and worked as a stripper for a few months. She spent some time modelling and six months at drama school, and worked in cabaret in Spain before travelling around the world for a year. On her return, Candy secured the job as Miss Belfridge. Other television credits include *The Two Ronnies* and *The Comic Strip.*

In the mid-1980s she achieved a Masters degree and taught in Asia for four years, then in America. She returned to England two years ago, and continues to teach.

NINA FRANCIS
(b. London)
Role: Miss Ainsworth,
Mr Rumbold's Secretary
(episodes 12 & 13)

Nina, who feels she was never cut out for a full-time television career, worked at Chichester – her first professional stage job – and performed all the classics, but after marrying and raising a family, she decided to concentrate less on acting and more on producing.

After leaving drama school she worked in rep before making several TV appearances, including *Science is Simple,* an educational programme which she presented, and playing a therapist in *The Life and Loves of a She Devil.* She also compiled and presented her own poetry show for Tyne Tees, and filmed numerous commercials. Today she concentrates on producing and freelance journalism.

DEBBIE LINDEN
(b. Glasgow)
Role: Old Mr Grace's Secretary
(episodes 49, 50, 51, 52 & 53)

Debbie was only 36 when she died tragically in 1997. She started her showbiz career at seventeen, playing a schoolgirl in the film *Home Before Midnight.* She appeared as Roy Kinnear's secretary, Doreen, in Thames's comedy *Cowboy* in 1980, the same year she was seen as a schoolgirl in *The Wildcats of St Trinian's.*

Debbie was also seen in EMI's 1983 haunted-house spoof, *Bloodbath at the House of Death,* and appeared in several popular TV shows including *The Bill, The Professionals, Bergerac,* a *Just Good Friends* special, and the BBC series *The Kid,* as well as working with, among others, Benny Hill and Dick Emery.

Besides acting, Debbie was a model and appeared in several commercials.

MELITA MANGER (b. Neath)
Role: Monica Hazlewood, Mr
Rumbold's Secretary (episode 26)

Melita, whose first TV role was playing a waitress in *Dad's Army,* always wanted to be a dancer and after leaving school studied at Brighton School of Music and Drama. Pantos and summer seasons followed, but she soon turned to acting, her first professional appearance being in a production of Arnold Ridley's *The Ghost Train.* Small TV parts began arriving, including *Doctor on the Go* and *The Basil Brush Show.*

Throughout the 1970s, Melita was also busy in commercials. After getting married she took a break from acting to bring up her family. Today she helps run the family business in Wales. Her last television appearance was in *Waiting for God.*

STEPHANIE REEVE (née Gathercole) (b. Croydon) *Role: Mr Rumbold's Secretary (episodes 1, 3, 4, 6 & 10)* Stephanie began her working life as an English and Drama teacher but, harbouring dreams of working in theatre, left to become an ASM at Leatherhead. During her first summer season at Croydon she was spotted by David Croft and his wife, Ann, then an agent.

She first worked for Croft in *Hugh and I Spy* before several years in rep. Other early television work included *Man Hunt* and playing a bird sitting on a golf course in *The Marty Feldman Comedy Machine*. She also worked on radio.

After getting married and bringing up her family, she returned to teaching nine years ago. She was Head of Drama in a secondary school for five years, but now works with the dyslexic, as well as being a freelance speech and drama teacher. Stephanie is also responsible for the voice-over on the *Are You Being Served?* signature tune.

ISABELLA RYE (b. Newbury) *Role: Mr Rumbold's Secretary (episode 23). She had been a member of Young Mr Grace's personal staff, but when he suffered a heart attack the doctor suggested she be transferred because she was bad for his blood pressure.* Isabella, who was brought up in Switzerland, worked in all facets of the business. In her early career she even spent two seasons in Tom Arnold's circus.

She trained at the Italia Conti stage school and RADA before working in numerous reps, including Nottingham and Rotherham. She made the most of her height by spending time as a Bluebell girl touring South America. Her first television role was with Eric Barker and Deryck Guyler, but other appearances quickly followed, including several episodes of *Crossroads* in 1969. Her biggest small-screen role was in *Manhattan Towers* in the US.

In later years, Isabella, who mostly worked in theatre, qualified as a London Blue Badge tourist guide, utilizing her many languages.

Other Secretaries

Two other secretaries were employed by Grace Brothers. MOIRA FOOT, who played Mr Rumbold's temporary secretary in episodes 17, 18 and 19, now runs her own production company. Moira, who went on to play a semi-regular role as one of the Resistance fighters in *'Allo, 'Allo*, had to leave *Are You Being Served?* because she was already booked for an appearance in *The Benny Hill Show*.

PENNY IRVING, who first appeared in the fourth series, was Young Mr Grace's longest serving and most loyal secretary. Later credited as Miss Bakewell, she was seen in over twenty episodes. During a twenty-year spell, she regularly popped up on the screen, including appearances as one of the Birds of Paradise in *Carry On Dick*, Chiquita in *Percy's Progress*, Sandy in the film version of *The Likely Lads*, in *Vampira* with David Niven, and as a serving wench in *The Bawdy Adventures of Tom Jones*. Her TV appearances include playing a chambermaid in *Dad's Army* and Mary in several episodes of *Hi-De-Hi!*

The Lift Girls

Like so many department stores of the period, Grace Brothers employed a number of lift girls. Smartly dressed in their brown uniforms, the girls were given the heady responsibility of controlling all the floor buttons in the shoe box-sized store lifts: customers simply told the girl what floor they wanted, then waited until their arrival at the chosen destination was greeted by the lift girl's announcement.

The lift girls at Grace Brothers were always seen but never heard, except in one episode, 'Anything You Can Do', when Belinda Lee and Sue Bishop managed to creep on to the bottom rung of the credits, thanks to some dialogue in a canteen scene. This was the only other place you could spot the girls in brown, who occasionally doubled up as non-speaking sales assistants. In the canteen, they would be seen seated at background tables whispering to each other. But like all members of the cast,

While the shop floor staff natter, the lift girls occupy their customary position in the canteen at a background table.

they played their part in the overall success of the show. Jo Austin, production assistant on two series, valued their contribution. 'They were very good and had to stay on the ball. Even though they were just shepherding people in and out of the store and didn't have much to do, the girls had to look right and play their part properly. It was difficult for them because they weren't wandering around the store consciously doing something; we had to rely on them to work off their own bat, to look natural and get on with their job – you had to have thor-ough trust in them. They only came in on the day of recording, but I'd like to think they felt part of the show.'

Jo remembers numer-ous hassles getting the lift doors to open. 'Those lift doors!' she exclaims. 'They were always playing up. The trouble is, we never knew whether they'd work

or not. The lifts were a complicated part of the set. When they were being assembled the balance mech-anism had to be just right or they'd jam.

'There were several times, even while recording, when a voice was heard wailing: "I can't get out!" We always made sure someone was hanging around the back just in case the girls needed help.'

Appearing as a lift girl in the last three series was Taryn Kay, who had previously worked for David Croft and Jeremy Lloyd on *Oh, Happy Band!* with Harry Worth in 1980. After finishing filming one day, David offered Taryn a lift back to Television Centre. She recalls: 'On the way we had a chat about my acting career, and it wasn't long after that I was offered a part in *Are You Being Served?*'

Although it was only a small role, Taryn, in her early twenties when she appeared, was happy to be involved. 'It was a tiny part,' she says, 'but I got the opportunity to dance, which I really enjoyed. I would liked to have done more, but it wasn't appro-priate because the lift girls had a specific job to do.'

Other actresses hired for the role included Sue Bishop, Sandy Leggatt, Jackie Bristow, the late Diane Holt – a well-loved member of the cast who died tragically of multiple sclerosis – and Belinda Lee, who loved her time in *Are You Being Served?* She stayed with the show throughout the ten series, and had previously worked for David Croft as a nun in *Dad's Army*. 'It was a wonderfully close-knit team, and a pleasure to be part of.'

Like most of the lift girls, Belinda was also a dancer. 'We were all multi-talented,' she explains, 'which meant we could get involved in the dances that happened occasionally in the series.'

David Croft explains that he tried to employ dancers whenever possible. 'We'd often finish a series with a production number and wanted some girls who could join in and dance, and it all worked very well.'

The fact that she usually had no dialogue didn't bother Belinda or her colleagues. 'We didn't mind because they were so good to us, never making us feel like outsiders. I always felt part of the team.'

As far as the canteen scenes are concerned, Belinda has vivid recollections of the food dished up for the cast. 'It was real but dreadful stuff,' she laughs. 'All the food was hot when it was brought on. The prop boys were very good and tried getting dishes everyone liked. But we tended to pick at the food because we never wanted to eat it.'

The biggest bugbear for everyone connected with the Grace Brothers lift, as Jo Austin has already explained, was the unreliable doors, and

Belinda remembers many a tussle over the years. 'We'd often end up closing them ourselves, while trying desperately to look like we were coolly pressing a button to the side. Often we'd have someone tucked away out of sight who'd pull them across by rope, but if he was inexperienced, we'd end up in all sorts of problems.'

Belinda, who was amazed at the number of people who believed that the lift was genuine, found that standing around in her thick brown uniform was hot work. 'It was like an oven behind those doors,' she says. 'The designers tried making it look as real as possible and it was like a small box. It was hot at the best of times, but if the doors jammed it was sweltering.'

Even though her role restricted her to mainly background scenes, Belinda, and the rest of the girls, still received fan letters. 'One man wrote saying I was a wonderful actress, which surprised me bearing in mind all I did was open a lift.'

TARYN KAY
(b. Clacton-on-Sea)
Role: Lift Girl
(series 9 & 10)
Taryn, whose parents ran a hotel in Clacton, trained as a dancer and began working professionally in variety shows and pantos. Eventually she was offered small parts in television shows, including *Oh, Happy Band!* with Harry Worth. She also appeared as a dancer in a Gary Glitter video. After *Are You Being Served?* she worked mainly in

weekly rep and musicals, and during the early 1990s she became a cheerleader for the London Monarchs, an American football team. Today, as well as acting – she recently played Bob Hoskins' wife in *Parting Shots* – she works in corporate hospitality.

BELINDA LEE
(b. London)
Role: Lift Girl
(all ten series)

Belinda did ballet training in Richmond straight from school, but she'd been appearing in commercials since she was a girl. Plenty of work in pantomimes, stage shows and catalogue work came her way before she moved more into television, though the medium wasn't unfamiliar to her. As a teenager she had appeared in many BBC productions, including *Jackanory.*

In the 1960s she was seen as a young mum in *Z Cars*; other TV credits include *I, Claudius, Terry and June* and a policewoman in *EastEnders*. Because she owned her own uniform she was often cast as policewomen.

Belinda moved away from acting in the 1980s and joined Thames TV's costume department. In 1988, disillusioned with the acting world, she began working as a freelance costumier. She worked for Anglia Television on the children's show *Knightmare*. Today she continues to work freelance as well as appearing in the occasional commerical, her last job being an advert for Asda.

Episode Guide

SERIES NINE

REGULAR CAST MEMBERS

Mrs Slocombe	Mollie Sugden
Mr Humphries	John Inman
Captain Peacock	Frank Thornton
Miss Brahms	Wendy Richard
Mr Rumbold	Nicholas Smith
Mr Spooner	Mike Berry
Mr Harman	Arthur English
Miss Belfridge	Candy Davis

57. *THE SWEET SMELL OF SUCCESS*

(Transmitted: Fri. 22/4/83, BBC1, 8.30pm)

ALSO APPEARING:

Canteen Manageress	Doremy Vernon
Mrs Peacock	Diana King
Handsome Customer	Michael Sharvell-Martin
Military Customer	Rex Robinson

With the wage cuts hitting hard, Mrs Slocombe lets the staff in on a secret: to help her finances, she makes home-made perfume and has developed a brand that attracts the opposite sex. Eager to earn a few quid, everyone sells it under the counter. Even Captain Peacock tries his luck, with alarming consequences!

WHAT A SCENE!

(While Mr Rumbold is talking to Mr Harman, Miss Belfridge arrives for her first day.)

MR HARMAN: Cor, blimey. 'Ere, you don't 'alf pick 'em. Where d'you get her, page three of *The Sun*?

MR RUMBOLD: (*pointing his finger*) That will do, Mr Harman. Miss Belfridge stood out from all the other applicants.

MR HARMAN: I'm not surprised.

58. CONDUCT UNBECOMING

(Transmitted: Fri. 29/4/83, BBC1, 8.30pm)

ALSO APPEARING:

'Tights' Customer ....Frances Bennett

Woman ....Gilda Perry

Mr Wagstaff ....Tony Sympson

Mr Humphries' behaviour is cause for concern, and when he opens his heart and explains that he's been kicked out of his home after having a tiff with his mother, everyone is sympathetic. But when he returns drunk from the pub at lunchtime, and money is missing from the till, the finger of suspicion points his way. To sort the matter out, a Board of Enquiry is called.

WHAT A SCENE!

(At the canteen, Mrs Slocombe boasts about how she used to attract men.)

MRS SLOCOMBE: You might not realize it, but when I was younger I had men coming out of the woodwork.

MR SPOONER: She used to spray on Rentokil to keep them off!

59. MEMORIES ARE MADE OF THIS

(Transmitted: Fri. 6/5/83, BBC1, 8.30pm)

ALSO APPEARING:

Canteen Manageress..............................Doremy Vernon

Mr Walpole...Jess Conrad

Fisherman ....Ballard Berkeley

Everybody in the sports department – except the fit Mr Walpole – has been taken ill and all the goods are transferred up to Peacock's floor. Everyone is up in arms until it transpires that Walpole, the golf pro, will be moving with the department, which pleases Mrs Slocombe, Miss Brahms – and Mr Humphries. While helping Peacock improve his golf swing, Mrs Slocombe is hit, loses her memory and travels back to her childhood, with the usual chaos.

60. CALLING ALL CUSTOMERS

(Transmitted: Fri. 13/5/83, BBC1, 8.30pm)

ALSO APPEARING:

Truck Drivers ....Nosher Powell, Ron Tarr

CB Voices ....Vicki Michelle, Robbie Coltrane

Sales are down to critical levels, so a commercial on Citizens Band radio is planned. All the staff submit ideas, and Miss Belfridge, who has an O-level in English Lit., judges the submissions. When they are asked to appear in Mr Harman's effort, there is uproar – until they realize they'll earn a hundred pounds each. As soon as Mary Whitehouse complains about the new commercial, and lorry drivers storm the store, everyone realizes they're attracting the wrong type of listener.

61. MONKEY BUSINESS

(Transmitted: Fri. 20/5/83, BBC1, 8.30pm)

ALSO APPEARING:

Mr Kayoto ....Eiji Kusuhara

Secretary at Number Ten ....John D. Collins

Fur Coat Customer................................John Biggerstaff

His Secretary ....Lisa Anselmi

Mr Yamoto ....Kristopher Kum

Monkey...Rusty Goffe

Voice of Mrs Thatcher ....Jan Ravens

The staff don't get a pay rise, and are so desperate that, when Rumbold isn't prepared to pursue the matter, they take their case up with the Prime Minister. But when they hear talk of a Japanese take-over, their anger is fuelled even more. Sadly, when the PM is running late for eetings and Mr Humphries wastes valuable time discussing his mother's washing, they realize they've missed their opportunity.

Memories

'I appeared in this episode dressed as a monkey who'd escaped from the zoo. It was great fun to do, and although I was only hired for a small part, I never felt like I was encroaching. The whole team was fabulous. The costume was hot but I'm used to dressing up as animals, so it didn't cause any problems.'

RUSTY GOFFE

62. LOST AND FOUND

(Transmitted: Fri. 27/5/83, BBC1, 8.30pm)

ALSO APPEARING:

Canteen Manageress..............................Doremy Vernon

Mr Winston ....Peter Cleall

Customer...Norman Mitchell

Mrs Slocombe's life is turned upside-down when she loses her pussy, and when its clockwork mouse is found at the edge of a well, she becomes distraught. Mr Humphries offers a shoulder to cry on, but she takes more advantage than the dandy salesman anticipated. Her colleagues buy her a new cat and when Humphries presents the gift, Mrs Slocombe gets the wrong idea, claims he's the new love in her life and plans their wedding day.

Memories

'I've supported Brighton football club since I was seven, and 1983 was the year they reached the FA Cup Final. I couldn't get any tickets for love or money for me and my children – I'd tried everywhere. During a break in rehearsals I was talking to Arthur English and he said: "I can get them for you, Pete, I'm a director of Aldershot." So he got me two tickets, and although I couldn't go, my two sons loved it.'

PETER CLEALL

WHAT A SCENE!

(A customer wants to buy some underwear.)

CUSTOMER: I don't want anything fancy, just a pair of Y-fronts.

MR HUMPHRIES: Sorry, sir, we're right out of Y-fronts. We do have a new range which are X-fronts.

CUSTOMER: X-fronts? I've never heard of them.

MR HUMPHRIES: (*laughs*) You are behind the times – we've actually got a pair of W-fronts.

CUSTOMER: What's the difference between W, X and Y fronts?

MR HUMPHRIES: About two octaves!

SERIES TEN

REGULAR CAST MEMBERS

Mrs Slocombe.......................................Mollie Sugden

Mr Humphries ....John Inman

Captain Peacock...............................Frank Thornton

Miss Brahms ....Wendy Richard

Mr Rumbold ....Nicholas Smith

Mr Harman..Arthur English

Mr Spooner ....Mike Berry

Miss Belfridge ....Candy Davis

63. GOODBYE MRS SLOCOMBE

(Transmitted: Mon. 18/2/85, BBC1, 8.30pm)

ALSO APPEARING:

Canteen Manageress..............................Doremy Vernon

Miss Featherstone ....Joanna Dunham

Customer ....Elizabeth Stewart

Mrs Slocombe returns after a two-week illness to find that Grace Brothers have lowered the age of retirement and she has to go. Before Captain Peacock can find the words to tell her, the canteen manageress blurts out the news. Determined to stay, Mrs Slocombe tries a new image, but it's no good, Rumbold has already decided on Miss Featherstone from Toiletries as her replacement. In her desperation to stay at Grace Brothers, Mrs Slocombe tries her hand at cleaning and cooking. But when Miss Featherstone's snooty attitude towards customers and colleagues alike causes unrest, the staff plot to oust her from her job, and it's not long before Mrs Slocombe is back where she belongs.

Memories

'It was great fun playing Miss Featherstone, with her bouffant hairstyle and terrible glasses. I wore my hair down when I arrived at the studio, but the make-up girl did such a good job that no one recognized me at first when I went on set. Although this was transmitted first in the final series, it was actually the last one recorded. It had earlier been postponed because of a strike, which means I actually got paid twice. And being involved in the last one, I was invited to the farewell party.'

JOANNA DUNHAM

64. GROUNDS FOR DIVORCE

(Transmitted: Mon. 25/2/85, BBC1, 8.30pm)

ALSO APPEARING:

Miss Bagnold .... Maggie Henderson

Mrs Peacock .... Diana Lambert

Customer .... Philip Kendall

Captain Peacock is having an affair with Miss Bagnold, a recent recruit in Accounts. But when he agrees with his wife to give their marriage one more try, Peacock tries desperately to avoid Miss Bagnold, without much success. The staff rally round Captain Peacock, trying to help, but it's his unusual attire that finally frightens off his pursuer.

WHAT A SCENE!

(Rumbold confronts Captain Peacock about his lateness, but Peacock's having none of it.)

MR RUMBOLD: You've been late three times this week, and a fourth time would have meant a severe reprimand.

CAPT. PEACOCK: Oh, what poppycock! We're not still at school, you know.

MR RUMBOLD: Really, Peacock. I won't be spoken to in that manner in front of the staff.

CAPT. PEACOCK: And neither will I. And if you continue to get up my nose I shall be forced to mention the number of days you leave early by the back entrance.

MR RUMBOLD: Peacock, you're pushing my patience to its limits.

CAPT. PEACOCK: Really.

MR RUMBOLD: I may seem a good-natured person but I must warn you I'm capable of blowing my top.

CAPT. PEACOCK: *(looking at Rumbold's bald pate)* Judging by the appearance, you've already blown it!

65. THE HOLD-UP

(Transmitted: Mon. 4/3/85, BBC1, 8.30pm)

ALSO APPEARING:

Burglars .... Michael Attwell, Paul Humpoletz

Policeman .... Ian Collier

The staff are staying late for stocktaking, but when Mr Harman bursts in announcing the store is being robbed, the staff set about capturing the villains. When Miss Brahms is taken hostage, action is needed quickly. Peacock disguises himself as a deerstalker-wearing policeman, with Spooner as his sidekick, but this fails, and it's down to Mrs Slocombe, Mr Humphries and Mr Harman, dressed up as The Gumby Gang, to save the day.

WHAT A SCENE!

(Mr Humphries is measuring a pair of trousers.)

CAPT. PEACOCK: Mr Humphries, Mr Spooner, have you nearly finished your stocktake? Uh! You're supposed to count them, not measure them.

MR SPOONER: Well, there's no label on it, we've got to know what size they are.

MR HUMPHRIES: Yes, now this inside leg is 28, and this inside leg is 15.

CAPT. PEACOCK: Well that can't be right.

MR HUMPHRIES: Oh. Of course, it's all coming back to me now. It was a special order by a Welsh sheep farmer who lived on the side of a very steep hill.

66. GAMBLING FEVER

(Transmitted: Mon. 11/3/85, BBC1, 8.30pm)

ALSO APPEARING:

Canteen Manageress.............................Doremy Vernon

Customer...Harriet Reynolds

Seymour ....Keith Hodiak

To help the fight against shoplifting, closed-circuit TV is installed on the shop floor again. It's also bonus day. Influenced by Mr Harman's talk of betting on the horses, the staff gamble their bonuses. While Rumbold is at the bank, the staff use the CCTV to watch the race. But when they lose their money they decide to pawn their valuables in a desperate attempt to retrieve their loss.

WHAT A SCENE!

(When closed-circuit TV is installed, the staff discuss the waste of money.)

CAPT. PEACOCK: Why they installed that instead of better air-conditioning, I shall never know.

MRS SLOCOMBE: I know, it's like an oven in here. I mean, look at my face. My foundation cream is beginning to crack.

MR HARMAN: Yes, and if you were a block of flats you'd be condemned by now!

67. THE NIGHT-CLUB

(Transmitted: Mon. 18/3/85, BBC1, 8.30pm)

ALSO APPEARING:

Canteen Manageress.............................Doremy Vernon

Seymour ....Keith Hodiak

Men in Cinema..................Ray Gatenby, Ronnie Brody

Young Mr Grace allows the staff to use the shop floor at night for any money-making schemes they can dream up, so long as he takes ten per cent of the profits. So it's ideas time again: Mr Spooner suggests a roller disco and bowls, Mrs Slocombe a snack bar, but it's decided to open a night-club, *The Club Rendezvous*. Mr Humphries arranges advertising when his friend – the manager of the local cinema – agrees to a free advert, to be filmed by the staff. When everyone turns out to see the end product, little do they expect their screen debuts to be shown during a sex film!

Memories

'David and Jeremy were both very good, they'd always consider any ideas from the actors. But it seemed that whenever I suggested a gag, David would say: "That's very good, Frank, but give it to Mr Humphries." I seemed to be better at inventing lines for Mr Humphries than for Captain Peacock.'

FRANK THORNTON

WHAT A SCENE!

(Mrs Slocombe, knowing she'll be late home, phones her cat.)

MRS SLOCOMBE: Ah! I forgot to tell Tiddles that I was going to be late; she'll be ever so upset. I'd better go and phone her. *(She walks over to the phone.)*

MISS BRAHMS: You don't mean to tell me you can communicate with that cat of yours?

MR SPOONER: Well, why not? They do with monkeys. They show 'em things like pictures of vegetables and numbers, and the monkeys point at 'em and make up a sentence.

MR HUMPHRIES: How do you know that?

MR SPOONER: Well, I watch nature programmes on the telly. I've learned quite a lot.

MISS BRAHMS: Oh. And when do you take your exam to go in the zoo?

68. FRIENDS AND NEIGHBOURS

(Transmitted: Mon. 25/3/85, BBC1, 8.30pm)

ALSO APPEARING:

Canteen Manageress..............................Doremy Vernon

Mrs Peacock ....Diana Lambert

Mrs Rumbold ....Jean Challis

Lady Customer.....................................Carol Cleveland

Cedric ....Felipe Izquierdo

The staff are hard up and demand a travel allowance, or else they'll look for work nearer home. Mr Humphries' willingness to act as spokesman sees him get the sack. After reconsidering, Mr Grace reinstates him and offers the vacant apartments at the top of the store at discounted rates. But it's not long before the staff realize that it's all right working together, but living together is another thing.

Memories

'I nearly didn't make the recording because I was extremely ill. I'd been fine during rehearsals, but the day before recording I'd eaten in a canteen before heading off to an audition for a musical. I got worse and worse and ended up being rushed to hospital with gastroenteritis. I was being violently ill and all I could think about was that tomorrow was the recording. Although I wasn't well and had to drag myself in, I made it to the studio, so it was a memorable job!'

CAROL CLEVELAND

69. THE POP STAR

(Transmitted: Mon. 1/4/85, BBC1, 8.30pm)

ALSO APPEARING:

Canteen Manageress..............................Doremy Vernon

TV Presenter ....Nick Ross

Seymour ....Keith Hodiak

TV Director...Charles Nicklin

Sam, the Director's Assistant....................Suzy Aitchison

Cleaners...............................Mary Bradley, Joan Dainty

Mr Spooner's consistent lateness leads to him being demoted to lift boy. He's cold-shouldered in the canteen, but when his recent performance in the London Department Stores' annual concert is hailed by the local rag, and a record company want to sign him up, the rest of the gang are keen to get back on his good side so they can be his backing group.

Memories

'The lines I said had been written for two cleaners, but they made it into one character for me. I wanted to play my character differently from your typical cleaner on TV, so I wore high heels and chewed gum for all I was worth. It was great fun.'

MARY BRADLEY

An Episode-by-Episode Guide to Every Character

The following information explains what every character did in the series. From a customer in the pilot to the TV director in episode 69, every actor who appeared on the credits of this classic sitcom, except those mentioned in more detail elsewhere in the book, is listed. If a particular episode is not mentioned, it is because only main cast members appeared, or the performers are described more fully within other sections.

THE PILOT
Customer (Michael Knowles) – the store's very first customer, who only wants the loo.

EPISODE 2
The 40" Waist (Robert Raglan) – a customer persuaded into buying a jacket that doesn't fit.
The 28" Inside Leg (Derek Smith) – a customer interested in buying a jacket.

EPISODE 3
The Returned Glen Check (Peter Needham) – a customer who returns a jacket and spoils Lucas's sales figures.

EPISODE 4
The Scot (James Copeland) – a customer who wants some hardwearing tweed trousers.
The 38C Cup (Anita Richardson) – a customer who comes out of the changing room in her underwear, requesting a lower-cut bra.
The Large Brim with Fruit (Pamela Manson) – a customer who tries on a large hat but doesn't buy it in the end.

The Man with the Large Bra (David Rowlands) – a timid customer buying a bra for his fiancée.
The Leatherette Gloves (Colin Bean) – a customer buying gloves for his brother-in-law.

EPISODE 5
Miss French (Joanna Lumley) – the glamorous saleswoman from the perfumery, selling *His and Hers* perfume.
The Customers (Margaret Flint & Evan Ross) – customers who show interest in the perfume.

EPISODE 6
Mr Humphries' Customer (Elizabeth Larner) – an indecisive customer who wants to buy a jumper for a surprise present, but can't decide.
Wealthy Customer (Hilary Pritchard) – a customer who loses her ring while buying gloves for her husband.
The Outsize Dress (Janet Davies) – a customer who is pressurized into buying an outsize dress.
Mr Humphries' Friend (Vicki Woolf) – a woman who visits Humphries in the store. It's discovered that she used to be a man before the operation!

EPISODE 7
The Check Jacket (John Ringham) – a customer buying a £30 jacket that's too big.
The Bridal Veil (Dorothy Wayne) – a customer who buys a veil that's so thick, she can't see anything.
Mrs Grainger (Pearl Hackney) – Mr Grainger's wife, who attends his 65th birthday dinner.
Elsie (Hilda Fenemore) – a cleaner.
The Trio (Avril Fane, Barbara and Dorothy Loynes) – the OAPs who form the orchestra for Mr Grainger's 65th birthday dinner.

EPISODE 8

Elsie (Hilda Fenemore) – a cleaner.

Gladys (Helen Lambert) – a cleaner.

Footwarmer (Robert Mill) – a customer who wants some trousers, but ends up buying two pairs of footwarmers as well.

The Large Hat (Carolyn Hudson) – a customer interested in buying a hat.

The Fur Gloves (John Baker) – a customer buying imitation rabbit gloves.

EPISODE 10

Mr Clegg (Donald Morley) – the newly-appointed security chief, who used to work for the CID.

Dr Wainwright (Robert Raglan) – a doctor who visits Mr Rumbold.

The Underwear Customer (Joyce Cummings) – a customer who wants to buy some bloomers, but can't decide.

The Scarf Customer (Stella Kemball) – a customer who wants a scarf.

EPISODE 11

The Ready-Made Suit (John Clegg) – a customer who wants a ready-made suit but finds it's not what you'd call ready-to-wear.

The Dressing Gown (Stuart Sherwin) – a customer who wants a dressing gown.

The Irish Lady (Helen Dorward) – a customer who buys a shamrock-green hat.

EPISODE 12

Mr Kato (Eric Young) – a Japanese customer who wants a raincoat but annoys everyone because he constantly bows and says 'so'.

Lady Customer (Therese McMurray) – a customer who's interested in a £4 crocheted hat.

EPISODE 14

The Forty Maternity (Donald Hewlett) – a customer who buys a frock for a fancy-dress party.

The Bold Check (Michael Knowles) – a customer who is interested in buying a jacket, but ends up with Hewlett's coat by mistake.

The Clip-On Bow (Jeffrey Segal) – a customer buying a clip-on bow tie.

The Captain's Fancy (Maureen Lane) – a customer browsing in the shop.

EPISODE 15

Daphne (Hilda Fenemore) – a cleaner.

The Blue Alteration (Ann Sidney) – a woman who tries on a blue dress and doesn't like it, but is pressurized into buying it by Mrs Slocombe.

Sister (Joy Allen) – the firm's Sister, who is called up to the department to check Mr Lucas's temperature.

The Fawn Trousers (Gordon Peters) – a customer who wants some fawn trousers.

Drooping Derrière (Pamela Cundell) – a customer who is unhappy with a suit she bought the previous day: the problem is that the seat droops.

Forgetful One (Bill Martin) – a customer who can't remember what he came in for, so he refers to a shopping list but rushes out of the store when Mr Lucas starts foaming at the mouth.

EPISODE 16

The Small Handicap (John Clegg) – a wig-wearing customer who wants a golfing jumper and is fooled into buying one that's much too long.

Miss Robinson (Sandra Clark) – works in the jewellery department and brings a tray of rings to Young Mr Grace. She is the girl Mr Grace was interested in marrying before changing his mind.

The Trousers (Jay Denyer) – a customer wanting some trousers.

EPISODE 17

German Customers (Ernst Ulman & Joanna Lumley) – customers who visit the store during German Week, but are annoyed when all they can buy is German goods.

The Lady for 'the Ladies' (Anita Richardson) – a woman who only wants to use the toilet but is mistaken for a customer.

EPISODE 18

The Returned Wig (Kate Brown) – a customer who returns a £4.50 wig after washing it.

The Honeymoon Couple (Jonathan Cecil & Hilary Pritchard) – a couple looking for sweaters.

EPISODE 19

The Gent for 'the Gents' (Felix Bowness) – a man who wants the gents.

EPISODE 20

Lady Templewood (Betty Impey) – appears on the credits but her scene appears to have been cut.

EPISODE 21
Ivy (Hilda Fenemore) – a cleaner.

The Wedding Hat (Hilary Pritchard) – a woman who wants a wedding hat, but is in a hurry because she's late for work.

The Large Gloves (Stuart Sherwin) – a customer who buys a pair of gloves.

The Check Suit (John Bardon) – a customer who buys a check suit.

Husband (Gordon Peters) – the husband of Anne Cunningham's character. His wife is buying an evening dress but they end up arguing in the store.

Wife (Anne Cunningham) – a woman who wants to buy an evening dress, but ends up in tears.

The Raincoat in the Window (Reg Dixon) – a customer with arms of uneven length, who wants a £28 overcoat that's displayed in the shop window.

EPISODE 22
Mr Ludlow (Peter Greene) – works in the design/electrical department and helps set up the new lifelike dummies on the shop floor.

EPISODE 24
Interpreter (Ahmed Khalil) – the Emir's private interpreter.

The Emir (Ahmed Osman) – a customer who buys trousers for his wives to wear in the harem.

Head Wife (Melody Urquhart) – the Emir's chief wife.

Firemen (Hamish Roughead & Ken Barker) – firemen who arrive when a fire breaks out in the store's basement.

EPISODE 25
Claude (Tony Sympson) – an old man wanting beachwear for his holidays.

Mrs Claude (Mavis Pugh) – Claude's snooty wife.

The Six-Pound Fox (Diana Lambert) – a customer in the store.

EPISODE 26
Mr Hazlewood (Michael Stainton) – Monica Hazlewood's father, who brings in a wedding cake and smashes it over Mr Grainger's head, mistaking him for Peacock.

EPISODE 27
The Plastic Umbrella (Jeanne Mockford) – a customer buying an umbrella.

The Boy (Donald Waugh) – a boy who chooses which member of staff will play the store's Father Christmas.

EPISODE 28
Ivy (Hilda Fenemore) – a cleaner.

Customer (Geoffrey Adams) – a customer who wants some trousers for his au pair, Helga.

Customers (Jennifer Lonsdale & Elizabeth Morgan) – two ladies wondering whether to buy a bra.

Customer (Jeffrey Gardiner) – a customer who wants to buy some gloves, but decides against it.

Customer (Raymond Bowers) – a customer who wants a beige cashmere sweater.

EPISODE 29
The Red Indian Father (Terry Duggan) – a man who brings his son into the store for an Indian's suit.

The Bridal Doll (Jacquie Cook) – a woman who buys a talking bridal doll for her daughter.

EPISODE 30
The Two Fur Coats (Tim Barrett) – a customer who wants two fur coats: one for his wife, the other for his mistress.

The Top-Pocket Handkerchief (Bill Martin) – a customer who only wants a hankie, much to Mr Lucas's annoyance.

The French Underwear (Carolle Rousseau) – a woman with a little poodle who buys a complete set of underwear.

Miss 38-22-36 (Jenny Kenna) – a woman who was supposedly interested in a secretarial job and was interviewed by Young Mr Grace; but it was all a ruse to get Mr Grace into the room.

EPISODE 31
The Afro Pants (Jeffrey Holland) – a man who wants a pair of trousers.

Cynthia (Bernice Adams) – a woman who wants a pair of tan pantihose.

EPISODE 32
Lady Weeble Ablesmith & Henry Grant Hopkins (Mavis Pugh & Donald Bisset) – shareholders attending the take-over meeting.

EPISODE 33
The Corset Customer (Peggy Ashby) – a customer who wants a very strong corset to keep her figure under control.

EPISODE 34
The Ten-Pound Perfume (Ferdy Mayne) – a suave Frenchman buying perfume for himself.

Mr Crawford (Raymond Bowers) – the cameraman from the Photography department who films the commercial.

The Porter (Freddie Wiles) – Mr Harman's assistant.

EPISODE 35
Ivy (Hilda Fenemore) – a cleaner.

Lady Customer (Joy Harington) – a customer who wants a suit for town, but gets annoyed when she thinks Miss Brahms is imitating her posh voice.

EPISODE 36
Roger's Master (Raymond Bowers) – a man who buys a made-to-measure coat for his poodle.

Roger's Mistress (Mavis Pugh) – the poodle's owner.

Flexibra Customers (Dominique Don & Tony Brothers) – the female customer buys a new Flexibra, while the man buys matching pants.

EPISODE 37
Wendel P. Clark (Norman Mitchell) – Mrs Slocombe's uncle from America, who comes over for her wedding.

Mr Tomiades (Gorden Kaye) – a friend of Mrs Slocombe's fiancé, who breaks the bad news that he's already married.

The Matching Pantaloons (Felix Bowness) – a customer who wants to buy some trendy underwear for his girlfriend.

Greek Band Leader (Stelios Chiotis) – a man who plays at the fake wedding on the shop floor.

EPISODE 39
Lady Customer (Jan Holden) – a woman who complains about some stockings that run when she puts them on.

Typist (Bernice Adams) – a typist who is fired by Young Mr Grace for not possessing the looks to set off his stress indicator.

EPISODE 40
Fairy Prince (Michael Halsey) – another member of staff who dresses up as the Fairy Prince in an identical costume to that of Mr Humphries for Mr Grace's birthday celebrations.

EPISODE 41
Mr Webster (Tony Sympson) – one of the applicants for the junior's job. Previously worked in a pet shop.

Mr Beauchamp (Jeffrey Gardiner) – a talkative, over-the-top applicant for the junior post.

Ivy (Hilda Fenemore) – a cleaner.

Customers (Harold Berens, Morris Barry & Bernard Stone) – all friends and ex-customers of Mr Goldberg who help boost up his commission.

Warwick (Jimmy Mac) – Mr Harman's assistant who helps at the interviews.

EPISODE 42
Ballet Mistress (Amanda Barrie) – a friend of Mr Humphries, who helps the staff get in shape by providing ballet lessons.

Staff Nurse (Joy Allen) – helps the doctor during the staff medicals.

Doctor (Imogen Bickford-Smith) – the doctor who carries out the medicals.

The Dressing Gown (Geraldine Gardner) – a woman who buys her husband a dressing gown for their wedding anniversary.

Second Customer (Jennifer Guy) – a customer who can't decide about a purchase, but ends up buying a 'disco fever' dancing skirt and a pair of fluorescent tights.

EPISODE 43
The Blazer (Jeffrey Holland) – a customer who tries on a £120 blazer, but ends up buying a tweed jacket for £140.

EPISODE 44
Miss Comlozi (Avril Angers) – Edna from Cosmetics who helps Mrs Slocombe choose soap for the executive bathroom when she's temporarily placed in charge. We later learn she has been sacked for being rude to customers.

The Plastic Mac (Gorden Kaye) – A Scotsman who works as a magazine photographer and wants a plastic mac.

First Customer (Derrie Powell) – a posh customer who makes a purchase.

EPISODE 45
Mr Franco (Jackie 'Mr TV' Pallo) – works in the sports department and was responsible for spreading the news that Peacock has a boil on his backside.

The Shrunken Sock (Raymond Bowers) – a customer who returns non-shrink socks one week and one wash later.

EPISODE 46
Signor Balli (Ronnie Brody) – a chef in the canteen at Grace Brothers. He goes on strike with the rest of the kitchen staff.

Warwick (Jimmy Mac) – Mr Harman's assistant, who compliments Mrs Slocombe on the quality of the food.

Mohammad (Mohammad Shamsi) – another of Mr Harman's assistants who praises the food, particularly the curry.

EPISODE 47

Mr Patel (Renu Setna) – works in Accounts. He instructs the staff in the new procedures for issuing the weekly wages.

The Long Sweater (Jeffrey Segal) – a customer who complains to Mr Humphries about his new jumper that has stretched to his knees.

Mrs Maxwell (Peggy Ann Clifford) – the wife of one of the directors, who returns a dress only to be insulted by Mrs Slocombe.

Amanda (Marcella Oppenheim) – a new girl in the restaurant, who is grateful to Mr Goldberg for getting her the job through his employment agency.

EPISODE 48

Ivy (Hilda Fenemore) – a cleaner.

EPISODE 49

Doctor (John D. Collins) – the doctor who arrives in a protective suit and confirms that Mr Humphries has contracted the rare marines' disease.

EPISODE 50

Tramp (Jack Haig) – a tramp who enters the store and makes a racket with his violin to earn a few pennies. Mr Humphries is feeling generous and donates 10p.

EPISODE 51

Man with Moustache (Michael Sharvell-Martin) – a man buying a funny £10 wig for a party.

Miss Hurst (Jennifer Guy) – a raver from Novelty Candles, who takes part in the beauty contest.

Miss Hepburn (Dawn Perllman) – an employee from Bathroom Fittings, who lives in Ilford and takes part in the beauty contest.

Miss Coleman (Denise Distel) – another contestant for the beauty contest. She works in Haberdashery and lives in Hatfield.

EPISODE 54

Mr Fortescue (Gorden Kaye) – the effeminate director, a friend of Mr Humphries, who directs the firm's advert.

Head Waiter & Second Waiter (Nicholas McArdle & John D. Collins) – staff who work at the restaurant where Lord Hirly plans to meet Miss Brahms.

Lord Hirly (John Oxley) – the man who is so infatuated with the deep, seductive voice he believes belongs to Miss Brahms that he invites her to dinner.

Rabbi (Marty Swift) – meets Mr Humphries at the restaurant.

Lady Customer (Margaret Clifton) – a woman who buys an extra strong bra with additional supports.

EPISODE 55

Old Man (Jack Haig) – dapperly-dressed man who is interested in dating Mrs Slocombe after spotting her advert in the 'lonely hearts' column – until seeing what she looks like.

Lady Customer (Brenda Cowling) – a customer who complains when her ribbed cardigan shrinks.

EPISODE 57

Mrs Peacock (Diana King) – Captain Peacock's wife.

Handsome Customer (Michael Sharvell-Martin) – a white-suited man who is attracted by Mrs Slocombe's perfume.

Military Customer (Rex Robinson) – a customer wanting a military tie.

EPISODE 58

'Tights' Customer (Frances Bennett) – a woman who buys twenty pairs of tights for her Italian holiday.

Woman (Gilda Perry) – Mr Humphries' next-door neighbour, who brings his Paddington Bear into the store when he rows with his mother.

Mr Wagstaff (Tony Sympson) – an employee attending Mr Humphries' Board of Enquiry only because Mr Harman, who gives the old man a lift to the bus stop, is involved.

EPISODE 59

Mr Walpole (Jess Conrad) – works in the sports department and joins Rumbold's floor when the rest of his department are hit with flu.

Fisherman (Ballard Berkeley) – a customer who wants some fishing equipment ready for the new trout season.

EPISODE 60

Truck Drivers (Nosher Powell & Ron Tarr) – lorry drivers who visit the store after hearing the advert on CB radio.

CB Voices (Vicki Michelle & Robbie Coltrane) – the people the staff make contact with on CB radio.

EPISODE 61

Mr Kayoto (Eiji Kusuhara) – Mr Yamoto's assistant who interprets for him during the visit to Grace Brothers.

Secretary at Number Ten (John D. Collins) – the secretary who shows the Grace Brothers staff through to a meeting room while they wait for the PM.

Fur Coat Customer (John Biggerstaff) – a customer who wants to spend £5000 on a fur coat for his secretary.

His Secretary (Lisa Anselmi) – called Miss Percival, she's the secretary who doesn't end up getting the fur coat she was expecting.

Mr Yamoto (Kristopher Kum) – A Japanese man who visits the store to consider whether it's worth buying.

Monkey (Rusty Goffe) – a runaway monkey from the Pet department.

Voice of Mrs Thatcher (Jan Ravens) – all you see is her arm, but the voice is supposed to be that of Maggie Thatcher at 10 Downing Street.

EPISODE 62

Mr Winston (Peter Cleall) – a writer for the staff magazine.

Customer (Norman Mitchell) – a customer who wants some Y-fronts.

EPISODE 63

Miss Featherstone (Joanna Dunham) – the bespectacled assistant from Toiletries, who takes over Mrs Slocombe's position until she's reinstated.

Customer (Elizabeth Stewart) – a customer who tries on lots of hats but leaves with the one she came in with.

EPISODE 64

Miss Bagnold (Maggie Henderson) – the woman from Accounts who fancies Captain Peacock.

Mrs Peacock (Diana Lambert) – Captain Peacock's wife, who storms into the shop when she hears of his supposed affair with Miss Bagnold.

EPISODE 65

The Burglars (Michael Attwell & Paul Humpoletz) – the villains who hold up the store during the stocktaking.

Policeman (Ian Collier) – the policeman who helps sort out the hold-up.

EPISODE 66

Customer (Harriet Reynolds) – a friend of one of the shareholders, who wants a hat for Ascot.

Seymour (Keith Hodiak) – Mr Harman's assistant.

EPISODE 67

Men in Cinema (Ray Gatenby & Ronnie Brody) – men in the audience at the cinema showing the Grace Brothers advert.

EPISODE 68

Mrs Peacock (Diana Lambert) – Captain Peacock's wife.

Mrs Rumbold (Jean Challis) – Mr Rumbold's wife.

Lady Customer (Carol Cleveland) – a customer who is interested in hats and brings her dreadful son, Cedric, with her.

Cedric (Felipe Izquierdo) – a brattish schoolboy who visits the store with his mother. He is celebrating his birthday and enjoys firing his water pistol into Captain Peacock and Mrs Slocombe's faces.

EPISODE 69

TV Presenter (Nick Ross) – the presenter on *Around London*, the show that features Mr Spooner singing his song.

Seymour (Keith Hodiak) – Mr Harman's assistant, who helps by taking a photo of Spooner and his backing group.

TV Director (Charles Nicklin) – the director of *Around London*.

Sam, the Director's Assistant (Suzy Aitchison) – the assistant on *Around London*.

Cleaners (Mary Bradley & Joan Dainty) – the cleaners who listen to Mr Spooner sing after the doors shut at the store.

The Stage Show

Venue: Winter Gardens Pavilion, Blackpool
Dates: June to October 1976
Written by Jeremy Lloyd and David Croft
Production supervised by David Croft
Directed by Roger Redfarn
Set and Costumes designed by Saxon Lucas

Starring: John Inman (Mr Humphries); Mollie Sugden (Mrs Slocombe); Frank Thornton (Captain Peacock); Wendy Richard (Miss Brahms); Nicholas Smith (Mr Rumbold); Michael Mundell (Mr Lucas); Larry Noble (Mr Grainger); Stuart Sherwin (Mr Mash and Carlos); Barbara Rosenblatt (the Lady Customer and Teresa); Petra Siniawski (the Nurse and Conchita) and Raymond Bowers (the Male Customer and Cesar)

The long, hot summer of 1976 marked a period in David Croft's life that couldn't have been sunnier. Not only was he enjoying the heat wave like everyone else in the country, he was also celebrating the success of not one, but two shows in the popular seaside resort of Blackpool. When *Are You Being Served?* began its successful run, the stage version of *Dad's Army* had recently opened at a nearby theatre.

His success was foreseen, albeit very late, by a fortune-teller whom David and Jeremy visited at the end of Blackpool pier. David remembers the day well. 'She told me the world hadn't yet given me the success I deserved, but that it was just around the corner – and there I was with two successful shows on at the same time. I told my wife about it. She asked whether I was wearing my old mackintosh at the time. When I told her I was, she said: "No wonder she thought you were struggling in life!"'

Co-writer Jeremy Lloyd remembers another amusing incident at Blackpool. One morning in their hotel, a crossed telephone line afforded Jeremy the ideal opportunity to pull a prank. 'David came through to my phone by mistake. It was about 10 a.m. and he was ordering eggs and bacon for his breakfast, so I pretended to be a member of the kitchen staff and shouted: "You're not welcome in this hotel if you're going to make these sorts of demands on the kitchen." He got very cross, it was hilarious,' laughs Jeremy.

The success of the television sitcom had triggered plenty of requests from companies wanting to produce a stage version of the show, but it was Bernard Delfont Limited that finally agreed terms with Lloyd and Croft. 'They commissioned us to write the show, which took as long as three TV episodes would have,' says David. 'Sadly, we had to reduce the cast because the budget wasn't substantial enough to pay for everyone.'

Soon after opening, *Are You Being Served?* was beating David Croft's other production, *Dad's Army,* hands down. 'Within a few days we'd taken more money than *Dad's Army* had in a whole week,' recalls David. 'Each morning there was a queue at the box-office, and as the days passed the queue got longer and longer. It was an enormous success.'

The local paper, *The Evening Gazette,* raved about the show. Reviewer Janet Graves wrote: 'The audience at last night's opening of *Are You Being Served?* ... were chuckling even before the curtain went up.' Graves was very impressed with the performance of John Inman. 'It's a show that began with a full house and will pack them in till the last curtain if Mr Humphries ("I'm free") has anything to do with it. From the moment he struts, stiff-legged and limp-wristed, on to the stage he has the audience screeching at his outrageous mannerisms.'

Tipping the production to become the town's top show of the season, Graves summed it up by saying: 'There are some downright hilarious moments in a show in which double entendres, the hidden meaning and the unsaid reign supreme.' She added: 'It is rude and crude certainly, but audiences have a fair idea of what they are in for if they have seen the television series.'

Even though it enjoyed a packed house for every performance, David failed in his attempt to put the show on for a second season. 'I had billing problems within the cast which I couldn't sort out. And the Delfonts had realized by this time that John Inman was so hot they didn't need anyone else; they could put a show on just with him and it would do good business – and that's what happened.'

Although the show's run wasn't extended, Jeremy was still amazed at its success. 'It was sold out before it even opened,' he says. 'I thought it was terrific, but very expensive and complicated as far as the sets were concerned. It was a big production; we even had tents on stage.'

Jeremy and David have received numerous offers to take the show to America, but the logistics have proved prohibitive. 'We were recently asked to put it on in San Francisco but the stage wasn't big enough,' says Jeremy. 'But if we could get the cast over there and find a venue big enough, I'm sure we'd fill the place many times over, it's that popular there.'

Directing the show in Blackpool was Roger Redfarn, who enjoyed every minute of it. 'My job was made easier by Jeremy and David delivering a very polished script,' he says. Roger was also impressed with the set. Not having to face the logistics headaches often associated with touring meant that the designers were able to construct a set that became one of the show's attractions. 'The designers did a wonderful job.'

Playing two roles in the show – a customer and Cesar, the revolutionary – was Raymond Bowers, who also appeared in the movie and several episodes of the television series. He has nothing but fond memories of his time at Blackpool. 'It was fantastic,' he enthuses. 'It was 1976, the year of the heat wave, which can often keep people away, and there were lots of good shows in Blackpool at the time, so we had plenty of competition. But our show was always chock-a-block.

'What I remember more than anything else was the laughter. The Winter Gardens is a big theatre, but the laughter was so loud and genuine that you felt you'd earned your money.'

Raymond, who worked for several years with John Inman, got on well with the other cast members, particularly Wendy Richard. 'On Sundays Wendy often had a leg of lamb. She doesn't like cold meat and would throw away anything spare. I told her of my love for cold meat, so whenever she had meat at the weekend, she'd bring in the leftovers on the Monday. It was wonderful in sandwiches and usually lasted the entire week. So I always associate Wendy Richard and me with cold legs of lamb!'

The Movie

First shown on British television on Monday, 22 December 1980. Transmitted on BBC1 between 9.55pm – 11.30pm.

THE CAST

Nat Cohen presents for EMI Film Distributors Ltd

Mollie Sugden	Mrs Slocombe
John Inman	Mr Humphries
Frank Thornton	Captain Peacock
Trevor Bannister	Mr Lucas

Also starring:

Wendy Richard	Miss Brahms
Arthur Brough	Mr Grainger
Nicholas Smith	Mr Rumbold
Harold Bennett	Young Mr Grace
Arthur English	Mr Harman

GUEST STARS

Andrew Sachs	Carlos
Karan David	Conchita
Glyn Houston	Cesar

With: Sheila Steafel, John G. Heller, Monica Grey, Jennifer Granville, Derek Griffiths, Nadim Sawalha and Penny Irving.

PRODUCTION CREDITS

Written by	Jeremy Lloyd and David Croft
Producer:	Andrew Mitchell
Director:	Bob Kellett
Executive Producers:	David Croft and Jeremy Lloyd
Director of Photography:	Jack Atcheler, BSC
Production Associate:	Richard Du Vivier
Production Manager:	John Wilcox
Art Director:	Bob Jones
Editor:	Al Gell
Assistant Director:	Vincent Winter
Continuity:	June Randall
Camera Operator:	Wally Byatt
Casting Director:	Weston Drury, Jnr.
Sound Recordist:	Bruce White
Assistant Art Director:	John Lagell
Set Decorator:	Harry Cordwell
Dubbing Editor:	Ian Fuller
Re-Recording Mixer:	Bill Rowe
Wardrobe Supervisor:	Ivy Baker
Make-Up:	Robin Grantham
Hairdressing:	Joan Carpenter

Made at EMI Studios, Elstree, London in 1977.

The staff of Grace Brothers head for the sun, courtesy of Young Mr Grace. While the store is closed for redecoration, everyone is offered a low-budget break. The ladies and menswear departments plump for the Don Bernardo Palace Hotel, on the Costa Plonka. Even before packing their bags, Mrs Slocombe has her heart set on Captain Peacock, particularly when she discovers his wife isn't coming; but Peacock, frosty towards Mrs Slocombe's advances, fancies his chances with the shapely Miss Brahms.

Before their departure there's another day's business to attend to, while Mrs Slocombe places her pussy in the safe hands of Grace Brothers' Pussy Hotel, selects her favourite snaps for her passport and is finally inoculated – in the rear!

On the Med temperatures hit the nineties, and checking in at the hotel meets with expected chaos, thanks to Carlos, the manager, getting confused as to why a booking for Grace Brothers can possibly include two females; but their problems deepen when it's discovered that rooms won't be available for another day, so there's no choice but for everyone to spend a night under canvas.

During the evening Carlos receives an unexpected visitor: his brother Cesar, a terrorist who has killed with his bare hands. He's planning a bloody revolution, but not before he has satisfied his immediate needs: a bed for the night, and a woman to share it – a role for which Carlos suggests Mrs Slocombe.

Meanwhile, in an attempt to woo Miss Brahms, Mr Lucas sends a saucy letter to her during dinner, only to see it accidentally end up in the hands of Mrs Slocombe, who wrongly believes its author is Captain Peacock. By the end of the evening, the much-travelled note has also left Peacock looking forward to a night of passion with Miss Brahms, and Mr Humphries expecting a visit from 'Sexy Y-fronts'!

The confusion continues when a large insect causes Miss Brahms, Mr Humphries and Mrs Slocombe to partake in tent-swapping, with the limp-wristed Mr Humphries receiving an unexpected visit from Cesar, mistaking him for the blue-rinsed Mrs Slocombe – certainly a holiday to remember!

When EMI approached David Croft and Jeremy Lloyd about making a big screen version of *Are You Being Served?,* they didn't have far to look for a story-line. 'We already had a good plot, thanks to the stage show,' says David Croft, 'so using that as the basis of the film seemed the logical thing to do, rather than develop a whole new scenario.'

The job of directing the film went to Bob Kellett, who had worked on numerous comedy pictures at Elstree Studios. 'At first the cast found it strange having someone intrude into their happy family,' says Bob. 'But they were a wonderful team and quickly got used to me as the director, particularly when they began realizing that working on a film requires a different discipline and I could help.'

Throughout the filming period, David Croft and Jeremy Lloyd were ever-present on the set, which Bob appreciated. 'I thought it was admirable because it can't have been much fun standing around watching, particularly as it was a *fait accompli:* the cast had already done the show on stage, so David and Jeremy knew how it would pan out.'

One thing Bob Kellett regrets is that the budget didn't stretch to a sunny Mediterranean location. 'Money was tight so we couldn't go abroad; all the exteriors – apart from a quick trip to Heathrow for the airport scenes – were shot on the set at Elstree. Everything had to be completed in six weeks; it was very frenetic getting it finished on time and within budget, but that's all part of the fun.'

The solitary day's filming at the airport made a welcome change from the confinement of the studio. John Inman remembers the day well. 'We borrowed the training plane, where they coached the cabin staff. It was a very windy day, so windy that my big white sun-hat had to be stuck to my head. I even had to keep it on during lunch because we were doing some reverse angle shots in the afternoon and it had to remain in the same position.'

During lunch, John and Mollie nipped across to the departure lounge for a quick drink. 'I was wearing this big white hat, fancy clothes and so much make-up, I couldn't believe it when a fella said: "Hello, John, are you going far?" He actually thought I was off on holiday – and dressed like that!'

Actor Frank Thornton also felt the film suffered under the tight budget. 'I didn't think it was very good; there wasn't enough money spent on it. In the film the characters had to sleep in tents because all the rooms were full, but when you see the dining-room or the reception desk, the place is empty – there could at least have been a few other visitors strolling around making it look less deserted.'

The 1970s was the decade when several popular TV shows were adapted for the movies, often with disappointing results. As many production companies found to their peril, small-screen popularity doesn't always translate to box-office success. Bob Kellett was well aware of this when he undertook the task of directing the *Are You Being Served?* movie.

'The British cinema was winding down so fast: audiences were falling and studios were closing because no one was investing money anymore. So as a last desperate fling to get people into cinemas, companies tried making films out of TV series. Many of them didn't work, but *Are You Being Served?* was good fun. It was made at the very end of this '70s whirl of TV spin-offs, and although it will never be regarded as a great movie, it was fairly successful.

'The artists missed the studio audience, though, partly because it's much more difficult timing the comedy without the reaction of the audience. But I was pleased with the results; it wasn't what you called mainstream movie-making because it was a stylized form of comedy – but there were lots of gags.'

John Inman was one of those who found it strange working without the audience. 'We'd rehearse a scene and the crew would howl with laughter, but then we'd do it for real and there was no reaction at all, complete silence. It was a weird experience.'

But despite the hectic schedules and lack of funds, Bob Kellett had a happy time on the film.

Except for a day at the airport, the film
was shot entirely in the studio.

He recalls one memorable scene involving John
Inman and an inflatable bra. 'John was dressed up
and being pursued by the villain, played by Glyn
Houston. The boobs were air-inflated, and there
was a lovely moment during rehearsals when one
grew bigger and bigger until it exploded and blew
John's wig off! If you rehearsed for ever you could
never catch that sort of moment again. It happened
unexpectedly and, of course, everybody collapsed in
laughter.'

Another incident occurred during the final
scenes, but this time it was something he'd rather
forget. 'Just as we were about to shoot, one of the
most important cameras started indicating we were
running out of film. It was the end of the afternoon
and everybody was waiting to go home. In those
days, you couldn't just arbitrarily say, "We'll all
work until we finish," so we had to quickly get on
with the filming. Reels of film were 400 feet and we
were at the end of the footage counter; we were
running on whatever extra, if any, was left on the
roll. Seconds after the scene finished, the film ran
out – it was a very fraught day.'

As well as the main cast, several guest stars
were called in. Playing Carlos, the hotel manager,
was Andrew Sachs, who had made his name as
everyone's favourite Spanish waiter, Manuel, in
Fawlty Towers. 'I'd just finished the first series
of *Fawlty Towers,* so I presume that's the reason
the casting director wanted me,' he says. 'Luckily,
the character was different from Manuel because he
was brighter and much more precise. It's the only
time I've accepted a part that's come right off the
back of another. I was rather green in those days
and thought it would be nice doing a film.'

Andrew, who nowadays avoids Spanish roles,
enjoyed working on the film. 'Everyone was so
friendly and I got on well with them all. But it's a
shame it was done so cheaply. We didn't get anywhere near Spain; it's silly doing a film like that with
such a restrictive budget. It's difficult transferring a
successful show from the small screen in your living-
room to a big screen in the cinema, and I don't think
the film worked very well. In fact, I don't know of a
TV show that's converted successfully to the cinema.'

David Croft, who wrote the script with Jeremy
Lloyd, was also disappointed with the outcome. 'It
was made entirely in a studio and it shows. It didn't
make much money, but if it had been handled differently, I believe it could have. I felt it was badly
distributed. But even though it wasn't terribly well
made, it was funny.'

As for Jeremy, he was interested to see the TV
series adapted for the cinema, even if the end product wasn't top-drawer material. 'When you're writing for a tightly-packed half-hour programme
everything is fine, but when the jokes are spread
thinly throughout a movie, it isn't the same.

'But it was moderately successful, even if it didn't
make us much money.' In their contracts, David
and Jeremy opted to take a cut of the profits rather
than a large initial fee; sadly, they haven't received a
penny since that original fee.

Useless Facts About
ARE YOU BEING SERVED?

This book would not be complete without some of those useless facts and statistics that do nothing to enrich one's life or liking for the show, but provide a moment of interest nonetheless.

As well as the customers who appeared on the credits and uttered some dialogue, there were others who strolled in and out without a murmur. Just how many ventured on to the shopfloor?

MRS SLOCOMBE'S HAIR COLOUR

Hair colour	*Number of times in the entire series*
Brown	● ● ● ●
Pink	● ● ● ● ● ● ●
Grey	● ● ● ● ● ● ● ●
Green	● ● ● ● ● ● ● ● ● ●
Purple	● ● ● ● ● ●
Mauve	● ● ● ● ● ● ●
Blue	● ● ● ● ● ● ● ● ●
Rust	● ● ●
Turquoise	● ●
Multi-coloured	● ●
Yellow	● ● ● ● ●
Fawn	●
Peach	● ● ●
Orange	● ● ● ●
Burgundy	●

The most frequently seen hair colour was green, followed by blue, with pink and grey tying for third place.

CUSTOMERS IN THE STORE

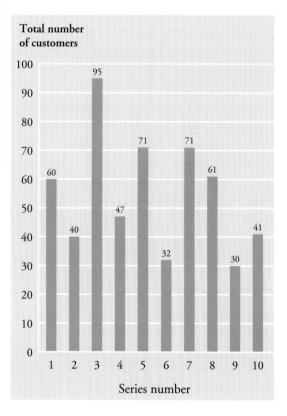

Total no. of customers in the entire ten series = 548
Average no. of customers per episode = 8

Are You Being Served?
AMERICA AND BEYOND

The history of British television is littered with home-grown shows which seem to suffer travel sickness. Although the shows achieve success in this country they don't travel well. What programmes foreign viewers will take to their hearts, and which ones they'll brush aside, is anyone's guess.

There's no secret formula for worldwide acceptance as far as the TV world is concerned. To prove the point, just consider the high regard the American public has for *Are You Being Served?* Who

Mr Humphries is brighter than ever thanks to his garishly-coloured suit.

would have thought that a British sitcom about an aged, traditionally-run department store would be welcomed so ardently across the Atlantic? After all, some critics classed the show as smutty, shallow, weak, over-packed with *double entendres*. But the popularity of *Are You Being Served?* in the United States is phenomenal.

One person who has experienced this mania at

first hand is former actress Elizabeth Reiss, née Lisa Anselmi, now a scriptwriter living in New York. She only appeared in one episode of *Are You Being Served?*, playing a secretary in 'Monkey Business', but is forever reminded of it.

'After many different theatre and TV roles, I'm known by friends and neighbours as "the girl who was in *Are You Being Served?*". It's that popular over here. If I show people my CV, two years in the West End means nothing; it's my role as the secretary that everyone's interested in.

'The show's popularity is quite incredible. I'm writing a show at the moment which we're trying to sell to Europe. People keep saying they don't know whether Europeans will like it. My answer is that if *Are You Being Served?* can cross the ocean and be as popular as it is over here, anything can happen.'

What Lisa finds interesting is that the show appeals to a broad spectrum of people from all walks of life. 'Friends who are stockbrokers, lawyers

With Royal visitors expected, Captain Peacock and Mrs Slocombe step into their regal shoes for a rehearsal.

and doctors, people I never thought would like it, watch it over and over. Part of the success must be that Jeremy and David got the formula right: it's very naïve and innocent in many respects. No one really hurts each other; although the characters insult one another, they all stick together.'

Television channels across the States, particularly PBS (Public Broadcasting System) stations, report a constant demand from viewers for repeats of Lloyd and Croft's classic. Many channels haven't taken it off the air for years. A spokeswoman for Dallas's KERA station said: 'It's hugely popular with our viewers. We're currently showing it at 10.30 p.m. on Saturday and 11 p.m. on Sunday – that's two prime slots for us.' The public enjoys the show so much; people regularly write to the TV station. 'Viewers are always saying how much they love the programme, as well as warning us not to take it off the air!'

Like the rest of the cast, most of John Inman's fan mail originates from the States. He can't believe how successful the show has been 'across the pond'. 'Before I found out for myself just how much the show means to the Americans, friends returning from there would phone saying that I was never off the television. By the time I holidayed in New York in 1988 the reaction was alarming. It had become so popular. I went to see a show at the theatre and was waiting in the foyer when suddenly all these people spotted me – I couldn't get away.'

Most summers John is invited by TV stations to tour American cities talking about the show. 'I call it my "Hello, folks!" tour. The crowds are amazing at these events. People are so nice over there, even the big fat ladies, who ask: "Hey, John, can I get a hug?" And then nearly squeeze you to death!'

People all over the globe have been able to sample *Are You Being Served?* As well as both sides of the Atlantic and Down Under, viewers as far afield as Hong Kong, Zimbabwe, Slovenia and Israel have tuned in to events at Grace Brothers. Even airlines, whisking their customers off to distant places, often screen the sitcom as part of the on-board entertainment.

However, Jeremy Lloyd isn't surprised that his creation is viewed with warm affection around the world. 'It has universal appeal,' he says, 'because most people have been inside a shop and can, therefore, relate to it. The only place it hasn't reached yet, as far as I know, is India; I think they'd love it because it's a country that still has that sort of pecking order.'

In Australia the original episodes were so well received that in 1979 Jeremy Lloyd and David Croft were approached by a television company wanting to make its own version of *Are You Being Served?* As part of the deal, John Inman was required to step back into the shoes of Mr Humphries, a challenge he relished. 'I had a smashing time. It wasn't as good as the original, but it was wonderful being there. I went on to do my own stage show and would happily go again, even for a holiday.'

David Croft was planning to travel to Australia himself, but when other commitments prevented him doing so, Jeremy Lloyd and director Bob Spiers travelled instead. With the help of Jim Burnett, Jeremy adapted many of his original scripts for the Australian market. 'It was new territory as far as the show was concerned,' he admits. 'John Inman was the linchpin of the new show; although they wanted Australian actors for the rest of the characters, John playing Mr Humphries was vital.'

The plot centred on Humphries arriving in Australia to work in Mr Bone's department store, where the faces are not dissimilar to those left behind at Grace Brothers. Two series were transmitted in 1980 and 1981, and the show was a success as far as the Australian market was concerned, although it didn't travel out of the country.

Working on the Australian version wasn't a particularly joyous time for Jeremy. 'I didn't find it an easy job,' he admits. 'I think some people involved resented an English writer working over there on the show; I felt one or two of the actors were put out. I'd hear words like "bloody pom!" occasionally.'

The success in America happened later in the

show's life and continues to amaze Jeremy and David. It took time and a lot of effort before *Are You Being Served?* was released on the American networks. 'Aware that other British shows were being shown in the States, we'd been pressing the BBC for ages to sell *Are You Being Served?*,' says Jeremy, 'and eventually they were successful.'

The show made a quiet entrance on to the Amer-

ican screen, taking a while to catch the audience's attention, as Jeremy confirms. 'It started slowly, with only one or two stations persuaded to take it, but then snowballed and before long it was being shown all over the country and everybody was talking about it. An example of its popularity today is that members of the cast are still flown over to make TV appearances. There are even Mrs Slocombe look-alike contests, with people turning up with stuffed cats – it's incredible!'

As in Australia, the Americans were keen to film their own version of the show, and a pilot entitled *Beans of Boston* was recorded in 1979. Sadly, it flopped and was never picked up by a television channel. Jeremy Lloyd feels there were several reasons. 'A lot of writers were involved in the production, all of whom had a bit to say,' he says.

Fundamental changes were also made to the structure of the characters, on which the British

success had been founded. 'It was decided that the old man should be younger and Miss Brahms in love with the Mr Lucas character – it didn't work.'

Jeremy Lloyd was nearly cast as Captain Peacock. When John Hillerman didn't turn up for a read-through, producer Gary Marshall asked Jeremy, who obviously knew the character inside out, to step in. 'I did a very good imitation of Peacock and was offered the part on the spot,' he enthuses. 'I would love to have done it, but David didn't think it was a good idea; so I was offered a part in *Happy Days* instead, which I couldn't do because it wasn't for another 21 weeks.'

Although the show didn't take off, Jeremy had an unforgettable time in the States. 'It was wonderful,' he says. 'We interviewed all sorts of people for the parts, including one of the Ritz Brothers for Young Mr Grace, and Robin Williams for the Mr Lucas character, in the days when he was looking for work. He was a remarkable character but we couldn't fit him in.

'It was a lovely time, what with our suites at a top hotel and meeting at the pool-side to discuss story-lines in the event that the show took off. But, alas, it didn't – it's very hard beating the original.'

LEFT Young Mr Grace's first nurse was Patricia Astley, who gave up acting and modelling to move back to Blackpool, where she was born. BELOW When everyone is summoned to the boardroom in episode 29, they discover that a change is as good as a rest!

LETTER FROM AMERICA

I can still remember the excitement I felt when my agent first told me that I'd got a small part in 'Monkey Business', an episode of *Are You Being Served?* ('Small part' – who am I kidding? I was Miss Percival, the mistress who ended up without the fur coat! I only had two lines, but delivered extremely well!) It was my first professional acting job.

One of the reasons for the show's great success was the way David and Jeremy assembled a cast similar to a company at a repertory theatre – actors who would work together on a daily basis with a different script every week. Part of the show's magic came from the fact that the actors had a great deal of theatrical experience. By working together every week they could develop their characters to perfection. At the same time, the director and cameramen learned when to capture Mollie Sugden pursing her lips or John Inman raising an eyebrow. Of course, when you hand talented actors wonderfully creative scripts, you have a winning combination. I was very lucky to work with such a gifted company.

Leaving my acting career in England behind, I married an American and moved to Washington, DC, a city full of actors, drama and high-profile performances. I was reintroduced to *Are You Being Served?* after trying, and failing, one day to entertain my two small children by simulating a marching band around the kitchen wearing a saucepan on my head and banging two lids together. While recovering from my headache, I turned on the television and was greeted by Mollie Sugden's blue hairdo! My children loved it! You have to remember that the show was competing with *Barney* and *Sesame Street*, so I realized that *Are You Being Served?* is truly family entertainment.

This is why the show is so wildly successful in the United States. First, it is suitable for the entire family. It depicts a collection of warm-hearted, if slightly eccentric, people who form their own sort of family. They share their pet peeves, oddities and whimsies with each other, alternately soothing and irritating each other. But we are in no doubt that under all the office politics, they truly care about each other. It is the sort of place we would all like to work.

Also, they are not above poking fun at each other. Indeed, one of David and Jeremy's great insights into human nature was how each person's foibles – from Captain Peacock's haughtiness to Mr Humphries' vanity to Mr Grace's innocuous skirt-chasing – make the character *more*, not less, appealing. And not least, especially for an American audience, any Mollie Sugden reference to her 'cat' is a sure-fire way to get a laugh!

Happy 25th birthday to *Are You Being Served?*!

LISA ANSELMI
New York, 1998

Grace and Favour

When fans of *Are You Being Served?* waved goodbye to their beloved sitcom in 1985, no one could have dreamt that the cast would resurface seven years later in *Grace and Favour*. For Jeremy Lloyd and David Croft, however, it was always an intention to retain the characters but change the setting. 'We never wanted to lose the cast,' David explains. 'Their time had expired as far as the store was concerned – there was no more we could do in that set. In fact, we probably did about two series too many. We always had it in our minds to do something with them again and, with no Young Mr Grace, the idea for *Grace and Favour* was an obvious development.'

Within the rustic setting of Gloucestershire, the cast rekindled their friendship, and with the injection of some new blood, Croft and Lloyd's latest comic creation began. Whereas *Are You Being Served?* had been a series, *Grace and Favour* was written as a serial, with story-lines overlapping into subsequent episodes. 'The trend for sitcoms was heading that way; if you had a group of people there was bound to

be a serial element in the story,' says David. 'Even with *Are You Being Served?*, although one couldn't regard that as a serial, there was always a hangover from previous episodes; it was inevitable.'

David Croft can be regarded as the doyen of British sitcoms: he's written or been involved in many of the country's top shows, but rates *Grace and Favour* as one of his favourites, even though it only ran for two seasons. 'I liked it very much,' he says. 'One of the aspects I enjoyed was being able to develop Mr Humphries: no sooner had he moved to the country house than he found a girl who was not only mad about him, but kept nipping into his bed.'

The country home that doubled as Millstone Manor was Chavenage House, an Elizabethan property near Tetbury, Gloucestershire. David Lowsley-Williams, who owns the house, was over the moon when the BBC picked his property as the setting for the sitcom, although it wasn't the first time it had been chosen for location filming. The house and its grounds have been used for *The House of Eliott, Casualty, The Comedy of Errors* and other productions. 'It was great fun having the crew and cast around. They were all very nice. Wendy Richard even bought a puppy from the daughter of a woman working here.'

David Lowsley-Williams recalls meeting Fleur Bennett, who played Mavis Moulterd in the show. 'I heard the doorbell go one day, and there was Fleur Bennett covered in manure. She had just filmed a scene and asked whether she could have a shower, and I agreed. Then she looked down at herself and said: "I can't come through the house covered in all this muck, so if you look the other way I'll strip off and run up to your shower." And that's what she did.'

Fleur remembers the scene well. 'The dresses I wore were all period, and the costume department couldn't find material to match the print; there wasn't enough time to make another dress, so I ended up with just one. We did the scene twice, with me falling back into what was supposed to be

cows' muck, and afterwards I rushed off to have a shower. The stuff was everywhere: up my nostrils, in my eyelashes – so having a wash was ery welcome.'

David also remembers an incident involving Mollie Sugden that later resurfaced on *It'll Be Alright on the Night*. 'Mollie was given a leg up by John Inman into a little pony trap, and she sat

Confiding in Mavis about his dreadful childhood brings tears to Mr Humphries' eyes.

down rather heavily, breaking the seat of the trap. She fell over backwards with her skirt and legs everywhere, frightening the little pony in front, who galloped off with Mollie still in the trap!'

Grace and Favour concentrated on the characters' lives post-Young Mr Grace, who bit the dust while scuba diving with his nurse Miss Lovelock. When her bikini top popped off, so did the ancient owner of Grace Brothers department store.

Mr Grace left most of his fortune to his favourite charity, a home for fallen women, while investing the company's pension contributions in some dodgy enterprises. He also bought property, and as the staff of the Ladies' and Gentlemen's Ready-to-Wear departments were the sole survivors on the final day of the closing-down sale, they were made beneficiaries of the pension fund and allowed to use Millstone

ABOVE Discovering the remains of an 18th century cat in the attic brings a run of bad luck to the staff at Millstone Manor.

OPPOSITE Sharing his bed with friendly Mavis (Fleur Bennett) was never on the agenda when Mr Humphries moved to the country!

Manor for their own purposes. But there was one drawback: Mr Rumbold was running the place as manager, a welcome distraction for him since his wife ran off with Mr Prentice of Tools and Hardware.

All the actors enjoyed reuniting for the show, especially as it involved location shooting. Nicholas Smith was looking forward to working with the cast again, but wondered whether the professional rapport they'd built up during the years at Grace Brothers would automatically click into being. 'As soon as we read the first script and started rehearsals it was as though we'd recorded the last *Are You Being Served?* the day before – it was extraordinary.'

Nicholas even felt *Grace and Favour* was better than *Are You Being Served?* 'We were given a larger budget, and consequently could afford to go on location; this gave it an additional dimension with lovely farmyard and country scenes – it wasn't restricted like *Are You Being Served?*

'Another reason I preferred *Grace and Favour* was that the scripts contained a little pathos and realism.

There's a lovely scene when Mr Humphries explains what a ghastly childhood he's had. Admittedly, the scene is quickly brought back to comedy, as it must be, but that element of sadness worked well.'

The change of setting also opened up the scope for costumes, something else Nicholas liked. 'In *Are You Being Served?* there was little opportunity to appear in anything but work clothes, while in *Grace and Favour* the characters were also seen in their off-duty outfits.'

Producer Mike Stephens, who'd previously worked with David Croft on a series of *Hi-De-Hi!*, and with Jeremy Lloyd on *'Allo, 'Allo* felt the locations brought a freshness to the production. 'The world they were living in was totally unreal: it was an idyll that couldn't really exist, but it was a warm, sunny, cosy world that audiences liked. The locations afforded the chance for more practical humour, and broadened the horizons as far as the production was concerned.' Mike had great fun making the show. 'It was terrific,' he enthuses.

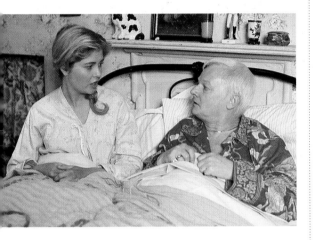

The introduction of some new faces was also welcomed by everyone involved in the show. 'Fleur Bennett was excellent,' says Nicholas Smith, 'and Billy Burden and Joanne Heywood were very good as well.'

Fleur, who played country-girl Mavis Moulterd, was excited to be offered the part, particularly as she'd watched *Are You Being Served?* as a child. 'It was an institution in my family, and we watched it for years,' she says. 'Every week my family visited my great grandmother, and after tea we'd watch *Are You Being Served?* before going home to bed.'

She remembers her audition well: with the character of Mavis being described as buxom, Fleur was determined to match the requirements. 'I decided to wear a padded bra,' she smiles, 'and I remember thinking: "Oh well, that's as buxom as you're going to get."'

Fleur must have impressed at the audition, because she was invited back for a second interview, and was asked to read another scene. 'It was where Mavis shared Mr Humphries' bed for the first time,' she says. 'I was sitting in the chair, so I said the lines and turned around in the chair as if I was in bed. Jeremy Lloyd then threw his glasses down on to the table, and this apparently – so he told me afterwards – was the sign that I was right for the part. When I was offered the job I nearly fell off the chair, I was so excited.'

In her early twenties when she joined the cast, Fleur felt at home playing Mavis – who was a perfect foil for John Inman – and found it easy adopting the country accent, having been brought up in Cornwall. 'I had to change some of the vowels because my father in the show, played by the lovely Billy Burden, came from Tiverton. But it worked well.' Billy died in 1994, while Fleur was holidaying in the Maldives. She'll never forget receiving a worrying phone message. 'I was on an island in the middle of nowhere and got this message saying: "Call Wendy Richard urgently." She broke the sad news to me. Billy and I were very close; I couldn't believe it when I heard he'd died.'

Fleur found the cast good to work with, particularly John Inman. 'He was very giving, and would always offer advice on how I could play the part better – it was a good learning ground for me.'

Just like its older relation, *Grace and Favour* is popular in the States, and she receives letters every week from American fans. 'I get a lot of books sent to me about baking bread!' she laughs. 'Because Mavis was always in the kitchen cooking, people feel I might find a copy useful.' She also receives more unusual presents and requests. 'Somebody sent me a pair of knickers, I don't know why, and another person sent a lock of their hair and wanted a lock in exchange – it's quite funny, really.'

Another addition to the team was Joanne Heywood, who'd worked for producer Mike Stephens in the series *First of the Summer Wine* and an episode of *The Brittas Empire*. Playing Jessica Lovelock in *Grace and Favour*, she was the glamorous nurse whose bikini mishap brought on the death of Young Mr Grace.

Joanne Heywood, who played the glamorous Miss Lovelock, had great fun appearing in *Grace and Favour*.

'*Grace and Favour* was great fun, and I enjoyed working for Mike again,' says Joanne, who learnt how to ride a horse for the show. 'I hadn't ridden a horse before, so I needed a few lessons beforehand; thankfully, the production crew made me look more competent than I was.' The character was also keen on motorbikes, but a stunt double stepped in for any scenes involving the bike. 'It was too heavy for me on my own,' Joanne explains.

It was Jeremy Lloyd who suggested the title *Grace and Favour*, but David Croft wasn't so enthusiastic. 'I didn't want the show to be called that,' he says. 'I tried to get it altered to *Are You Being Served? Still!* or *Are You Being Served? Again!,* which is what it was called in America, but to no avail.'

But both writers enjoyed working together again. 'Everyone was happy returning to their characters,' says Jeremy, 'and we had great fun. David and I thought the two series were good, and many viewers felt the same way, but the BBC didn't pick us up for another run. We were all disappointed.'

David was very surprised a further season wasn't commissioned. 'We offered to do more, but it was the beginning of a new era in sitcoms and, in my view, the BBC was against the popular *Carry On* element that existed in *Are You Being Served?* and obviously carried over into *Grace and Favour*.'

Producer Mike Stephens agrees with David. 'Without being snobbish, *Are You Being Served?* and *Grace and Favour* contain a very working-class style of humour: an ordinary, accessible *Carry On* style and, possibly, the BBC wanted more alternative comedy than anything else – it's all about fashions. But I think the public are yearning for something like it again.'

The success of recent *Are You Being Served?* repeats has astonished everyone, including the BBC, and David Croft believes *Grace and Favour* could be just as successful. 'I think we could see it repeated in the future, and I'm confident it would be another big hit.'

New Faces

FLEUR BENNETT

Born in St Ives, Cornwall, Fleur – who played the attractive Mavis Moulterd – completed her A-levels and joined drama school. After graduating she travelled to Frinton and gained valuable experience in weekly rep. She'd only been out of drama school nine months when offered the role in *Grace and Favour*.

Since playing Mavis, Fleur has appeared on television as a maid in BBC's *The Prisoner*, Melanie in *Nelson's Column*, Nina in an episode of *Cracker*, *The Bill*, a TV reporter in *Animal Ark* and Laura Forester in the television film *The Rag Nymph*.

She has also been busy in the theatre, her most recent role being Daphne Stillington in *Present Laughter* with Peter Bowles. Her other credits include Bianca in *The Taming of the Shrew* and Phyllis in *Mrs Cinders*

Fleur, whose interests include horse riding and motorbikes, divides her time between London and St Ives, where her parents still live.

BILLY BURDEN

Billy was a comedian and actor, who spent most of his career in variety. Born in Dorset in 1914, he spent much of his fifty-year career playing straw-hatted country yokels, and built up a loyal following who never tired of his comic style.

He began his career as an amateur before turning professional and appearing regularly at summer schools and in pantomimes. Preferring to work in the South of England, where he knew his audience, he was hugely successful in his own shows, regularly topping the bill on the Moss Empires circuit. He also spent more than a decade as a special guest in Clarkson Rose's legendary revue at Eastbourne. Although he was not a regular on television, his credits include appearances in *Oh Happy Band!* and a play, *The Children of Dynmouth*. He also appeared in Cannon and Ball's 1983 film, *Boys in Blue*.

Billy, who was loved and respected in the profession, died of a heart attack in 1994, aged 79.

JOANNE HEYWOOD

Born in York, Joanne attended drama school at Guildford, having already completed a business studies course. After graduating in 1986, she embarked on a very busy two-year period: she appeared in an episode of *Brush Strokes,* a musical in Sheffield, *High Society* at the Haymarket in Leicester and for a year in London, before the first series of *First of the Summer Wine*.

Since *Grace and Favour*, Joanne has appeared in several shows, including *Artrageous,* a children's art show for BBC, two episodes of *Coronation Street,* as a parachute instructor, *The New Statesman* and an episode of *The Prince Among Men*. In between acting jobs, Joanne, whose hobbies include dancing, works for a temping agency as a secretary.

MICHAEL BILTON

Michael – who appeared as the antiquated solicitor, Mr Thorpe – was born in Yorkshire. A well-loved jobbing actor, he turned professional after the Second World War and spent his early career in rep. He made several film appearances, but was busiest on television, appearing in a lot of comedy shows, including *The Fall and Rise of Reginald Perrin,* as a customer, *Waiting for God,* as Basil, and *To the Manor Born,* as Ned the gardener. Michael was also the gardener in the popular Yellow Pages advert.

Michael – who enjoyed playing the stock market – suffered from arthritis but never let it affect the work he loved. He was busy working until his death from cancer.

SHIRLEY CHERITON

Shirley appeared in four episodes as Miss Prescott, Mr Thorpe's secretary. Born in London, she trained at the Italia Conti stage school before building a successful career for herself, largely on the small screen. She is best remembered by many for playing nurse Katy Betts in *Angels* and Debbie Wilkins in *EastEnders,* but her TV credits also include *Crown Court, Within These Walls, The Cuckoo Waltz, Z Cars, Bless This House, General Hospital* and *Three Up, Two Down*.

Episode Guide

PRODUCTION TEAM

(Unless otherwise stated, members of the production team worked on both seasons.)

SCRIPTS: Jeremy Lloyd and David Croft

TITLE MUSIC: Roy Moore and David Croft

COSTUME DESIGNER: Mary Husband (season 1, episode 1, & season 2); Carol Lawrence (season 1, except episode 1)

MAKE-UP DESIGNER: Denise Baron (season 1, episode 1); Pauline Cox (season 1, except episode 1, & season 2)

GRAPHIC DESIGNER: Everol McKenzie (season 1, episode 1); Joanna Cheese (season 1, except episode 1, & season 2)

CAMERA SUPERVISOR: Ken Major

RESOURCE CO-ORDINATOR: Steve Lowry

VISION MIXER: Hilary Briegel (season 1, except episode 6, & season 2, episode 5); Anne Stanley (season 1, episode 6, & season 2, except episodes 5 & 6); Hilary West (season 2, episode 6)

PROPERTIES BUYER: Jeffrey Witts (season 1, episode 1); Amanda George (season 1, except episode 1, & season 2)

PRODUCTION ASSISTANTS: Margaret Hulse and Frances Mable (season 1, episode 1); Christine Gernon (season 1, except episode 1); Christine Gernon and Antonia Rae (season 2)

ASSISTANT FLOOR MANAGER: Simone Dawson (season 1, episode 1); Simon Foster (season 1, except episode 1); Paul Hastings (season 2)

SOUND SUPERVISOR: Graham Wilkinson (season 1); Mike Felton (season 2)

VIDEOTAPE EDITOR: Roger Martin

PRODUCTION MANAGER: George R. Clarke (season 1, episode 1); Peter R. Lovell & Amita Lochab (season 1, except episode 1); Amita Lochab (season 2)

LIGHTING DIRECTOR: Harry Bradley

DESIGNER: Stephan Paczai (season 1, episode 1); Richard Dupre & Stephan Paczai (season 1, except episode 1); Richard Dupre (season 2)

PRODUCER & DIRECTOR: Mike Stephens

REGULAR CAST (SEASONS 1 & 2)

Mrs Slocombe	Mollie Sugden
Captain Peacock	Frank Thornton
Mr Humphries	John Inman
Miss Brahms.	Wendy Richard
Mr Rumbold	Nicholas Smith
Miss Lovelock	Joanne Heywood
Maurice Moulterd	Billy Burden
Mavis Moulterd	Fleur Bennett

SEASON ONE

EPISODE 1

(Transmitted: Fri. 10/1/92, BBC1, 8pm)

ALSO APPEARING:

Miss Prescott	Shirley Cheriton
Mr Thorpe	Michael Bilton
Secretary	Penny Gonshaw

The staff return from Young Mr Grace's funeral to discover they are beneficiaries of the company's pension scheme. Mr Grace invested the funds in some suspect business ven-

tures in far-off places such as Rangoon and the Falklands. He also invested in bricks and mortar, and as beneficiaries they're entitled to use Millstone Manor, a Tudor manor house which is being run as a country hotel. But to everyone's chagrin Mr Rumbold is the incumbent manager.

Their arrival in the country is met by the news that, except for country yokel Mr Moulterd and his daughter, the staff have been frightened off by Rumbold's infamous man-management skills. There's also a surprise in store for Mr Humphries when he finds a girl in his bed!

EPISODE 2
(Transmitted: Fri. 17/1/92, BBC1, 8pm)
ALSO APPEARING:
Miss Prescott ....Shirley Cheriton
Mr Thorpe...Michael Bilton
Joseph Lee ....Andrew Joseph
Fox Hunter ....Martyn Townsend

Deciding to continue running Millstone Manor as a country hotel, everyone settles into their new abode. While Mr Humphries tries stoking the boiler, Mrs Slocombe is thrown in jail for stealing a gypsy's cart and Captain Peacock is caught speeding. But country life is doing wonders for Mr Humphries: as well as lighting Mavis's fire, he practises his massaging skills on Miss Lovelock.

EPISODE 3
(Transmitted: Fri. 24/1/92, BBC1, 8pm)
ALSO APPEARING:
Miss Prescott ....Shirley Cheriton
Mr Thorpe...Michael Bilton
Usher...Roger Winslett
Clerk...James Walker
Sir Robert..Eric Dodson
Lady Magistrate ....Diane Holland
Police Inspector ....Geoffrey Greenhill
Joseph Lee ....Andrew Joseph

It's the day of Mrs Slocombe's court case. Arriving at court in style, on the back of Mr Moulterd's pig cart, no one gains much confidence from their solicitor, Mr Thorpe, who suggests Mrs Slocombe pleads guilty. But she has other ideas, even though her case isn't helped when star witness Captain Peacock sends the magistrate to sleep with his waffle. But Mr Moulterd saves the day and gets Mrs Slocombe off the hook.

EPISODE 4
(Transmitted: Fri. 31/1/92, BBC1, 8pm)
ALSO APPEARING:
Gypsy ....Andrew Joseph
Car Driver ....Jeremy Lloyd
Mrs Cleghampton..................................Maggie Holland
Mr Volpone ....Gordon Peters
Mr Frobisher..Gregory Cox

Mavis is making a new man of Mr Humphries, who seems to have acquired a zest for life since moving to the country. The first booking is also received: a group of Americans are touring England's old ruins and will arrive at the weekend; but there's still a lack of staff. Finally some applications arrive for the vacant jobs at the Manor, but no one's up to scratch, so it looks as if Peacock and Co. will have to roll their sleeves up and run the hotel themselves.

EPISODE 5
(Transmitted: Fri. 7/2/92, BBC1, 8pm)
ALSO APPEARING:
Mr Frobisher..Gregory Cox
Mr Maxwell...Paul Cooper

With a photographer arriving at 6 p.m. to take a staff photo for the Manor's new brochure, there's a major problem to resolve: where to get the staff. As a last resort, Captain Peacock becomes the waiter and Mr Humphries dons the barman's jacket, while Mrs Slocombe and Miss Brahms are forced into becoming chambermaids.

EPISODE 6
(Transmitted: Fri. 14/2/92, BBC1, 8pm)
ALSO APPEARING:
Mr Frobisher..Gregory Cox

The Americans arrive and the staff try their best in their new roles, although Miss Brahms burns the omelettes and Mr Rumbold, who is temporarily demoted to porter, doesn't have enough newspapers to go round. But there are no major catastrophes and everything ticks along until the staff discover to their horror that the agreed itinerary entails a church service and a Harvest Thanksgiving dance.

SEASON TWO

EPISODE 1
(Transmitted: Mon. 4/1/93, BBC1, 8pm)
ALSO APPEARING:
Riot Policeman ....Steve Whyment
Inspector ....Roger Sloman
Sergeant..Richard Lumsden
Colin ....Steve Edwin

With the Americans gone – but their chewing gum left behind and causing problems for Mrs Slocombe's pussy and Mr Rumbold's foot – life continues as normal at Millstone Manor. Mavis is besotted with Mr Humphries, which begins to worry the rest of the staff.

But any concerns pale when a pistol is discovered in the bureau drawer and the police are called. With Royal neighbours living just over the hill, the local constabulary take the matter seriously, especially when they believe Captain Peacock is a terrorist brandishing a loaded gun.

EPISODE 2

(Transmitted: Mon. 11/1/93, BBC1, 8pm)
ALSO APPEARING:
Mr Lubitch ....Leonard Lowe
Celia Littlewood ....Diane Holland
Mr Thorpe...Michael Bilton
Miss Prescott ....Shirley Cheriton
Jessie ....Joe Hobbs
Malcolm Heathcliff ....Andrew Barclay
Sir Robert...Eric Dodson

Mr Rumbold, wearing his manager's hat again, and Captain Peacock are still rubbing each other up the wrong way – but what's new? As another group of tourists departs, an invitation to form a team for the local cricket match arrives. As expected, Rumbold takes charge by appointing himself captain, picking the team, and opening the batting himself. It's a glorious day for Millstone Manor, with victory sealed when Mr Humphries hits the winning runs.

EPISODE 3

(Transmitted: Mon. 18/1/93, BBC1, 8pm)
ALSO APPEARING:
Cecil Slocombe ....Donald Morley

The guests are just as sparse as the customers were at Grace Brothers. But there's one unwanted visitor to the Manor: Cecil Slocombe, Mrs Slocombe's ex-husband, who now runs his own leisure company. It's 42 years since he slipped out to buy some butter at Sainsbury's and was never seen again, and Mrs Slocombe doesn't want to see him now. When it transpires that he's a prospective buyer of Millstone Manor, the staff set out to put him off.

EPISODE 4

(Transmitted: Mon. 25/1/93, BBC1, 8pm)
ALSO APPEARING:
Museum Attendant..Roger Avon
Museum Curator ....Patrick Fyffe

While repairing the attic, Captain Peacock and Miss Lovelock discover the remains of an eighteenth-century cat behind a wall, and decide to donate the petrified pussy to the local museum. But the staff of the Manor soon rue their decision when Maurice Moulterd reminds them of the local saying: 'Take a cat from the wall, bad luck shall befall'. When the cow dries up, the cistern nearly falls on Rumbold's head and lemon foam oozes from the oven, it's time to return the cat to its resting place.

EPISODE 5

(Transmitted: Mon. 1/2/93, BBC1, 8pm)
ALSO APPEARING:
Malcolm Heathcliff ....Andrew Barclay
Henry Heathcliff ....Paul Humpoletz
Policeman...Nick Scott
Landlord ....Colin Edwynn

When Rumbold takes issue with Peacock for constantly undermining his authority, it's decided that the Manor should be run more democratically, with everyone involved in the decision making. The staff receive a challenge from the local pub to a darts match; tempers boil over when Mavis's ex-boyfriend, Malcolm, confronts Mr Humphries and a scuffle ensues; but Mrs Slocombe is the hero of the day, flattening the local bully.

EPISODE 6

(Transmitted: Mon. 8/2/93, BBC1, 8pm)
ALSO APPEARING:
Malcolm Heathcliff ....Andrew Barclay
Mr Thorpe...Michael Bilton
Mrs Cleghampton....................................Maggie Holland
Miss Long Wee ....Akemi Otani

The staff at Millstone Manor have to scrimp and save. Since a party from Outer Mongolia booked for a cultural visit, their country's currency has nose-dived, leaving the staff with no alternative but to cut costs. When it comes to offering a display of British culture, Mrs Slocombe and Captain Peacock perform an extract from an operetta, Miss Brahms recites Shakespeare, while Mr Humphries and Miss Lovelock plump for Romeo and Juliet.

Glossary

advert
commercial

annual do
a party that takes place every year

ASM
Assistant Stage Manager

BAFTA
an award given by the British
Academy of Film and Television Arts

Beeb
another name for the BBC
(British Broadcasting Corporation)

biscuits
cookies

bitch
female dog

block of flats
apartment building

boot
throw

bowls
a game where large wooden balls are
rolled towards a small ball to try to
bring them as near to it as possible

brimming a hat
where a customer's hat is exposed to
steam and a shop assistant runs their
wrist over one side of it to get a
rakish curl on the brim

call-boy
someone who summoned actors
from their dressing-rooms in time
for them to appear on stage

candy-floss
cotton-candy

cardigan
a sweater that opens down the front

Carry-On films
a series of popular comedy films made
in England that were packed with
double-entendres and bawdy jokes

chock-a-block
chock-full

civvy street
refers to ordinary life and work which
is not connected with the armed forces

cockney
a person who comes from London,
particularly the East End of the city

demob
when a person is discharged from
the armed forces

drawers
can be used to mean underwear, but
also part of a desk, or other piece of
furniture, which can be pulled out
so that you can put things in it

dressing gown
bathrobe

electric fire
electric heater

ENSA
Entertainments National Service
Association (an organization during
the war that provided entertainment
for the troops at home and abroad)

estate agent
real estate agent

FA Cup
the Football Association Cup,
a soccer tournament

fancies
likes

fire brigade
an organization which has the job
of putting out fires

fish and chip shop
a shop where you can buy fish and
chips (sliced potatoes) to take away
and eat

frock
dress

general drapery
a business that sells cloth and goods
made from cloth

Harrow Road style
a style that represents a less upmarket
type of store, associated with shops
in the suburbs

holiday gear
clothes taken on holiday

jumper
sweater

junket
a sweet dessert food made
with milk and rennet

keen
enthusiastic

kisser
the face

knickers
underwear

labour exchange
a place where people out of work
register and look for jobs

LAMDA
London Academy of Music
and Dramatic Art

lift
elevator

lift boy/girl
a person who operates the lift
in shops, offices, etc.

lift gate
a gate that is closed on an elevator
as a safety precaution

loo
toilet

lorry
truck

mates
pals

moggie
an informal word for cat

muck in
help out

national service
compulsory service in the armed
forces, no longer in existance in
Britain

navvy
a person who is employed to do hard
physical work

nursery
a place where children can be looked
after while their parents are at work,
shopping, etc.

OAP
old age pensioner

on holiday
on vacation

palmist
palm reader

panto/pantomime
a funny musical play for children,
that is usually based on a fairy tale
and normally performed at
Christmas

pantomime dame
female character in a pantomime,
traditionally played by a man

pants
underwear

perks
something extra you might receive

pinch
steal

PM
the Prime Minister

poof
an offensive word used to describe an
effeminate man especially a male
homosexual

prams
strollers

Punch and Judy
a comic puppet show for children,
in which Punch, a small, hook-nosed
puppet, fights with his wife Judy.
These shows are normally performed
at fairs or at the seaside

puddings
desserts

queue
line

RADA
Royal Academy of Dramatic Art
(a drama school in London)

regimental tie
an identifiable tie worn by members
of a particular regiment in the British
army

REME
Royal Electrical and Mechanical
Engineers, part of the British army

RSC
Royal Shakespeare Company

scent
perfume

sherbet
a fruit-flavoured powder

silly ass
a fool

sister
a senior nurse

situations vacant
a section in a newspaper where jobs
are advertised

spiv
a man who lives by his wits, without
doing any honest work

squatters
people who live in an unused
building without having a legal right
to do so and without paying any rent

stroppy
angry

sucks up
trying to please someone by
flattering them or doing things
to help them

suspenders
garter belt

table tennis
Ping-Pong

take the mickey
make fun

temping agency
temporary employment agency

Tiller Girls
a weel-known dancing troupe

Toby jug
a jug that is shaped like a person or
a face, often collected as ornaments

Tube
an underground railway in London

wide boy
an astute or wily person, especially
one prone to sharp practice

Y-fronts
a style of mens underwear

Index